Workbenches

From Design & Theory to Construction & Use

Christopher Schwarz

Workbenches. Copyright © 2007 by Christopher Schwarz. Printed and bound in China. All rights reserved. No part of this book may be reproduced in any form or by any electronic or mechanical means including information storage and retrieval systems without permission in writing from the publisher, except by a reviewer, who may quote brief passages in a review. Published by Popular Woodworking Books, an imprint of F+W Publications, Inc., 4700 East Galbraith Road, Cincinnati, Ohio, 45236. First edition.

Distributed in Canada by Fraser Direct
100 Armstrong Avenue
Georgetown, Ontario L7G 5S4
Canada

Distributed in the U.K. and Europe by David & Charles
Brunel House
Newton Abbot
Devon TQ12 4PU
England
Tel: (+44) 1626 323200
Fax: (+44) 1626 323319
E-mail: postmaster@davidandcharles.co.uk

Distributed in Australia by Capricorn Link
P.O. Box 704
Windsor, NSW 2756
Australia

Visit our Web site at www.popularwoodworking.com or our consumer Web site at www.fwbookstore.com for information on more resources for woodworkers and other arts and crafts projects.

Other fine Popular Woodworking Books are available from your local bookstore or direct from the publisher.

11   10   09   5   4   3   2

Library of Congress Cataloging-in-Publication Data

Schwarz, Christopher, 1968-
  Workbenches : from design and theory to construction and use / by Christopher Schwarz.
     p. cm.
  Includes index.
  ISBN-10: 1-55870-840-5 (hardcover : alk. paper)
  ISBN-13: 978-1-55870-840-2 (hardcover : alk. paper)
  1. Workbenches--Design and construction. 2. Furniture making. 3. Woodwork--Equipment and supplies. I. Title.
  TT197.5.W6S34 2008
  684.1'8--dc22   2007020662

Acquisitions editor: David Thiel
Senior editor: Jim Stack

fw
F+W PUBLICATIONS, INC.

Designer: Terri Woesner
Production coordinator: Jennifer W. Menner
Interior Photographer: Christopher Schwarz
Cover Photographer: Al Parrish
Technical Illustrator: Louis Bois

Metric Conversion Chart

TO CONVERT	TO	MULTIPLY BY
Inches	Centimeters	2.54
Centimeters	Inches	0.4
Feet	Centimeters	30.5
Centimeters	Feet	0.03
Yards	Meters	0.9
Meters	Yards	1.1

ABOUT THE AUTHOR

Christopher Schwarz is the editor of Popular Woodworking and Woodworking Magazine and is a long-time amateur furniture maker and handtool enthusiast.

He began working with wood at age eight when his family members built their first home on their farm outside Hackett, Arkansas, using hand tools because there was no electricity. After studying journalism at Northwestern University and The Ohio State University, Chris became a newspaper reporter but studied furniture-making at night at the University of Kentucky and joined the staff of Popular Woodworking in 1996.

In addition to his duties at Popular Woodworking, Chris writes about hand tools for The Fine Tool Journal and has four DVDs on traditional hand tool use produced and sold by Lie-Nielsen Toolworks. He teaches handwork at the Marc Adams School of Woodworking and Kelly Mehler's School of Woodworking.

He lives in Fort Mitchell, Kentucky, with his wife, Lucy; two daughters, Maddy and Katy; and at least three cats. This is his first book.

ACKNOWLEDGMENTS

I began writing this book as a manual for my students after explaining for the 100th time why their workbenches weren't working. It was written on the couch at night with the kids by my side, on weekends and in hotels from California to Germany.

Luckily for me, lots of people around me gave their time, effort and goodwill in generous measures. At the top of the list are my wife and daughters: Lucy, Maddy and Katy. They tolerated me being chained to my laptop without a single complaint.

John Hoffman, a fellow woodworker in arms, read every word of this book in both its rough and polished form, helped me shape the narrative and listened to untold hours of me droning on about workbench obscura. Also without complaint.

Louis Bois, a professional draughtsman and amateur woodworker, made all of the construction drawings in this book and also edited every chapter for style and substance.

Gary Roberts, who runs the excellent Toolemera Press web site (toolemera.com) provided many of the old photos and engravings from his personal collection. His web site is an excellent resource for anyone investigating the written record of early woodworking.

Other illustrations, photos and research materials came from a fair number of readers and woodworking friends, including: Michael Gladwin, Stephen Fee and Wiktor Kuc of the internet magazine *OldToolsShop.com*.

After the book was written and (basically) designed, Linda Watts, my art director at *Popular Woodworking* magazine, spent a few days cleaning up behind me. And Megan Fitzpatrick, the managing editor for the magazine, spent several of her lunch hours copy editing my book and rooting out numerous typographical errors.

And finally, I'd like to thank one person who probably doesn't know this is coming. David Raeside, one of my most enthusiastic students, suggested one day during a class on handwork that I should write a book. While I'd been asked several times by publishers to write books on a topic of their choosing (and then declined their offers) it was his suggestion that set me in motion. Without his casual remark, this book simply would not exist.

Contents

Workbenches

From Design & Theory to Construction & Use

Cabinetmaker's bench from the book
*Holtzapffel's Construction, Action
and Application of Cutting Tools.*

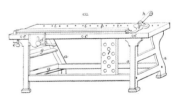

"Portable cabinet bench" from *Spons'
Mechanics' Own Book.*

NICE WORKBENCH (AND HAT): Note how the legs, stretchers and almost certainly the front edge of the benchtop are all in the same plane. This is one of the oft-missed fundamentals of workbench design. I've studied this photo for months. And the only explanation for the pose he is striking is that he is pulling the hand plane toward him. My guess is that's because the photographer asked him to.

Chapter One

Introduction: Functional Failures

Every piece of lumber has three kinds of surfaces: edges, faces and ends. A good workbench should be able to hold your lumber so you can easily work on these three kinds of surfaces. Any bench that falls short of this basic requirement will hold you back as your woodworking skills advance.

It took me years to come to this conclusion – years of frustrating fits and starts, observation and – eventually – success. And though this maxim above looks so obvious when written down, it sometimes eludes both the woodworkers who set out to build their own benches and the manufacturers of commercial workbenches.

To understand how I got to this modest epiphany, it's helpful to understand where I began.

It is 1976. I am eight years old and sport a bowl haircut that hasn't been fashionable since the Reformation. My grandfather has come for a visit to our house in Arkansas, and he's decided we should build a workbench together. I need a place to build my model airplanes that's away from my father's bench, and I am also taking an interest in woodworking, which is an obsession and hobby that runs deeply through both twigs of our family tree.

Grandad buys some white pine 2 x 4s for the legs and some plywood for the top. I can remember building it in our family's suburban garage. He held the nails as I drove them. The completed bench had a portable blue vise that clamped to the benchtop. The jaws were closed by a spindly chrome-plated handle. I clamped everything in that vise, regardless of the workpiece's shape or size. I didn't have bench dogs, a tail vise, a face vise or even a planing stop.

I wish I could tell you I built a Newport kneehole desk at that bench despite the primitive working conditions. But I didn't. I first built a tool tote for my hand tools. And I used my hand tools for that project because my father forbade me from using the table saw or radial arm saw. The tool tote was a sad piece of work. But I kept on working with those tools and found myself drawn to my workbench after school and on weekends.

I wanted to be an architect, so I pilfered my father's books on house building. At the time he was framing out two houses on our farm in nearby Hackett, Arkansas. In his library, there were two books I was fond of. I liked one (I can't remember the title) because the house-building process was narrated by a married cartoon couple

and in a few frames they were naked. I suspect that hippies were involved in the production of that book.

The other book was Graham Blackburn's *Illustrated Furniture Making*. In addition to houses, my father also built some furniture. But I suspect he had this book because Blackburn showed how to use hand tools, and we had no electricity at the farm as of yet.

I consumed Blackburn's book. I would stare at his drawings for a long time and then try some of the techniques. I remember attempting to raise a door panel with a block plane one day.

But my time at my bench began to decrease as I became interested in girls, guns, cars, guitars and (in time) college. By the time I left for college my grandparents had bought the house next door and my grandfather had dragged the bench into his garage so he had one.

During the next four years my parents got divorced, my father abandoned his home-building efforts, my grandfather died and the bench was likely sold during a garage sale while I was living in Ft. Lauderdale, Florida, squatting in a guy's garage and writing crime stories for a newspaper.

In on the Ground Floor

Of course, just a few years later marked the moment I was ready to build furniture, but I lacked the tools and a workbench. Again, my grandfather came to the rescue, though he was gone from this world.

"At its most basic we are only discussing a learned skill, but do we not agree that sometimes the most basic skills can create things far beyond our expectations? We are talking about tools and carpentry, about words and style ... but as we move along, you'd do well to remember that we are also talking about magic."

— Stephen King, *On Writing*

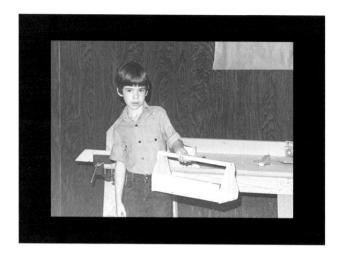

IT WAS THE 1970S: Even our garage was fully clad in ugly dark paneling (you should have seen my room). Here is my first workbench and the first project I ever built on it, a tool tote that probably fell apart within a few years – I can't remember its specific fate. Note the nice hammer marks on the bench's legs from my expert pounding.

HOLDS TOOLS BETTER THAN IT HOLDS WORK: I see a lot of workbenches in professional cabinetshops that look like these benches in our shop. They store a lot of tools below and are useful for piling stuff on. But if you ever want to plane or saw anything, you have to start improvising.

My grandmother called me one day and asked if I wanted Grandad's tools and workbench, which were still in the shop he kept in Connecticut. I rented a trailer and drove the contents of the shop to the house my wife and I had just moved into in Lexington, Kentucky.

I took classes in woodworking at the University of Kentucky. I started building furniture on our back porch. And I got a job as managing editor at *Popular Woodworking* magazine.

My fellow editors there were former tradesmen, and they had built workbenches for the magazine's shop that were suited to a commercial power-tool shop. Each bench consisted of a large base cabinet with doors that was topped with a thick walnut veneered slab. In a former life, the benchtops had been the doors in our building's cafeteria. All the benches had a quick-release metal vise, placed either on the front or the end of the benchtop. There were no dog holes or planing stops. Functionally, the benches were like my childhood bench.

I didn't have a bench at work at first, so I would work on one of the benches that wasn't being used. On my lunch hour, I would cut dovetails by hand to remember what I'd been taught at the University of Kentucky and stay in practice, and then I came to a rude conclusion: These modern workbenches stink for handwork. They are like trying to cut dovetails at your kitchen table. You can't saw on them. You can't plane on them. But you can sand stuff on them. You can clamp stuff to them for routing. And you can pile parts on them for later assembly on an assembly bench.

My grandfather's bench at home was a bit better. It had a face vise and dog holes, but it wasn't ideal for handwork. And there was other hope. One of the other editors, Jim Stuard, had trained under a German cabinetmaker and had used a European bench and a bench built for patternmaking. One year he built a nice bench that blended those two traditional designs. And whenever I got the chance to work on Jim's bench, I would. It was my first taste of a good bench.

Meanwhile, I was granted some space in the shop against the wall and was bequeathed a section of the walnut slab doors to construct a make-do bench. It was a door slab screwed to sawhorses with a couple vises and a dog hole or two. It was an improvement now that I didn't have to ask permission to work on a bench, but I was still miserable and soon asked to build my own bench from scratch.

But then I had to design my bench, and I was bewildered. I knew more about what I disliked about workbenches than I knew about what I wanted. So I retreated into books, both old and new. I designed the best bench I could at the time and used it for many years. I built four variations on it while touring around at woodworking shows. I built a smaller version designed to be tucked next to a table saw.

They were all decent benches, but each revealed occasional limitations. I suspected there was a better design out there. I considered copying a form from one of the recent books on workbenches, such as a Frank Klausz bench, a Shaker Bench or an Ian Kirby bench. But each was missing some function that I thought was critical.

So one night at a bar I started making lists. I first made long lists of all the functions I needed to perform to build furniture and cabinets. Then I made long lists of all the features and devices on a workbench that could be used to tackle these essential functions.

For example, one common function is to plane the face of a board that is less than 6" wide and 48" long. You can do this by working

10 Rules for Building Workbenches

RULE NO. 1: Always overbuild your workbench. There is a saying in boatbuilding: If it looks fair, it is fair. For workbenches, here's my maxim: If it looks stout, then make it doubly so. Everything about a workbench takes punishment that is akin to a kitchen chair in a house of 8-year-old boys.

RULE NO. 2: Always overbuild your workbench. Use the best joinery that you can. These are times to whip out the through-tenon, the dovetail, whatever you've got.

RULE NO. 3: You must remain married as you overbuild your workbench. Every project is a strain on everyday life. And when I build a workbench, I feel soreness in my joints and sorry for my family. If something isn't right on a project, I'll tear it out and start again. A bench has to be perfect – like a highboy, but in a different way.

RULE NO. 4: After you sketch out your workbench design but before you cut the wood, do yourself a favor. Compare your design with other historical designs of benches. If your bench appears to be a new design or looks unlike anything built before, chances are your design is flawed. I hate to be the one to stomp on innovation, but we're not talking about the latest fashions from Milan. We're talking about a table designed to grip bits of wood.

RULE NO. 5: Your bench design cannot be too heavy or too long. But its top can easily be too wide or too tall.

RULE NO. 6: All benches should be able to grip the wood so you can easily work on the faces, the ends and the edges. Submit your bench to what I call the *Kitchen Door Test*. Imagine a typical kitchen door that is ¾" thick, 15" wide and 23" long. How would you affix that door flat on your bench to level its joints and then sand (or plane) it flat? How would you clamp the door so you could work on the ends to trim the top rail and tops of the stiles so the door will fit its opening? And how will you secure that door on edge so you can rout its hinge gains and plane off the saw blade marks without the door flopping around? Does your bench pass this test? OK, now ask the same questions with a door that is ¾" x 15" x 38".

RULE NO. 7: Showcase benches made from exotic materials with a fancy finish are nice. No argument there. But focus on the functions before you work on the flash. I'd rather have a construction-lumber bench that followed these rules than a beautiful European beech Ulmia bench that skipped even one of these basic concepts.

RULE NO. 8: When finishing a workbench, less is more. A shiny film finish lets your work scoot over the bench. And a film finish will crack when struck by a hammer or dead-blow mallet. Choose a finish that is easy to apply, offers some protection from stains and doesn't build up a thick film. I like an oil/varnish blend (sold as Danish Oil) or straight boiled linseed oil.

RULE NO. 9: Avoid bolting your bench to the floor or the wall. You should be able to move your bench, but not too easily. Some operations require you to pull your bench away from the wall. However, a bench on a mobile base can be a problem. If the bench rests on casters (even if the casters lock) it will move too easily.

RULE NO. 10: Your bench is a three-dimensional clamping surface. Anything that interferes with clamping work to your benchtop (aprons, a drawer bank, doors, supports, etc.) will frustrate you in short order.

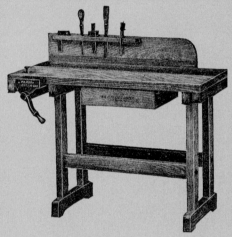

Fig. 2940

STILL SPINDLY: Modern manufacturers don't have the market cornered on workbenches that are small and puny. Check out this vintage example from a William P. Walters tool catalog. This bench would frustrate anyone who wanted to make anything other than small boxes.

No. 100

THE GNOME BRAND: This "bench" was one of Hammacher Schlemmer & Co.'s Gnome Brand benches. Why Gnome Brand? My guess is that the benches were too small for the average-sized woodworker.

against a planing stop or you can pinch the work between dogs using a tail vise, wagon vise, wedges or the Veritas Wonder Dog system. Pick one. They all work.

With these lists complete, I decided to use them as a way to either design a new bench or to find a commercial one that satisfied all of the workholding needs on my list.

I started looking at many of the inexpensive commercial workbenches at woodworking supply stores. I couldn't find a single one that did all the basic tasks for handwork. Plus, they lacked mass and would wobble. So I looked at some of the expensive commercial workbenches. These were better in many cases (especially when it came to mass), but I still couldn't find one that held my work so I could work on edges, faces and ends of boards.

By chance, I stumbled on a drawing of an 18th century French workbench and it was – no lie – like a religious conversion. It looked like nothing I'd ever seen before in stores or in workshops. I built that bench and began working with it. It was everything I'd hoped it would be, and it was simpler to construct than any other bench I'd encountered. Encouraged by my success, I started digging into other old books and found other forgotten forms of benches. I built those (they also were simple to make) and started making furniture on them. After three benches, I had to ask myself: Why are so many modern benches inadequate for basic handwork?

I don't have an iron-clad answer. But I have clues. My old-style workbenches were the dominant forms in the 18th and 19th centuries, before the Industrial Revolution. Before steam power. Before Manual Training (what we call shop class) was brought into schools.

These old benches were generally built by the woodworker. Some early books discuss the fact that there were commercial benches available (some with cast iron bases), but the forms offered in the books were for the craftsman to construct.

THE $175 WORKBENCH: This bench is an excellent first bench because you can modify the heck out of it without worrying too much about how much the raw materials cost. It's like customizing an old Volkswagen Beetle, I suppose. Chop it. Drop it. Paint flames on it if you like.

The Industrial Revolution changed how we made furniture and tools and even educated a citizenry. Furniture, tools and almost everything else became a factory item instead of bespoke. As we moved into the machine age, some thoughtful individuals became worried that people would lose touch with handwork as the nation industrialized, and so the Manual Training movement was born in our schools. This new generation of woodworkers needed workbenches, and factories could make them quickly. As the 19th century closed, workbenches begin to appear in great numbers in tool catalogs, many of them labeled as ideal for Manual Training.

And these Manual Training benches are pretty sorry. Many are spindly and lack key features. But they can be broken down and shipped flat by rail, unlike the traditional old benches, which are unsuited for factory production.

Why didn't the marketplace reject the spindly benches? My guess is that these benches were sold to schools and students who didn't know the difference between a good bench and a bad one. It's a problem still today. (These factory benches are usually called *European Benches*, but that is generally an insult to the old form – usually a German form – that they are based on.) Eventually these factory benches became the dominant form and they still are today.

And that's too bad. The older shop-made benches are simpler to make and do all basic woodworking tasks with ease. But they are, for the most part, forgotten relics in dusty books.

STARTING SPINDLY: When you look at old catalogs of workbenches, they would list a line for pros and a line for *Manual Training*. The manual training benches, such as the one above, were almost always lacking. A bench like this isn't a tool for your shop. It's a challenge to overcome.

DON'T FORGET THE EDGES: Your workbench is a three-dimensional clamping surface, so don't give up the ability to clamp items vertically against your legs, aprons (shown above) or a sliding deadman.

This book is an attempt to walk you through the bench-design process and help you design a bench that works for you. I think you'll find that if you follow this advice, you'll build a bench that resembles a classic historical model, even if you are a router and biscuit-joinery woodworker. I came to this same conclusion, and it is a testament to the fact that woodworking processes haven't changed much, just the tools and the technology that produces the tools. The work is the same: We all cut, shape, smooth and assemble wooden parts.

Beware the New — Fight Progress

I hope this book also will prevent you from venturing down unnecessary paths. If you can see in your mind's eye a workbench device that no one has ever invented before and that you think you need, then I caution you. Chances are that someone has come up with a way to do what you want to do, and they used simple technology to do it. Or your particular need is so specialized and narrow that few people would ever need to do that to a piece of wood. So take a moment to look around at what already exists before you build a triple-screw vise with pneumatic suction panels. Or a bench that is attached to a barber's chair (yes, that one exists). Or a bench that is 42" high with vises on all four corners.

Whenever I build a bench, it's inevitable that someone on our magazine's staff will ask me if this is the last bench I'll ever build. They ask if I have found perfection. I don't think there's an answer. Since I started woodworking at age eight, my needs as a woodworker have changed. And they will continue to change.

But the benches I have now – the two benches I show you how to build in this book – fulfill all the basic needs of a furniture maker. I have yet to stumble into any serious limitations of either design. Would I change things if I built them again? Sure. Would that change they way they functioned? No, not really.

So these benches are a good place to begin. And that's what this book is for: To give you a head start in the craft by building a bench that is capable of doing things you might not be ready to do yet. And when you are ready, your bench will be willing and waiting.

The Most Common Workbench Questions (and the Answers)

When woodworkers approach the question of building a bench, they usually have a series of questions that generate quite a bit of debate among veteran craftsmen. Here are some of the most common questions, and the answers (from my experience).

1. SHOULD I BUILD OR BUY MY WORKBENCH? This gets to the heart of many questions in woodworking (buying used tools v. new tools, buying rough lumber v. surfaced stock). Whenever I face a question such as this, I answer: "What do you like to do? Work wood or fix up old tools? Spend a week at the planer or cut joints? Let your answer be your guide." But with workbenches, my semi-Socratic method falls apart. I think you should build your workbench, even if you aren't looking for a career in workbench building. Building a workbench teaches you a lot about woodworking, including: traditional joinery, integrating hardware into a design, balancing form and function and making assemblies that are demonstrably flat and square. And you get to learn all this on a piece of furniture that doesn't have to go in the living room and embarrass you if you stumble.

2. WHAT STYLE OF WORKBENCH SHOULD I USE? Workbench purists will push you toward building a copy of a tested or classic design. I know craftsmen who have built benches that are doppelgangers of benches built in the 19th century. I say that you should use your good judgment instead. While you shouldn't re-invent the wheel when you build a workbench, you shouldn't be afraid to combine elements of different benches, as long as the result meets the minimum requirements for size, mass and workholding. Then I think you'll have a fine workbench. Most workbenches (even the holy relic ones) are hybrid designs with features from other cultures. (The earliest workbench that I know of is an Egyptian rock. That one has mass in spades, but the workholding is lacking.)

3. CAN I MAKE MY BENCH MOBILE OR HEIGHT-ADJUSTABLE? Unless your bench is bolted down, it is already mobile. Every mobile base I've seen for benches has wheels that are too small, a mechanism that is too complex, a design that makes the bench unstable or a price tag that has too many zeros. I move my bench all the time and it weighs 350 pounds. Push. Shove. Done. Height-adjustable benches are for hospitals. If you need to get closer to your work to see details, buy a stool and sit down. Build your bench so it's comfortable for common operations then adjust yourself up or down for the uncommon ones. Few people need a height-adjustable bench unless they also do dentistry or barbering there, too.

4. HOW HIGH SHOULD MY BENCH BE AND WHAT WOOD SHOULD I USE TO MAKE IT? OK, now you're getting ahead of the class. Turn the page and we'll dissect those two questions like frogs in a high school biology class.

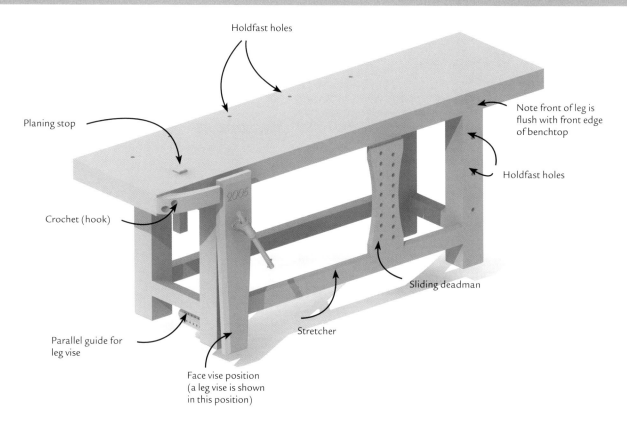

Holdfast holes

Planing stop

Note front of leg is
flush with front edge
of benchtop

Holdfast holes

Crochet (hook)

Sliding deadman

Parallel guide for
leg vise

Stretcher

Face vise position
(a leg vise is shown
in this position)

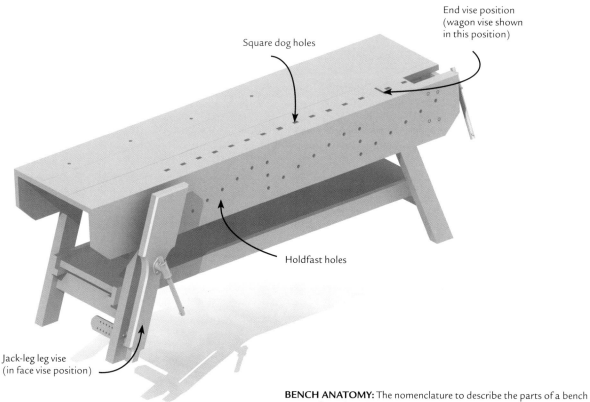

End vise position
(wagon vise shown
in this position)

Square dog holes

Holdfast holes

Jack-leg leg vise
(in face vise position)

BENCH ANATOMY: The nomenclature to describe the parts of a bench
can confuse (though it's not as tricky as understanding your own preteen
children or the geometry of sawteeth). Here's the most important thing
to remember: the terms *face vise* and *end vise* refer to the position of the vise
on the bench. A quick-release iron vise is a face vise when it's mounted on
front, and it's an end vise when it's on the end.

Chapter Two

The Basics of Workbench Design

Few people dispute that the workbench is the single most important tool in the workshop, yet there is surprisingly little written about the details that are critical to its design, construction and — most of all — its use.

There are plenty of books that offer a guided tour of workbenches built by contemporary woodworkers around the globe. They offer plans for a handful of handsome workbenches. They show you photographs of the woodworkers using the benches and discuss how some have added a sailing ship's galley of storage to the bench. Or a lift mechanism that raises the benchtop like a dentist's chair.

I own those books and like them. But this isn't that kind of book.

This book is everything that I've always thought was missing from the other workbench books. This book focuses on how you solve everyday problems with a workbench that resides in your garage or basement. Professional woodworkers who I know use either rudimentary workbenches designed for production work or specific purpose-built workbenches that solve a thorny problem that crops up every day in their work. In other words, the professionals I know use benches that are designed for that person's business, which might be kitchen cabinets, millwork, veneering panels or laying up butcher-block tops. Such benches as those are not for the generalist.

Workbench Design

It's my belief that the enthusiastic modern-day home woodworker needs a workbench that has much in common with the workbenches used by 18th- and 19th-century craftsmen. Home woodworkers tend to build a wide variety of projects (shelves one month, chairs the next, followed by picture frames). So they need a workbench that excels at the garden-variety woodworking tasks and yet is flexible enough to be adapted to the oddball stuff.

Old-school workbenches are well-suited for a jack-of-all-trades woodworker.

So the chapter on workbench design isn't about how a Shaker-style workbench is different from a Tage Frid-style workbench. Instead, it's about how the construction details of a workbench — any workbench — affect the way you work. Workbenches are far more than a strong table. When designed, built and used properly, a workbench is a four- (sometimes five-) legged dance partner that will add fluidity and speed to your work. A poorly designed bench is one of the most frustrating obstacles in the craft.

Here are some of the critical points to consider as you design your own workbench or buy a commercial one:

· The species of wood.
· The size of the top and the amount of its overhang.
· The size, location and existence of a tool tray.
· The placement of the completed bench in your workshop.
· The placement of the legs — flush or recessed from the top's front edge.
· The selection and placement of vises.
· The addition of dog holes and stops in the benchtop and legs — including their size, shape and composition.
· The height of the benchtop from the floor.
· The use (or misuse) of the space beneath the top.
· The design of the support structure beneath the benchtop.
· And most of all, designing a workbench around the tasks you need to perform instead of designing a workbench around ideas or names or nationalities. Here, we'll list all the typical things you can do with a workbench and match them to the devices and features above. That is the heart of this book. Many woodworkers end up building several benches as their skills grow and they realize their first bench-building efforts were inadequate. By understanding all the common tasks performed on a bench, you can draft a workbench you will never outgrow — even if you've never taken hammer in hand.

"He (the wheelwright) had no band saw to drive, with ruthless un-intelligence, through every resistance. The timber was far from being prey, a helpless victim, to a machine. Rather it would lend its own special virtues to the man who knew how to humour it."

— George Sturt, *The Wheelwright's Shop*
(Home Farm Books)

Building a workbench is simple. The joinery is straightforward. The materials are inexpensive and plentiful. There is a wide variety of hardware available. I've built 10 workbenches and worked on many commercial benches as well, everything from Ulmia to Sjoberg to Lie-Nielsen to no-wonder-it's-got-no-name.

Choose a Good Material

The first question that bench builders ask is what sort of material they should use for making a workbench. It's the first barrier: "Where will I get the wood? And what kind of wood?" There's a lot of confusion on this topic. Most European benches were built using beech, and sometimes fine-grained steamed European beech. And so a significant number of woodworkers go to lengths to purchase precious beech for their workbenches. After all, who wants to argue with several hundreds of years of tradition?

I do. European apprentices, cabinetmakers and joiners didn't choose beech because of some magic quality of *Fagus sylvatica*. They chose it because it was dense, stiff, plentiful and inexpensive. In the United States, beech is dense, stiff, hard to find and (sometimes) a bit spendy. You can, of course, use it to build a bench (it's your bench, not mine), but you will pay for the privilege. And it will have no demonstrable advantage over a bench built from a cheaper species.

Other woodworkers, tacking toward the sensible I suppose, use hard or soft maple for their benches, rationalizing that it's like the beech of the New World. And indeed, the maples have all the desirable qualities of a species for a workbench (save its expense – boy howdy, it's expensive in the United States).

Maple is stiff, resists denting and can span long distances without much of a support structure below it. But so can other species. In fact, if you went by the numbers from the wood technologists alone, you'd build your bench from shagbark hickory, despite its difficult nature. Once you look at the characteristics that make a species good for a workbench, you see that white oak, Southern yellow pine, fir, poplar or just about any species (excepting basswood and the soft white pines) will perform brilliantly. The real challenge is in how you scale and assemble the parts (which we'll discuss) to increase the top's stiffness or its resistance to loading.

So don't get hung up on the species of your material. There are many other workbench properties that are more important than the particular species.

Here's one important property: How stiff is the wood? You want the wood to remain stiff over long spans so you don't have to build a complex undercarriage that could impede clamping things to the top. And a monolithic top is the way to accomplish this. Among the wood scientists there are several ways to describe the stiffness of a board, including, most critically, the modulus of elasticity. Tip: *modulus* is just a fancy word for *measure*.

I don't intend to get technical here, but I do want to say that I think one of the most striking failures of woodworkers is that they don't understand the material. Wood's structure is complex, though no more complex than a plunge router. Years ago I read R. Bruce Hoadley's masterwork *Understanding Wood* (The Taunton Press) and it changed the way I looked at wood. Instead of seeing boards, I saw my shop filled with snippets of a cone-shaped organism. That is a big-

A HEAVY FRENCH MEAL: I move my bench at least once a week – and not for exercise. A tricky setup or clamping job can be easier with access to the rear. But sawing and planing are easier with the bench braced against the wall.

The Stiffness of Common Workbench Woods

SPECIES	E VALUE
Hemlock, eastern	1.20
Chestnut	1.23
White pine	1.24
Sycamore	1.42
Basswood	1.46
American cherry	1.49
Hemlock, western	1.49
Red oak (Northern)	1.49
Poplar	1.58
European beech	1.63
Red (soft) maple	1.64
Black walnut	1.68
American beech	1.72
Ash	1.77
White oak	1.78
Hard maple	1.83
Southern yellow pine	1.93
Douglas fir	1.95
Yellow birch	2.01
Hickory, shagbark	2.16

Source: *Understanding Wood* (Taunton Press)

ger shift in viewpoint than it might sound. I highly recommend the book for the mindful woodworker.

OK, back to numbers. The most important technical factor when choosing a species for a bench is its E value. The E value is the measure of stiffness, or how much strain a species exhibits under a certain amount of stress. The higher the E value, the stiffer the board. A board with an E value of 2 is twice as stiff as one with an E value of 1. When you dissect this chart, I think you'll understand why I choose Southern yellow pine or Douglas fir for workbenches (and joists). Use the chart at right to figure out how your local species fare on the stiffness scale.

Another characteristic of the wood that's important for building a bench is its weight. Unless you are building a bench that must be portable, a heavy bench is desirable. Heavy benches resist the pushing and shoving that comes with the craft. One of my first workbenches was an old walnut cafeteria door resting on a poplar sawhorse-style frame. It weighed no more than 70 pounds. During planing or sawing, the bench would inch down the wall until it kissed the drill press's table. Every few days I'd drag my bench back to the starting line.

There are definitely ways to make a lightweight bench function well. You can bolt it to (or through) your floor. You can capture its base using cleats that you attach to your floor with concrete anchors or screws. But these fixes prevent you from easily moving your workbench. And you will occasionally want to pull it from the wall or move it a few inches or a few feet. So the ideal bench is one that is difficult to move unless you are trying to move it.

My current French-style bench weighs about 350 pounds, all told. It does not move under any woodworking task. However, I can lift one end and pivot the bench to move it by myself within the shop. Two strong backs can move the bench onto a truck (we've done this several times). It is the heaviest bench I've ever used, and I'm well pleased with its weight.

The relative weight of wood is expressed by what is called *specific gravity*, which compares the weight of the wood to the weight of an equivalent volume of water. The larger the number the heavier the wood is. A wood that approaches (or exceeds) 1 will be heavier than water and will sink in water. That's heavy.

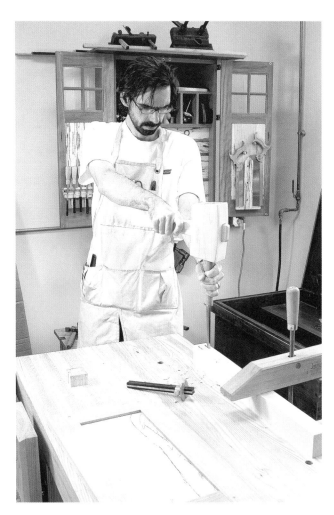

THE DAILY BEATINGS WILL CONTINUE: Even if you don't like nails (and I do) you'll find yourself whacking your benchtop. If you don't like dents in your pretty bench, choose a species for the benchtop that is high on the Janka scale.

The Weight of Common Workbench Woods

SPECIES	SPECIFIC GRAVITY
White pine	.35
Basswood	.37
Hemlock, eastern	.40
Poplar	.42
Hemlock, western	.47
Chestnut	.48
Douglas fir	.48
Sycamore	.49
American cherry	.50
Red (soft) maple	.54
Black walnut	.55
Red oak (Northern)	.59
Ash	.60
Yellow birch	.62
Hard maple	.63
American beech	.64
Southern yellow pine	.67
European beech	.68
White oak	.68
Hickory, shagbark	.72
Purpleheart	.77

Source: *Woods of the World*, a list of species at 12 percent moisture content, plus various industry publications.

Most texts tend to separate hardwoods and softwoods when they deal with specific gravity, but I think that's a taxonomic transgression. The difference between a so-called *hardwood* or *softwood* has nothing to do at all with the wood's woodworking properties. Instead, it has to do with how the trees reproduce. Yes, tree sex. Look it up if you don't believe me. Hardwoods are angiosperms, which means their seeds have a covering, such as an acorn. Softwoods are gymnosperms, which means their seeds don't. That's the major difference. Now, it's true that hardwoods are generally harder and denser than softwoods, but it's also an over-simplification. So don't discount the so-called softwoods when building a bench. Southern yellow pine is about the same density as European beech, and both species make a fine workbench.

Another important characteristic of wood is its resistance to blows and denting in general. Anyone who has purchased a white pine 2x4 bench from a home center can attest to this fact: These benches are easy to beat. They dent when you look at them wrong. A maple bench, on the other hand, won't dent even after you park a Ford F150 on it.

Is this an important trait for a workbench? That depends. I think that handwork is more likely to introduce a lot of pounding and beating on the benchtop. Chop a few mortises by hand and you might

agree. The power-tool workshop is much less reliable on percussion tools (such as mallets); the joinery is handled almost exclusively by cutting tools.

If you don't like dents, then you should get to know the Janka scale. It is a test that reveals the amount of force (in pounds per square inch) required to insert a .444"-diameter steel ball into a species of wood so that half of the pellet is buried in the wood.

If you study the chart, you'll note that some of the woods I've used for workbenches, such as Southern yellow pine, are pretty pitiful on the Janka scale. Truth is, I think that yellow pine is tough enough for a bench. I flatten my benchtops about once a year, and it's an opportunity to see how each top fared in use. I find very few serious dents in my yellow pine tops. Never do I see a dent from a clamp head. We use parallel-jaw clamps that can apply up to 1,000 pounds of pressure across the clamp's contact area. Occasionally I find a stray hammer mark, but all in all, yellow pine is tough enough to resist most percussion. In fact, it seems to get tougher with age.

So the bottom line is that you have a wide latitude when choosing a species with which to build your bench. In fact, almost any species will do. So select a species that is stiff, heavy, tough, plentiful in your area and affordable. And if you are strapped for cash, you can always

SHRINKAGE IS OK: When the top of my French bench shrank, it distorted the base into a slight A-frame shape. It's no problem to work on a bench with this shape, and it might add stability.

The Janka Scale for Some Common Workbench Woods

SPECIES	PSI
White pine	380
Basswood	410
Hemlock	500
Chestnut	540
Poplar	540
Douglas fir	660
Southern yellow pine	690
Sycamore	770
American cherry	950
Red (soft) maple	950
Big leaf maple	1,000
Black walnut	1,010
Yellow birch	1,260
Red oak (Northern)	1,290
American beech	1,300
European beech	1,300
Ash	1,320
White oak	1,360
Hard maple	1,450
Hickory/Pecan	1,820
Purpleheart	1,860
Ipe	3,680

invest the most money on the wood for the top and use construction-grade white pine lumber for the base, which doesn't have to be as stout. There's nothing wrong with a mongrel, mixed species bench. Most benches end up that way after user modifications anyway.

Wood for Workbenches: Somewhat Seasoned is OK

When building cabinets and other casework, you generally want your wood to be at equilibrium with your shop environment. In other words, you want it to achieve a state where it is not actively giving off (or taking in) large gulps of moisture from the air. Any change in moisture content of wood at equilibrium is related to the changes in humidity with the seasons.

The usual advice is to bring the wood into your shop and allow it to acclimate to the shop environment, checking its progress with a moisture meter. That's good advice for cabinets, however you can use wood that is still in flux for a workbench if you are smart about it.

Here's how: Once you bring your stock into your shop, check each piece with the moisture meter, writing its moisture content on the surface of the board (I use a grease pen). Then separate the stock into two piles: those boards that are close to the equilibrium moisture con-

tent in your shop and those that are way over (4 percentage points or more counts as way over). I've used stuff that is 9 points over, and I've tried using stuff that was even wetter. That was a bit of a disaster. The wood was Douglas fir and was probably 22 percent moisture. When I ripped it on the table saw, the blade sprayed a thin fan of water back at me, which was a weird way to work. When I'd leave the wood on a cast-iron surface for a couple hours, the iron would rust. So I try to avoid stuff that is too wet.

Once you have the two piles of wood, that's when you can start marking out your parts. First choose the driest parts for anything that will be a rail or a stretcher – anything that will have a tenon on the end of it. Now pick the wettest stuff for the legs or anything that will have a mortise bored into it.

Then set the other stuff aside as you build the base of the bench. As the legs dry out, the wet legs will shrink on the dry tenons (which won't change in size much). This will tighten your most critical joints. This is a basic chairbuilding technique used by green woodworkers to make their projects last for centuries.

Once you've selected the parts for your base and built it, go back to your pile of wood for the benchtop and check the stock again with your moisture meter. During the time it took you to make the base,

17

LONG ENOUGH: This 1910 photo shows a bench at the Bristol Aeroplane Co. in Filton, Bristol. It is likely 14' long. Note the drawer and the frame clamped on edge in the face vise. Photo courtesy of Michael Gladwin.

the boards for the top all should have moved closer (sometimes much closer) to the equilibrium moisture content in your shop.

This strategy has worked well for several of my benches. It allows you to get to work on your workbench, it makes your joints stronger and it doesn't cause any splitting that I've found.

The Size of the Top

With your wood species selected, you should start sketching the skeleton of your design on your computer, graph paper or a napkin. The first issue is the top. Its thickness, width and length are key. And their dimensions are not arbitrary.

My first revelation about the size of the top came from my own early experiences as an adult in working wood. I started on our back porch in Lexington, Kentucky, which was sagging and reeked of the sweet but nauseating smell of rotting possum. I had my grandfather's bench out in the shed, but I didn't move it to the porch for some reason, which is now lost to me. Instead, I assembled all the furniture I built on the floor of the porch. I even had the table saw out on the porch, which would have made a half-decent assembly surface. But instead, I would move all the parts to the floor for fitting. Ridiculous? Yes.

Fast-forward seven or eight years and I'm trying to teach some fellow employees at *Popular Woodworking* magazine how to do some basic woodworking operations. I walked them through all the critical power-tool operations that could sever a digit. But then I left them alone for a few minutes to adjust their joints and assemble some parts while I returned some phone calls.

I'm out of the shop for 10 minutes, tops.

When I walk back in they are all working on the floor. It looked like I'd barged in on circle time at the local kindergarten. In the shop we had six or seven workbenches and assembly benches the students

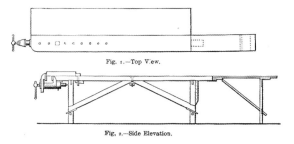

BENCH EXTENSION: This is an odd bench with an unusual position for the end vise. But what's interesting is the fold-down extension. Long benches were the norm, especially for house carpenters and joiners. From Carpentry and Building magazine, October 1882.

could have used. We also had three table saws, two with massive outfeed tables that would have been great assembly tables. Instead the students chose the cold, hard concrete floor. Why?

I suppose we gravitate toward the support and space offered by the earth. It is the infinite assembly table, after all. And it offers unerring support. You rarely run out of floor space when moving cabinet parts around down there. So when I make a workbench top, I make it imitate the best qualities of the floor. I think your benchtop should be as long as possible. Find the wall where your workbench will go. (Hint: Pick the wall that has a window.) Measure that space. Subtract four feet from that and that's a good length for the top. Note: The benchtop should be at least 5' long unless you build only small-scale items. Furniture-sized parts typically range up to 48" long and you want to be able to support these fully and have a little room to spare.

I've made tops that are 8' long. My next bench will be a 10-footer, which is the maximum that will fit in my shop at home. I dream of a 12' top. It is difficult to make or imagine a workbench that's too long. The same goes for thickness. It is the thickness that allows the top to

JUST WIDE ENOUGH: You can reach across a benchtop that is narrower than 30" to work on a typical cabinet. Benchtops that are wider than 36" force you to trot around them all day.

HAMSTER TOWN: The tool tray in Senior Editor Robert W. Lang's commercial bench gets cluttered during a project. His next bench will have a tool tray that is deep, removable and runs down the middle of the bench.

be that long. If you make the top really thick, 4 or more inches, then it will offer the unerring support offered by the earth and allow you to build your bench without any unwieldy support system beneath. The top can perch on your legs and will not sag under any normal weight.

But the width is a different matter. You can have benches that are too wide for a one-person shop. I've worked on benches that are 36" wide and they have some downsides. For starters, if you park them against the wall you'll have to stretch to reach the tools that are hanging on the wall or have scooted across the top and are cowering against the wall.

But there's more. Cabinetwork is sized in standard chunks. These sizes come from the human body; they aren't arbitrary. A kitchen's base cabinet is generally 24" deep and 34$\frac{1}{2}$" high. This is important for a couple reasons. First: It means you don't really need a bench that's much more than 24" deep to build cabinetry. With that 24" depth, you actually gain advantages, including the fact that you can clamp the cabinet to your bench from as many as three sides of your bench. That is handy. A deep bench will allow you to clamp your cabinets to the bench on only two sides (with a couple exceptions).

Here's the other thing to keep in mind: Kitchen cabinets are themselves a highly studied work surface. There's a good reason that kitchen cabinets are 24" deep. And, if you think about it, it's the same reason you don't want your workbench much deeper either.

The height of the kitchen cabinets (and your workbench) are another important dimension. Keep that 34$\frac{1}{2}$" in mind for now.

Now I'm not going to argue with you if you build really big stuff or have a bench that you share with another woodworker facing you; you might need more depth. But if you are like the rest of us, a 24"-deep bench is a powerful and right-sized tool.

These guidelines for bench sizes aren't random. Check out illustrations of early benches for cabinetmakers or joiners, who outfitted homes with sashwork and doors. These benches usually follow these rules, especially the ones on length and depth. The top's thickness is another matter, and it depends on whether the cabinetmaker was French or English. More on that later as we'll get into the different styles of benches.

The Tool Tray: Do You Need One?

In general I don't like discussing religion or politics, so I was tempted to ignore the topic of tool trays. This recessed area at the back edge of your bench – or down the middle in some designs – is the subject of much debate. It can be a good place to keep bench tools handy, according to some, and a great place to make a nest for the family hamster, according to others.

I've worked on all sorts of benches, with and without tool trays, and both perspectives are exactly right.

A BENCH IN THE BREACH: This bench has always interested me. It has so many qualities of 19th- and 18th-century benches, yet it has metal vise screws, the face-vise is built using finger joints (a machine-made joint) and the tools suggest it's an early 20th-century photograph. This bench was (and still is) a blend of old and new. Note especially how the top is flush with the legs and sliding deadman.

If you're going to have a tool tray in your workbench, make it deep. I'd say that 4" is right. The deeper the tool tray, the better it is at holding tools. Shoulder planes and right-angle drills will nest in a deep tray without poking up above the benchtop surface. Another excellent feature with a tool tray is to make the floor of it removable in sections. This cunning idea, which I first encountered in David Charlesworth's books, eliminates some of the features I dislike about tool trays. By removing the floor of the tool tray you can get a clamp in there to secure some work to the top. Plus, the tool tray is easier to clean of shavings and dust. The tool tray on my grandfather's bench has ends that are ramp shaped so you can sweep debris out of the tool tray – this also works, but the removable floor works better.

The most significant downside to tool trays of any design is that they reduce the amount of working and clamping surface you have available. There are times where you need the support of the benchtop right where the tool tray is located. I've encountered this obstacle a number of times when planing wide panels for case sides. I'll want to get a shim or wedge under the panel to make it sit firmly on the benchtop, but I cannot because of the tool tray. Also, a bench with a tool tray in the center is tricky to flatten.

Also, no matter how fastidious you are, your tool tray is going to be a junk magnet. Dust and shavings collect there among your tools, and you can end up having to root around like a pig hunting truffles for your marking knife or carpenter's pencil.

The Placement of the Bench in the Workshop
Where you place your bench in your shop might not seem like something you should be concerned about at the design phase, but it is.

Workbenches for handwork thrive when they're placed against a wall with a window. The wall braces the workbench as you are planing cross-grain and sawing. The light from the window points out the flaws in the work that your hand tools are trying to remove. (In fact, when I work with hand tools, I usually turn off the overhead lights in my shop. I can see much better with fewer light sources.)

There are some interesting theories about which direction your bench should face. One 19th-century maxim was that benches should stand so the length runs north and south. There should be windows at the north and south, with no windows east or west.

"I think that if I did not work with wood, my life would be a hollow emptiness. If I did not form and shape and build, what would I have done to leave my mark in this world? My eyes have been filled with the endlessly changing patterns of the grains. I have felt the warmth of a thousand suns in my hands every day. I have smelled the rich, tangy odors of the freshly hewn chips. These are the things that have made my life so fine. These are the most precious things I can leave for you, my son."

— Jonas Wainwright, Master Carpenter,
from a letter to his son, 1832

Benches from the Old Countries

People tend to personalize benches – a Tage Frid bench, a Frank Klausz bench, a Michael Dunbar bench. I tend to nationalize them instead.

We could start with the Roman workbench, a low table with four to eight legs that's built like a Windsor chair. It's just about the earliest form of workbench in the literature, but it's disappeared from the workshop. The French workbench shown in Andre Roubo's 18th century masterwork *Description Des Arts Et Metiers* has a thick slab top, massive legs and narrow stretchers.

Work-holding is simple and ingenious. There's a planing stop on the benchtop, plus holes for holdfasts in the top. Early French benches sport a crochet, a planing stop for working edges of boards. The wood is supported below by holdfasts in holes in the legs.

German- and Scandinavian-style benches share similarities with French benches, with some engineering added. These benches – sometimes called continental or European benches – generally have a slab top, though the top is more complex. It can be thinner in the middle and ringed by a thick frame. For workholding, you get a tail vise on the right side of the bench with a system of dogs for pinching the work. Some benches also have holes for holdfasts. And there is a shoulder vise on the left. The shoulder vise allows you to clamp pieces for dovetailing or tenoning without interference from screws from the vise. The undercarriage of the bench can have sled feet, and the legs are rarely flush with the front edge of the benchtop. Instead of relying on the legs to support long work, these benches would use a bench slave – a separate stand with an adjustable shelf.

And then there is what I call the English bench, which appears in Peter Nicholson's *The Mechanic's Companion* (1831). Nicholson calls out this bench as intended for joiners – workmen who made sashes, doors and fittings for houses. There is no discussion of furniture being made on this bench. (An earlier book by Joseph Moxon also insists its bench is for joiners. And so does Roubo, though the bench is shown being used for fine furniture work).

The English bench has a thin top supported by interior ribs, and at least one wide apron. The English bench has a face vise, a planing stop and pegs on the front apron to support long boards on edge.

There are rarely dog holes in the top surface or a tail vise, which would make working the faces of wide panels quite a challenge. But that is a task for furniture makers more than joiners.

It is a material-efficient design and the English form survived into mid 20th-century America. My 1947 edition of *Audels Carpenters and Builders Guide* (Vol. 1) shows some typical English benches for house carpenters, but one form has a sliding deadman; another has dog holes in the benchtop. But neither has a tail vise! How did they secure the work between dogs? My guess: Wedging.

These three basic bench forms – French, continental and English – are the basis for most Western-style workbenches, with latter-day bench designers mixing and matching their features to suit their work or whim. Sometimes the mongrel designs work; sometimes they don't. Examining why a bench design succeeds or fails is why this book exists.

THREE TRADITIONS: The French bench (top) is massive, the Continental workbench (middle) is the most complex (and it's the dominant form today), and the English bench is cleverly engineered.

ABOUT FACE: Though its jaws are wooden, this is a face vise because it is located on the face of the bench. Quick quiz: If this were a twin-screw vise, what would you call it? Yup, a twin-screw face vise.

FACING FACTS: The quick-release metal vise is perhaps the most common form of face vise on benches today. That doesn't mean it's the best thing for woodworking. Its guide bars interfere with clamping boards to work on edges and ends.

My bench at home is under a window that faces north, and the light is constant and even throughout the day. My bench at work is under a west window. There, the light is harsh at the end of the day. This produces glare on lighter workpieces and the color of the light is warmer than at mid-day. The work looks different at the end of the day – and that's not just due to fatigue or progress I've made that day.

Your particular shop space may determine the ultimate length of your workbench. If you have an 8'-long wall for your bench an 8'-long bench isn't going to work. You need access to the ends and room for your tools (particularly your long planes) to complete their strokes without striking a wall.

Your shop space can also affect what sort of vises you choose. If you have to wedge your bench into a tight space, then a twin-screw vise on the end of the bench is a bad idea. It will be unusable if you cannot get your body in front of it for sawing dovetails or tenons.

When working with power tools, I tend to pull my workbench away from the wall so I can work on all sides of it. When working with routers, you sometimes have to work with odd clamping setups to avoid climb-cutting. So access to all four sides of the bench is handy. Power tool setups thrive on overhead light – and lots of it. So being by the window is nice, but not as necessary as with hand work.

Because most shops use some sort of combination of hand and power tools, I bet you'll move your bench around a bit. Mine gets shifted a couple times during most projects. Keep this in mind when you settle on the ultimate length of the bench. Make it as long as possible while allowing the vises to work without hitting a wall.

Overhang: How the Top and Legs Interact

When you build a dining room table, the amount that the top overhangs the table's apron is a critical measurement. A well-sized overhang can add grace to the design. It's something I fuss over whenever I build a table. But when it comes to designing workbenches, I have concluded that the old ways are best. Here's exactly how much the old-timers let their workbench tops overhang the legs in front: zero.

Why? OK, erase from your mind that a workbench is a table. It's not a table. It shouldn't be built like a dining room table, and it shouldn't look like one either. Your bench is a three-dimensional clamping surface. If you're clamping work to the top only, you're missing out. The front of your bench (when made properly) is an amazing clamping surface. You can clamp an entryway door against the legs and top (if they're flush) to mortise in the hinges or lockset. You can clamp a carcase side for dovetailing. You can easily support long and wide boards to work their edges. Cabinet doors, face frames, tabletops – anything big and flat can be clamped there.

In fact, early French benches would even make the stretchers between the workbench's legs flush to the front of the bench. I have to agree here with the French – this feature has come in handy in my shop. English woodworkers also knew this trick. English workbenches have legs that are flush to the front of the bench and also have an enormous front apron that is flush to the legs and top. The apron offers unparalleled vertical clamping (it also gets in the way of clamping things to the workbench top).

The Placement and Selection of Vises

Vises confuse many workbench builders. Vises are especially bewildering if you've never spent much time working at a bench developing a

RACKED WITH A WEAK GRIP: Many face vises, wooden or iron, will rack when pressure is applied on one end only. This racking saps your clamping power. You need a vise block (actually, you need several), that will even out the pressure on both sides of the vise's screw.

Face Vise

The face vise is so named because it goes on the front face of a workbench. Almost any vise can be a face vise, though most people associate the term with a cast iron vise or a similar wooden-jawed vise. Right-handers generally place the face vise on the left side of the bench; lefties put it on the right. It is typically the workhorse of a modern bench. It will hold small pieces of work, generally up to about 24" in length, for a variety of handwork and power-tool tasks.

Smart woodworkers will take the extra time to fit the rear jaws of a cast iron face vise into the front edge of the workbench top. This arrangement allows you to use the front edge of your workbench's top to support long boards.

The garden variety cast iron face vise has charms and challenges. First the good stuff: A face vise will generally open and close rapidly and smoothly, sometimes by pulling a trigger on the screw, or sometimes by rotating the main vise screw counterclockwise for half a turn or so. These vises, called quick-release vises, can adapt to parts of wildly varying size in a jiffy.

More good stuff: The jaws are cast iron or malleable iron, which makes them fairly stiff and robust. Cast iron face vises generally require little upkeep and are quick to install.

All these nice features make the cast iron face vise popular. In fact, in all the commercial shops I've been in, virtually every workbench had one. And when I started work at *Popular Woodworking* in 1996, every bench had an iron quick-release face vise. And so did my grandfather's bench. And my father's. In fact, I was unaware that any other vises existed.

But here's the truth: The typical iron face vise has serious limitations that are rarely discussed. It's not a conspiracy cooked up by vise manufacturers. I just think that woodworkers have adapted to the form and developed clever ways to work around its warts.

So what's wrong with them? The biggest problem is they don't excel at clamping long boards vertically – like when you want to cut dovetails or tenons on an end. The vise's screw and parallel bars interfere with the clamping capacity of the vise. You're lucky if you can reliably clamp anything wider than 5". And if you try to use one corner of the vise to clamp something wide and long, you're in for a rude shock. The jaws will rack under pressure, so you can't clamp the work securely without putting a vise block (a block of wood that has the same thickness as your workpiece) on the opposite corner of the vise. And even with a vise block, you still can only grab one edge of the work and the other edge is free to shake about. So you clamp that side to the front edge of your workbench – assuming the jaws of the vise and the front edge of your bench are in the same plane.

And that's just for starters. You really should line the vise's jaws with something softer so you don't mar your work. Some people glue leather to the jaws. Other people secure plywood *skins* to the cast iron jaws. The jaws themselves can be a liability. I've scratched a number of plane soles on the iron jaw, chipped a few chisel edges and extracted a few saw teeth.

The best solution I found to these myriad issues was to add a long, thick wooden jaw to the movable jaw of the vise. This gave me more clamping capacity thanks to the added length of the jaw, and it kept my work surrounded by some extra wood, which protected the tools.

taste for the peccadilloes of all the idiosyncratic forms out there. There are a lot of weird configurations in the world, from a table with no vises at all to the bench with a vise on every corner.

So let's start with first principles when you consider a vise. I think the first question you need to ask yourself is not how many vises you need, but if you need a vise at all.

Early benches didn't have the quick-release, iron-and-steel behemoths we use today. Early woodworkers used gravity, force and simple machines to solve workholding challenges, and they solved those problems well. Working on a bench without a vise is an interesting experience. A crochet on the left corner constrains work on edge; a series of pegs or a sliding deadman supports the work from below. For working on the faces of boards, a planing stop does the dirty work with the benchtop supporting the length of your board.

So why do vises exist if you don't need them? They're handy, though not as useful as you might suspect. They can pinch small work to hold it for sanding, planing, rasping or chiseling, but when it comes to other common tasks, metal bench vises are a challenge you have to work around. So with that in mind, let's take a look at the most common metal vise around. Most people call it the face vise.

THE NEXT FRONTIER: My next bench will use these wooden vise screws. They feed remarkably fast and have less slop in the mechanism than my metal vise screws. They also are more fragile, harder to come by and require you to fabricate some basic vise parts.

So why not buy one of those face vises that requires you to make the wooden jaw? These imported vises are rarely quick-release vises, but they are a bit less expensive. I've installed and used three or four of these and have found them OK, but not perfect. You need to install a long, thick and stiff jaw for them to be effective. That's not a big deal, but I have found them to be more prone to racking: I was reaching for the vise blocks more with a wooden face vise than I was with an iron face vise with an accessory wooden jaw.

If you're a real traditionalist, you might be tempted to try a wooden-screw face vise. You make these yourself with a screwbox and tap (and a few cottage industries will make them for you), or you can dig up a vintage one sometimes. These vises can have a couple idiosyncrasies. One is that they use a rectangular section of wood that's parallel to the screw to keep the vise jaws parallel to the benchtop. That's the theory, at least. The examples I've tried (and based on reports from my hard-core traditional woodworking buddies) are tricky to manage.

And some vintage versions of these vises lack a garter – this is a locking ring that keeps the screw married to the jaw. If you don't have a garter, then you have to manually slide the jaw back toward you after you back off the screw.

All in all, I think the cast iron face vise is a fair choice for a workbench. You can always remove it. But before you automatically choose one, it's good to look at what the other vises have to offer.

Shoulder Vises

The shoulder vise shows up on many European benches at the left end of the bench in the face-vise position. It is like a giant letter L that is stuck to the front of the bench. There is a clamping screw through the L that presses your work against the front edge of the benchtop.

It's a remarkable vise, particularly for dovetailing drawers. Because of the arrangement of the screw, there is nothing to interfere or obstruct clamping below the benchtop. That means you can clamp long work that goes all the way to the floor and work an end of the board with ease. With most of these shoulder vises, you have the ability to clamp right at the center of a 12"-wide board without racking the jaws – that's quite a feat for any vise. Once your boards get wider (and especially as they approach the width of a typical case piece) you are going to have to add a clamp to your setup to hold the piece against

the front of the benchtop. This arrangement is typical for most vises with a couple exceptions.

The vise also works as a typical face vise for holding one end of a long board for planing (a portable bench slave typically supports the far end of the board). And it handles small tapered pieces beautifully.

The only disadvantage I've ever pinned down on the shoulder vise is that it is more complex to construct and install than a quick-release vise or a wooden leg vise. Nor is the vise a simple retrofit to an existing bench. The vise generally requires its own (fifth) leg that is tied into the trestle base of the workbench. The cantilevered section of the vise is typically bolted to the benchtop with a very long threaded rod.

When I first used one, I was concerned that it would force me to lean forward when dovetailing. The vise assembly does, after all, stick out a foot from the front end of the main benchtop. But my concerns were for naught. I approached the work from the same position as I did with any typical vise. There is some close work that isn't as elegant as I'd liked. When chamfering or shaping the ends of boards, I would

WORTH THE EXTRA LEG: Woodworkers who like hand-cutting dovetails like shoulder vises, such as this version made by Louis Bois. These vises are much better as original equipment than they are as an add-on.

SUPER – TO A POINT: My twin-screw vise at the end of the bench is great for dovetailing – as long as I don't have stock that is wider than the space between the screws. Then I'm stuck.

sometimes strike the bench screw or the cantilevered section of the vise. There are probably ways to work around this problem, but I simply moved my work to a traditional face to finish the job.

Twin-screw Vises

Yet another style of face vise is the twin screw. I have hundreds of hours of experience with a twin-screw vise, and here is my short assessment. Twin-screw vises are a lot like my collegiate experiments with Southern Comfort: Both work sweetly on the mind and make you think that anything is possible (tapers, dovetails, tenons, a Pulitzer). But when you reach their limit, everything goes south in a hurry.

Twin-screws excel at clamping wide material for dovetailing right up until you reach the maximum space between the vise's two screws. If you cross that limit, you're kinda sunk. Regular face vises, leg vises and shoulder vises can be rigged with the help of a clamp or sliding deadman to clamp boards of any width, as long as you are willing to live with some extra steps and inconvenience. You can set a face vise on one edge of your work and then a clamp across the benchtop to hold the other edge of a wide board.

With a twin screw, you generally have little leeway once you reach the vise's limit. Clamping on the vise's corners outside the protective confines of the screws is a bit of a pain on many of these vises. And if you have the twin screw mounted on the end of the bench instead of the face, you're truly out of luck.

There are some other personality quirks to the twin screw. Releasing the screws can become a two-handed operation with some vises and some setups, and you end up using one of your knees to keep the work from dashing to the floor while you release the pressure.

The twin screws (even the modern ones with the screws linked by bicycle chain) can be a bit fussy to keep the jaws parallel and everything moving smoothly. And old-school wooden ones require a bit of skill to manipulate – some of them don't have garters and the screws operate independently.

It might not sound it, but I quite like twin-screw vises. When set up and used properly, they are a pure joy for dovetailing, tenoning and working the edges of boards. Lots of other woodworkers over the years have also agreed because this style of vise is a common sight on the left front corner of early benches in particular.

Leg Vises

You don't see a lot of leg vises on modern-day benches. Perhaps one reason is that they can require two separate adjustments for one clamping operation. As you advance the screw of a leg vise (one adjustment), there is a separate guide at the floor that helps keep the jaws parallel (the second adjustment). When you reach your desired clamping range, you insert a pin through one of the holes in the parallel guide and advance the screw some more. The jaw then pivots on your pin and is levered onto your work with remarkable force.

This type of leg vise requires some stooping and some extra movements, so it's little wonder that woodworkers and manufacturers came up with devices that eliminated the extra steps required by the parallel guide. Among the fancier leg vises, these enhancements took the form of a scissor device near the floor that kept the jaws in parallel. There were also some other devices that would do the job, including a second screw with a flat plate that spun on it like a jam nut on a drill press's depth stop.

Leg vises – which are almost always in the face vise position – have their rewards. They can clamp a flat piece against the bench's leg all the way to the floor. If you mount them on an angled leg, you can increase the width they can clamp all the way to the floor without hitting the screw – a 7"-wide leg vise at a 20° angle will clamp an 8"-wide workpiece vertically all the way to the floor. That's great for dovetailing drawer sides.

They are the best vise I've ever used for clamping doors, windows, face frames and long boards so you can work on their edges. They are inexpensive and easy to make. And you can simply unscrew them to remove them from the bench if you ever want to try a different vise arrangement. They also play nicely with a crochet for working on the edges of boards.

And as to the stooping, I don't have back problems so it's an irritation more than a pain. Usually, I'm working on $3/4$- or $7/8$"-thick materials, which use the same hole in the parallel guide. So I'm not futzing with the thing as much as I thought when I first built it.

Tail Vises – Sometimes Called an End Vise

An end vise can actually be a number of different kinds of vises. What they all have in common is that they are mounted on the end of the

AN IDEAL ANGLE: A leg vise that's angled at 20° can grip wide boards all the way to the floor. This one handles boards up to 8" wide – perfect for most drawers.

PERCHED FOR PLANING: You don't need a vise to work across the grain or at an angle to the grain. Thin wooden strips cinched by hold-fasts stop the work from sliding side-to-side. A planing stop at the end prevents the board from shooting into space.

NO WONDER THEY'RE POPULAR: The Veritas Wonder Dog is a good substitute for an end vise. There are limitations – they're tricky to use with thin work. But for the price and the simplicity, they're good workers.

bench and are in line with a number of dog holes in the benchtop. There are a number of forms. I'll deal with them in an evolutionary manner, starting with the simplest form: No vise.

I ran into this arrangement when perusing my old books on house carpentry and even older books on French woodworking. The early French books showed no familiar rows of bench-dog holes. Just a few holes for holdfasts and a planing stop or two. You work long boards using the forward and downward force of the tool (plus the sometimes-helpful gravity) to immobilize the work against the planing stop. This arrangement, which I have tried to master for some time, requires skill with the tool. It requires you to skew the plane as you work to keep the stock against the stop and not careening across the benchtop. Wider boards are harder than narrow ones to control.

How do you work across the grain? I've used thin wooden strips secured by my holdfasts to act as stops. It works, but not as well as some other solutions.

A house carpenter's bench in *Audels Carpenters and Builders Guide* offers only a long row of bench-dog holes. No vise mechanism at the end to pinch the work. And no text to indicate how the dog holes should be used. My first thought was that you could use a couple wedges and two dogs to secure your work. And you probably could.

More likely, however, is that the house carpenter would use a vise-like portable metal device that would attach to the benchtop and grip the work from behind when a lever was engaged. This hook-from-behind device – sometimes called a bench knife stop – is not made anymore. But it is the missing link to the next step in the chain: The Veritas Wonder Dog.

The Wonder Dog, invented in 1992 and patented in 1996 by Lee Valley Tools, is one of those few commercial products that lives up to (and perhaps even exceeds) its ambitious name. What is it? The Wonder Dog is a movable tail vise. It drops into any $^3/_4$"-diameter round dog hole in your benchtop. Once in place, you turn a small brass handle and it advances a screw that is attached to a rectangular dog. With a Wonder Dog, a round bench dog and a row of $^3/_4$" holes you can have an instant tail-vise setup that works for nearly all of your benchtop clamping needs.

Yes, the Wonder Dog has a couple inherent quirks in its design. First, the screw that advances and retracts the dog has a fine thread, about 14 teeth per inch. I wish the thing would advance and retract faster – I've spent a lot of time screwing and unscrewing. The second detail is that the movable rectangular dog sits $^5/_8$" above the benchtop. That's fine when planing $^3/_4$"-thick material, but a bit tricky when doing thin work. I've mounted accessory wooden jaws to the Wonder Dog, but you still have to steer carefully around the dog because a handplane sole is going to be 9" long or more with smoothing planes – even longer with jacks and jointers. These are minor flaws in the Wonder Dog system, all in all, especially if you stack them up against not having a tail vise at all.

UNUSUAL BUT EFFECTIVE: A so-called wagon vise does a lot of things that more complex end vises do. It clamps assemblies and can work as a spreader to take things apart.

KEEP YOUR DOGS CLOSE: It's tempting to space your dogs based on the maximum throw of your vise. Resist this lazy urge. Keep them 3" apart and you'll be messing with your vise less and working wood more.

Wonder Dogs also do a lot of other benchtop tasks: I've used them as spreader clamps to dismantle a door assembly. You can also (with a couple Wonder Dogs and regular dogs) clamp up many oddball shapes. I typically use them to secure benchtop tools, such as my router table, temporarily to the benchtop.

The next simplest kind of tail vise is called a wagon vise in some French accounts. It essentially is a movable dog that rides in a slot in the benchtop. This dog also is in line with a row of bench dog holes in the benchtop. It's not a common vise, though I have yet to understand why, especially after building and using a couple. The wagon vise's strength is its simplicity and the fact that it has but a few moving parts. You can move the dogs up and down to clamp really thin work – which gives it one advantage over the Wonder Dog. But the wagon vise serves only one line of bench dog holes and cannot be moved around the bench for unusual situations. To make one (which is shown later in this book), you need only purchase a metal bench screw, which is a little more expensive than a Wonder Dog. The remainder of the components are wooden.

Your next simplest option is a quick-release face vise. It can be mounted on the end of the workbench and function as a tail vise, if it is equipped with a dog. Even if it doesn't come with a dog, you can add an accessory wooden jaw to the vise (you really have to do this anyway to keep your work supported) and equip that with a dog or two. The advantage to using a quick-release vise is that it's an easy way to install a fully functional tail vise. And you get the additional bonus of being able to clamp your work between the jaws at the tail end of your bench. I've found that's a handy spot for some unusual sawing and planing chores.

The downside to this arrangement is mostly cost. Quick-release vises are going to set you back some coin. There's another disadvantage to this vise that you might run into if your dog holes are spaced far apart on your benchtop. When clamping some boards, you'll have to extend the vise's jaws out to the point that your work will be unsupported over part of its length. When planing thin material, this can be a problem. The solution is to keep your dog holes spaced closely together. I typically put them on 3" or 4" centers. One of my first benches had a quick-release vise as a tail vise and the jaws extended out about 10" or 12", once you took the accessory jaw into

consideration. In an attempt to be a clever (but lazy and foolhardy) boy, I drilled my bench-dog holes on 10" centers. As a result, some boards would have very little support. It didn't take me long to realize the error of my ways.

Some modern workbenches mount a twin-screw vise on the end of the bench and use it as an end vise. I've done this as well. The twin-screw tail vise usually has two or three dogs in the movable jaw, which can be in line with two or three rows of dog holes in the benchtop. This arrangement allows you to clamp circular work, primarily, though some plain-old odd-shaped work can be accommodated as well. (I've had great luck clamping Windsor arm bows with this rig.) You should keep your bench dog holes spaced closely together to avoid the same lack-of-support problem when using a quick-release vise in this position.

I also was told by some fellow craftsmen that using a twin-screw as an end vise is inherently bad for the vise. You end up stressing one of the vise screws most of the time with the other one racking the vise and not being under pressure. I scoffed at this notion until one day – after about five years of daily use – I advanced the screw on some work and heard a large thunk from inside the mechanism. I took the vise apart and found that one of the beefy screw heads that mounts the vise to the moving jaw had been sheared off. A defective screw perhaps? Or was it the result of my stressing out the vise? The rest of the vise appeared to be in good shape. I replaced the broken screw with a beefier one and went back to work. Two years later, no problems. Yet. Veritas, the manufacturer of my twin-screw, shows the vise being used in this position on the end of the bench and says nothing about stressing one screw.

"A simple bench is like Tuscan pasta soup. You think it will be better if you add more stuff. But getting the basics right is way more important, and the extras won't make up for poorly prepared stock."

—Adam Cherubini

PERFECT FOR PANELS: Tasking a twin screw to be an end vise is great if you work with wide panels or circular tabletops. If you use it only for clamping narrow boards you might be stressing the vise unnecessarily.

And then there is the classic tail vise: an L-shaped section of the bench that slides left and right at the end-vise position. It has a number of bench-dog holes (four to six holes is typical) that line up with the other bench-dog holes in the top. The vise opens and closes by turning a fast-moving screw. It keeps the work (almost) fully supported and you can even clamp some workpieces between the vise's big jaw and the benchtop – narrow drawers and drawer sides fit nicely. You also can use the tail vise as a spreader clamp, like the wagon vise or Wonder Dog vise setup.

On paper, a traditional tail vise looks like an obvious good choice. But once you try installing one, or work with one that droops, it doesn't seem so ideal. Such vises are the most complex forms available, and when they do droop, the work can shift around in undesirable ways. That is not to say that you should dismiss tail vises out of hand. They are both useful and popular forms. Instead, I encourage you to take a balanced view and investigate the merits and drawbacks of every style of end vise.

For all the forms of the tail vise or end vise, there is one thing you must be careful to avoid: overclamping. All the tail vise forms are capable of bowing your stock under pressure. Once you flatten the face of the board and release it from the vise mechanism, you'll find the board bows in the opposite direction. So snug the vise just enough to secure the work and no more. It takes practice, but it ensures your work will end up flat and true.

If you are having trouble getting things secured flat, try lining the faces of your bench dogs with some leather or suede. The leather adds grip and allows you to use less clamping pressure.

Sliding Deadmen and Slaves

Though a bench jack (sometimes called a sliding deadman) isn't usually a vise, it is for workholding. It slides along the front of a workbench and supports work that's too long to be held by the face vise alone. The jack can also be a stand that is separate from the bench entirely – sometimes called a bench slave – with some kind of height-adjustable mechanism so you can support boards of many widths.

Another typical setup is to have a board built into the workbench that slides back and forth on a rail between the front legs. The board has holes that receive a peg. You place the peg in a hole that will support the door or wide board that you want to work on and then slide

MIND THE GAP: When you clamp work with an end vise, the difference between correct clamping and over-clamping is a few degrees of spin on the vise handle. When clamping, tighten the vise until it doesn't move and isn't bowed. Then go to work.

the jack into position. Clamp one corner of your work in the face vise, and you can then work on the edge of the board or assembly.

English workbenches would approach this problem differently. Instead of a slave or jack, the bench would be built with a wide front apron. This apron would be bored with as many holes as needed for pegs. This front apron, of course, prevents you from applying a clamp to the top at the front of the bench.

There are other tricks that work quite well. The front legs can be bored with holes and you can secure long boards of scrap to the legs with holdfasts. Then you rest the work on the ledge of scrap. You also can use two handscrew clamps to support the tail end of the board with the front corner held by the face vise. Or, if you have your benchtop perched on a bank of drawers, you can pull a drawer out to support your boards. This works well.

Bench Stops

On a traditional workbench, the front left corner of the benchtop is home to a bench stop (sometimes called a bench hook, a confusing term that also means a jig for crosscutting small parts). The bench stop can be wood or metal and can be moved up and down in the benchtop with a lever, a screw or a mallet. The stop immobilizes your work while planing. Raise the stop a little to plane thin work. Raise the stop a great deal (mine goes up to 6" above the benchtop) to work

YOU SHOULD KNOW JACK: A sliding bench jack supports long and wide work from below. Sometimes called a deadman, it is infinitely adjustable.

SEPARATE SUPPORT: If your bench isn't capable of supporting long or wide work, you can make a bench slave to do the job. This one clamps in a tail vise; it also could be freestanding on a base.

PINCH IN A PINCH: Two handscrews can hold the tail end of your work. This isn't really the way you want to work, day-in and day-out. But it is a good trick to have when you are in a bind. Or need to get into a bind.

boards on edge. This is a nice feature: The work is fully supported by your benchtop and is easy to control as you work the edge.

Some of the stops are smooth. Some are toothed, which will bite into the end grain of your work. There are dozens of commercial versions that you might stumble upon at flea markets or on vintage benches. But the bench stop does not have to be a piece of toothed metal to be effective. In fact, the oldest bench stops were made entirely of wood, as were many of the British-style workbench appliances and jigs from the 19th and 20th centuries. Once you make a few wooden stops that clamp in your face vise or drop into dog holes, you'll probably put the metal ones aside. Why? Once you bang your plane into a metal one or scrape your plane's sole against the stop for the first time, I'm sure you'll consider the merits of wood. This is from hard-won experience.

That said, bench stops for thin work are (in my experience) ideal when they are metal. A couple screws driven into a workbench act as finely adjustable stops for thin work – down to about 1/8"-thick stock. Need to plane something thinner? Use escutcheon pins.

When you look at old drawings of bench stops, the illustrations typically feature one stop. This is ideal for narrow stock but is a trick to use when working on panels. Some benches will feature two stops: Raise one for narrow stock and two for panels. Working on wide panels is a task typically performed by the furniture maker. Joiners (who made doors, sash windows and mouldings for homes) could probably manage with one stop.

Another option is a planing board. These ingenious trays are essentially large flat surfaces with raised stops around the edges. They might have adjustable planing stops at one end. You'd mount the planing board to your benchtop, perhaps with clamps, holdfasts or dropping it into dog holes. Then you'd work against the planing stops when working with the grain, the far lip when working across the grain, or into a corner when working diagonally.

The other bonus to a planing board is that you don't have to worry much about your benchtop's flatness – just the flatness of the planing board. And if the planing board casts (another name for warp) you pitch it and make another.

Holdfasts and Hold-downs

Other bench accessories for the benchtop are devices that hold the work down using single-point pressure from above. The oldest form of this is probably some sort of rope that is cinched by the worker's foot. But the earliest furniture-making and joiner's books discuss the holdfast as the tool of choice.

Traditional holdfasts are a steel hook – many look like a shepherd's crook. The shaft drops into a round closely fitted hole in the benchtop. Pound the hook with a mallet. The hook wedges into the hole and secures the work. Pound the back of the crook and it releases its grip on your work instantly.

To the modern woodworker, this must seem like some sort of cruel joke. Modern holdfasts (with few exceptions) are worthless. We've had some come in that were made of cast grey iron (two strikes and they split). Some in ductile iron with a steel shaft (they seem like a good idea until you try to use them, and they don't work at all). Others are finely cast and seem to almost work. I'm speaking of the Jorgensen's here.

Style E

COMMERCIAL PERFECTION: If I didn't have to work on the edges of wide boards, this bench is a near-perfect specimen. In this old catalog, Hammacher, Schlemmer & Co. advertised this bench as handmade using 4"-square timbers. Sign me up.

The Stanley No. 203 – Better than a Peg

Usually a sliding bench jack uses a peg to support the work. This is pretty much all the support you need because when you are working on the edge of a board most of the forces involved are directed at the floor. However, the peg solution can allow the board to flop forward and back quite a bit.

Of course, there is an accessory from Stanley Works that solves this problem.

In 1915, Stanley patented a bench bracket that combines the support of a wooden peg with the holding power of an F-style clamp. It was manufactured as the Stanley No. 203 (also the number used for a Stanley block plane, by the way). And this item turns up at flea markets and on eBay. I bought a couple of them to try with the Roubo bench jack to see if they were useful.

The Stanley No. 203 works best in a 1"-diameter hole in an apron or bench jack that is ⅞" thick. Use thicker stock and the No. 203 won't grab. Use thinner and the bracket will not create a square ledge for your work. That was my first problem with the No. 203; my material ended up being a little under ⅞", so the clamp head came in at an angle to my boards. As a result, sometimes the head would dent the work on one edge.

While staring at the bracket, I noticed a small hole at the bottom of the device. It looked like there could be some sleeve of metal inside it. Could this small hole be used in some way to square the bracket in its hole? With no answers coming to mind, I decided to ask the U.S. Government. Patented devices have nice drawings and sometimes instruction-like information on file at the U.S. Patent Office. However, the interface to search there isn't the friendliest.

But there's help. The Directory of American Tool and Machinery Patents (DATAMP for short) makes looking up patented old tools easy. The DATAMP (datamp.org) is run by volunteers from the OldWWMachines and OldTools mailing lists. You can search patents very easily here. Type the patent date (usually cast into the tool) into the search engine. If you know the patent number, that will work, too. There are other ways to search the 30,000 patents in the Advanced Search function. (Google also has a patent-search function now that works just as well.)

I typed in the patent date (03-16-1915) and immediately had beautiful drawings of the No. 203, plus drawings of

IT SUPPORTS & SECURES: A Stanley No. 203 bench bracket is like a peg that supports long work. The clamping function presses the work against the sliding deadman. When used properly (watch that clamp pressure) it is effective.

a similar bracket that may not have been made commercially and two pages of details on how the bracket works. The small hole at the bottom of the bracket is for a nail, according to the application, "to steady the lower end of the clamp…." Hmmm, that's not my problem. So I made a little shim and am going to epoxy that to the bracket tonight. That should fix it. And the material in the hole that I thought could be a sleeve? Just junk.

After a couple years of experience, I have found the No. 203 to be useful. When I'm dovetailing boards that are too wide for my face vise, I use the No. 203 in the topmost pegs to clamp the workpiece to the bench jack. But mostly, I like the No. 203 because it holds wide boards or doors motionless and in perfect position when I am working their edges or mortising hinges in place.

One little detail: Don't clamp the No. 203 directly to your work. The pad on the vise screw will ding your work. I wish the pad would pivot. Use a small scrap of wood between the No. 203 and the workpiece – just like you would with a holdfast.

EDGE WORK ON THE TOP: Many times you can work the edges of individual boards by bracing them against the bench stop and planing the edge. This is faster than clamping the board up with a sliding dead-man – plus you get more support.

WHACK A HOLDFAST: These traditional holdfasts work by striking the hooked area. You release them by striking the back of the device. They work well – usually. Some workbenches have trouble with them but most do not. Just remember to keep your hole tight on the holdfast's shaft.

OLD SCHOOL STOP: This metal stop, made by a blacksmith, drops into a wooden bench stop. The toothed end will bite into your work, which is no big deal if you build period furniture where you hide the end grain. More modern work is trickier with this stop.

The best pound-'em holdfasts are those made from wrought iron or cold rolled steel by a blacksmith. I've had about six holdfasts made for me in a variety of patterns from wrought iron that was salvaged from the beaches of Northern California – how romantic – or cold rolled steel from a village blacksmith in Alaska.

The two common patterns are a holdfast with a pronounced curve and those that are basically an L shape. The curvy ones are great for holding work for mortising or sawing. Heck I use them to hold patterns to my benchtop for pattern-routing. The L-shaped ones are ideal for setups where a hand plane might be involved. The L-shaped ones keep a low profile to the bench, so you are less likely to plow into them with your plane. But mine don't seem to hold as tenaciously as the curvy ones.

Any blacksmith can make you a pair of holdfasts from scraps in about an hour. And it shouldn't be an expensive job either. If you go

this route, it's best if the smith has a workbench with some holes in it so you can try the holdfasts out yourself. When I got blacksmith Don Weber to make me a few, we were able to change the shape of each holdfast until it performed sweetly.

There also is a mass-manufactured holdfast that works well and is inexpensive. The *Tools for Working Wood* catalog sells a fine set under its Gramercy Tools line. They have a modern look but an old-school way of working. And the price is completely reasonable.

In general, here are the rules for holdfasts that require a beating: The thicker your benchtop, the less likely the holdfast will work. Holdfasts seem to work better in thin benchtops (though not too thin). Once you get a benchtop around 4" thick, the holdfasts get unpredictable. Really thin benches ($1^{1}/_{4}$" or so) also pose difficulties.

Second: The tighter the hole is on the shaft the more likely the holdfast will work. Loose holes require the holdfast to flex more before it will cinch down. A tight fit means the whole thing has to flex just a bit to get wedged in place.

Third: Holdfasts can be affected by the position of the stars, the humidity level or other factors outside your control. Sometimes (especially in thick tops) they simply will not work. When you come back the next day, they work fine. Sometimes, during a fussy period, I'll coax them to cinch down by angling them so they wedge against the end grain in the dog hole. Other times, this fails completely.

And so I keep a pair of Veritas Hold-Downs on my bench. These are bit slower to use than the holdfasts, and they aren't as showy as bashing a holdfast, but they always work. Turn the brass knob on top, and the ribbed shaft engages the hole. Turn the knob the other way, and the hold-down releases. Thin tops or thick tops, it matters not.

There are a bunch of other hold-downs on the market that are less expensive and also work using a screw principle, but they have major disadvantages. The main one is that you usually have to secure the hold-down to the benchtop with a threaded nut located beneath the benchtop. In truth, deep-throat F-style clamps are faster than these boys. But they are inexpensive. And now you know why.

NEVER FAIL: The Veritas Hold-Down never lets me down. The one thing I don't like about it is the barbs on the shaft sometimes hang up on the hole – making it hard to extract the Hold-Down. These are a bit slower to use than a hit-me harder holdfast, but speed isn't everything.

SECURED FROM THE SIDE: Battens are ideal for restraining your work from the side. This allows you to plane or saw across the grain without having to clamp down your work. Using the force of the tool to hold your work speeds you up.

A ROUND RETROFIT: When you add dogs to your workbench after its completion, you are typically limited to using round dogs. Round dogs are best at gripping stuff that's low to the bench, and at odd angles.

You rarely use a holdfast by itself and directly on the work. When securing pieces for mortising, a small scrap under the pad of the holdfast or hold-down protects the work from denting. When using a holdfast with planes, I generally use them in conjunction with scraps that are thin, narrow and long, typically ¼" x 2" x 18". I was turned onto these so-called battens by other woodworkers who have gone the old-style woodworking route.

A couple other readers of our magazine have pointed out to me that these battens – useful as they are – are not shown or discussed in early woodworking texts (except in one old plate I've found that's in Chapter 3 of this book). I couldn't imagine working without battens, but early woodworkers might have had a better way that relied more on skill than scraps. Sometimes these old drawings can be misleading. There are early engravings that show woodworkers using holdfasts directly on marquetry work without a pad to protect it – even though the text discusses using a pad. Illustrators make mistakes, too.

Holes and the Dogs that Inhabit Them

Most workbenches have some sort of dog-hole system. Usually this can be anything from a wide array of holes across the top to a couple holes in line with the face vise. The most typical arrangement is to have a line of holes across the length of the benchtop that is in line with whatever end-vise system is in place. The line of holes is usually nearer the front edge than it is to the centerline of the benchtop. This is ideal for securing boards of a typical cabinetmaking width (8" or so these days) without the boards hanging over the front of the benchtop.

The dog holes can be round (¾" diameter is the norm) or square with a rectangular section at the top where the dog emerges from the benchtop. The dogs can be metal or wood. So what's best?

The round holes are the best solution for any bench where the holes are a retrofit. It's a lot easier to bore a round hole with an auger bit than it is to chop an angled mortise for a square dog. If you are building your bench from scratch, you can consider both. I personally

COW MEETS DOG: A small scrap of leather adds gripping power to a wooden dog. I buy little scraps of leather or suede from the craft store or Tandy Leather stores. I never cut up my wife's shoes.

DOGS WITH BITE: The steel dogs with their pointy fangs do grip better, but sometimes at the expense of bruising your work. With practice, you learn their limits.

prefer square wooden dogs, if given a choice. Holes for square dogs can be built into a bench lamination during construction – routing slightly angled dados in the main top slab and the front apron before glue-up is a typical way to do it.

And why wooden dogs over the more durable metal ones? The wooden dogs won't damage your tools if you slip, and having four square dog faces to work against can be very handy. Plus, I've found that a well-made wooden dog with a wooden spring moves up and down faster than other breeds of dogs do. Some people contend that metal dogs hold better. Well, that's true. But when you are applying the maximum grip with a metal dog, I bet you are bowing or marring your work. I find that wooden dogs hold great. Here's a tip to make a wooden dog hold even better: Glue a rectangle of leather to the face of the dog (yellow glue works great). You will be impressed.

The round dog is typically metal, which can be a hazard to your tools. And it is a bit slower to move up and down in the round holes. Of course, speed isn't everything.

Benchtop Height

Many bench builders worry about the height of the bench's working surface from the floor. There are a wide variety of rules, guidelines and advice on the matter. The bottom line is that you have to make the bench fit you and your work. And in the end, there are no ironclad rules. Really. I wish there were. Some people like low benches; some like them high.

So consider this advice as a good place to start. After taking in my crackpot theories, your next stop should be a friend's house or a woodworking supply store to use their benches and get a feel for what feels like a right height (it could be as simple as having a bad back that prohibits you from a low bench, or a love for wooden handplanes that dictates you must use a 31"-high bench).

Here's how I came to my best bench height: I started with a workbench that was 36" high, which seemed right for someone who is 6'-3⅝" tall. And for machine woodworking I was spot-on. The high

bench brought the work close to my eyes, allowing me to see exactly what I was doing with the router as I wasted away hinge gains and mortised stock. I loved the high bench. Everything in the world was right by my eyes and I never stooped to work.

Then my love of handwork reared its ugly head.

Once you start getting into hand tools, a high bench becomes less attractive. I started out with a jack plane and a few smoothing planes. They worked OK with a high bench, but I became fatigued fast. My arms would get tired, weak and wobbly while planing, even after months of practice. I knew something was wrong because I'm not a weak fellow.

After reading the screed on bench heights, I thought about lowering the height of my 36" bench. It seemed radical surgery. But one day I got the nerve and sawed 2" off the four legs. Those two inches changed my attitude toward planing. Something serious in the equation had changed. I couldn't put my finger on it at the time, but here is how I see the world from 34".

The 34" bench height allowed me to do several things while planing. I could lock my left arm which grasped the front knob, and shift my weight to the tool, which held it down during the cut. And I could use my long leg muscles to propel the plane forward at that height. I found that I used my arms less to push the tool forward. The arm muscles kept the tool under control and on track. But it was the rest of my body that assisted in moving the tool forward.

Now, before you go to the shop and build your next bench at 34" high, stop for a minute. It might not be right for you. Do you use wooden stock planes? If so, you need to consider that the wooden body can hold your arms about 3"- 4" higher off the workbench than a metal plane can. As a result, a wooden plane user's workbench should be lower than one who favors metal-bodied planes. In my work with wooden planes, 31" is a good working height.

Also, if you use wooden-stock planes, a key part of using them correctly (according to my experience) has been to get on top of them to press them down against the work. This is as good a reason as ever to

GET OVER IT: Wooden planes work better (for me) if I'm able to use my body weight to press the tool down into the work. I have more control and less fatigue. The mass of a metal plane does some of this for you, but at the expense of being more weight to push around.

VANITY OR WORKBENCH? These workbenches are ideal for storing tools, but aren't designed for holding your work steady. You can do nice work on these benches, but you'll be solving workholding problems as often as you are woodworking problems that crop up during a project.

get to know someone who has a good shop you can visit and discuss your ideas with. You cannot make this decision on paper alone. You must make it with the help of a couple trips to a shop along with some thoughtful questions. The rewards are worth it.

But there are other factors you must consider when settling on the bench's height. How tall are you? If you are over 6' tall, as I am, you will be best served to try to scale your bench just a bit higher. Start a bit higher and cut it down if it feels too high after a while. And prop it up on some blocks of wood if it's too low. Experiment. It's not a highboy; it's a workbench.

Here are some other things to consider: Do you work with machinery? If so, a bench that is 34" from the floor – or a bit lower – is a good idea. The top of a table saw is typically 34" from the floor, so a workbench could be (at the most) a great outfeed table or (at the least) not in the way of your crosscutting and ripping.

Of course, everyone wants to know where to start. They want a ballpark idea. So here it is. Stand up straight and drop your arms against your sides in a relaxed manner. Measure from the floor to the place where your pinky finger joins your hand. That has been the sweet spot for me. It might not be right for you, but it is right for someone who uses metal-bodied planes, has really long arms and is 6' 3⅝". And likes cats and osso buco.

It's all very personal.

The Misuse of the Space Under the Top

We had a phase at *Popular Woodworking* magazine where we tried to design a cup holder into every project. It started innocently with a sling chair for the deck. Who doesn't want a cool beverage next to them? Then there was the dartboard. What goes better with darts than a beer? (Besides an adhesive bandage for the resulting puncture wounds, that is.) I think we came to our senses when we designed cup holders into a Gustav Stickley Morris chair reproduction. Do you really need a large-drink hole in your Morris chair? I didn't think so.

The point is to illustrate a trend in workbench design that's troubling. It's a knee-jerk reaction to a common American complaint:

We don't think we have enough space in our shops to store all our tools and accessories. And how do we solve this problem with our workbenches? By designing them like kitchen storage cabinets with a countertop work surface.

This design approach gives us lots of drawers below the benchtop, which is great for storing all the little tools and accessories you reach for everyday. What it also does is makes your bench a pain in the hinder to use for many common operations.

Filling the space below the benchtop prohibits you from using decent holdfasts or hold-downs. There's just not enough space below the benchtop, typically, to make a holdfast or hold-down function. Believe me, I've made this error myself when designing a bench for my home shop. It's agony to admit the stupidity of the mistake.

If you build drawers below the top, how will you clamp objects to the benchtop to work with them? Typically, the banks of drawers below the benchtop prohibit a typical F-style clamp from sneaking in there and lending a hand with the set-up. So you can't use a typical clamp to affix a router template to the bench. And the drawer bank prohibits you from clamping things to the workbench from above. There are ways around these problems (a tail vise comes to mind). But the tail vise can be a challenge to install, set and use.

You can try to cheat (as I have) and install the drawer bank so there is a substantial space underneath the benchtop for holdfasts and clamps. This can work with holdfasts, but clamps come in such a variety of lengths that it's hard to anticipate everything you will need to clamp there. And that's why I like workbenches that are wide open in the undercarriage department.

That said, you can incorporate some storage in your bench that will not compromise basic functions. Early 18th-century woodworking texts by A.J. Roubo illustrate a bench that has two drawers below the rails of the bench – essentially they are tucked between the floor and the bottom rails of the bench. This bank of drawers is unlikely to interfere with any clamping and will hold a fair number of tools.

And for those of you who have one single drawer below the bench, I've been there as well. It always seemed that the drawer was right

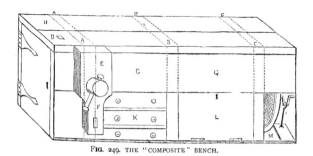

AH (BATHROOM) VANITY: This bench from the Wm. P. Walter's Sons 1888 catalog shows a bench I hope never to work on. There's no way (none) to hold boards for cross-grain work. There's no way to work edges. And that backboard stops you from clamping across the bench (a trick that usually gets you around other problems).

DIG A DEEPER HOLE: The storage cabinet below this benchtop holds lots of tools, but the holddown can't hold anything. The drawer bank is too close to the benchtop. So now what? Remove the drawer bank or get one of the inexpensive (and inconvenient) plastic holddowns.

NO NEED FOR CLAMPS: Wanting storage space in a bench is nothing new. This ridiculous bench – called the Composite Bench – was published in 1904. The authors suggest you mount a table saw in the top. It's proof that old designs can be as bad as new designs.

where a clamp needed to be. And one of the drawer sides happened to be under a dog hole, which wasn't my fault because it was a commercial bench. Plus the drawer filled up with sawdust that dropped through the dog holes. All in all, the one drawer was a bad idea.

The Support Structure Below the Top

Because wood seems expensive, it's tempting to build a bench with a thin top – or perhaps make the center of the top thin. If you look at inexpensive modern commercial workbenches, this is exactly the trend you'll see. The center section of the top is thin, just 2" or so, and there's a wide apron that bands the top and gives the illusion of beefiness. And the apron banding the top does indeed lend support.

Another common strategy is to build a thin top and then support it from below using a system of aprons, much like a dining table.

When you are drafting a plan for a workbench, these strategies seem sound and material-efficient. The problem is that a short period of work with these kinds of benches will point out a few limitations you should consider when you have an eraser nearby.

With the commercial benches that feature a thin top banded by wide boards, the risk is that the top can flex a little bit under heavy pounding or other loads. This is more of a concern with hand work than it is when using the bench with power tools.

However, it's also quite difficult to clamp your work to this style of benchtop using common F-style clamps. The wide edging around the top interferes with any clamping you might want to do that approaches the center of the benchtop. In fact, this thin top/wide apron configuration makes some setups almost impossible.

The thin top also reduces a workbench's weight – so the bench might be more likely to skitter across the floor under planing pressure – if you haven't bolted your bench to the floor.

The other sort of benchtop strategy, where you have a thin top supported by aprons (what I call the dining table workbench) has many of the same issues as the inexpensive commercial benches. The

aprons below the benchtop prevent the top from flexing without using a lot of material. But the aprons impede clamping. Maneuvering clamps around the aprons can be a challenge if the aprons are narrow; and clamping can be impossible if your aprons are wider than the length of the screw on the clamp.

So as you plan the support below your top, think of the benchtop as a three-dimensional clamping surface. Your clamps are going to interact with both the top surface of your benchtop as well as the underside. After working on benches built in both of the styles mentioned above (aprons below the top or a thin top banded by wider boards), I can say that these are the most frustrating benches to use, both with hand tools and with power tools.

That's why I usually prefer a benchtop that is thick (4" or so) and unsupported by aprons. This feature lends flexibility with clamping. It also allows you to retrofit vises to the bench easily. Say that you didn't add an end vise to your bench at first. If you wanted to add a quick-release vise to the end of the bench the aprons might get in the way of the screws and rods of the vise. If you don't have an apron, you only have to deal with interference from the legs.

There is, of course, an exception to every rule. The English-style workbench in this book breaks the above rules. It has extremely wide aprons and a thin top. You cannot clamp a thing with those aprons in the way. But because of the bench's system of dogs and its wagon vise you can clamp panels against the top. And with the help of holdfasts and the face vise, you can clamp boards on edge against the apron with ease. In short, it allows you to clamp boards to work faces, edges and ends. So it's a functional bench.

The English-style bench is what I prefer for woodworkers who need to make a bench that is material-efficient. The English bench uses less than half the wood of the similarly sized French bench in this book. Unlike your typical dining table workbench, the English bench doesn't have a top that overhangs the aprons, and that feature alone makes it a decent bench in my opinion.

Pl. 18

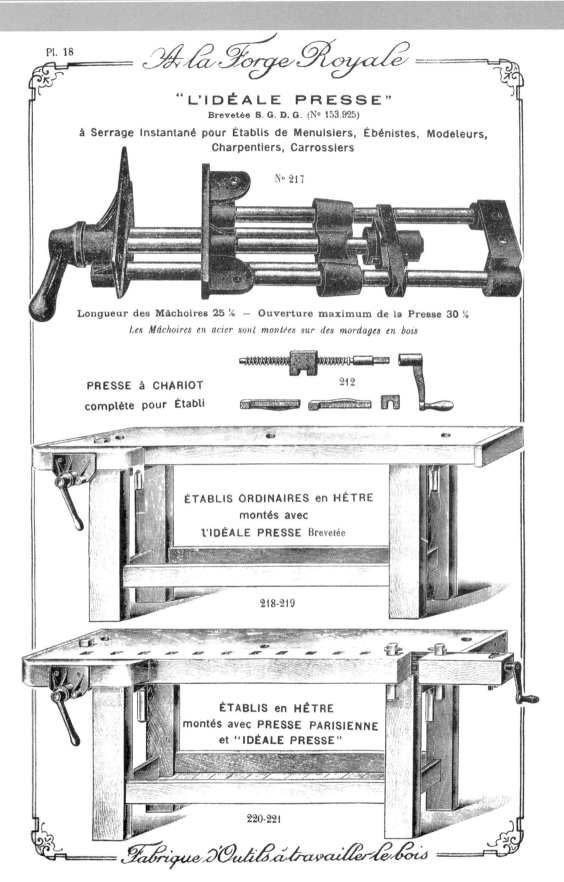

A la Forge Royale

"L'IDÉALE PRESSE"

Brevetée S. G. D. G. (No 153.925)

à Serrage Instantané pour Établis de Menuisiers, Ébénistes, Modeleurs, Charpentiers, Carrossiers

No 217

Longueur des Mâchoires 25 ‰ — Ouverture maximum de la Presse 30 ‰

Les Mâchoires en acier sont montées sur des mordages en bois

PRESSE à CHARIOT

complète pour Établi

212

ÉTABLIS ORDINAIRES en HÊTRE
montés avec
L'IDÉALE PRESSE Brevetée

218-219

ÉTABLIS en HÊTRE
montés avec PRESSE PARISIENNE
et "IDÉALE PRESSE"

220-221

Fabrique d'Outils à travailler le bois

IT'S A GIFT TO BE SIMPLE: There is a long list of vises you can put on a workbench. Perhaps that list is too long. Workholding should be as simple as possible. When you begin to devise jigs that fit in your workholding jigs, it's time to take stock of the way you grip your stock.

Chapter Three

Match Features to Functions

Here's the goal: Avoid unworkable workbenches. It sounds simple, but with all the different vises available, plus all the different designs for benches that are floating around, it's child's play to design a bench that is quite ridiculous.

Here's a quick example: I was talking to a guy who designs and builds custom workbenches, and he had a customer who wanted a workbench that had two twin-screw vises. One vise for the right end of the workbench that was matched to work with two long rows of dogs along the length of the benchtop. And the customer wanted the second twin-screw vise on the face of the bench that was matched to two more rows of dogs that were lined up across the width of the benchtop.

Now I'm certain that there are woodworkers who need this arrangement – perhaps someone who has to simultaneously work on a circular tabletop on one end of the bench and a Windsor chair seat at the other. And, in truth, I have seen a couple workbenches with two twin-screw vises (a quad-screw bench perhaps?) that made sense. But for most people who build cabinets and furniture, this setup is redundant in many ways and (as you'll see later in this chapter) neglects some functions of a bench that are critically necessary.

Making a misstep like this in designing a bench is common. When people begin working in the craft, the first thing they need to address is finding a place to work. Second on the list is obtaining a workbench to build things on (it's what all the books and magazines say you should do, and it beats building on the floor). If you haven't done much woodworking yet, your expectations and impressions of how a workbench should function and look will be colored by the fact that you haven't done much woodworking. So having two tail vises might seem logical. Or putting the face vise on the right corner of the benchtop might seem correct for an inexperienced right-hander.

To figure out the world of workbenches, you might take a class, go to a woodworking store to check out the commercial benches or even buy a book on workbenches. These are all good things to do, but these efforts might still lead you astray. Some woodworking schools and stores stock commercial workbenches that are designed to cost a certain number of dollars, even if they don't make sense. And many workbench books have designs in them that range from fantastic to fantastical, and it's up to you to figure out what is reasonable and what is the sideshow. The difference isn't always obvious. A hydraulic height-adjustable bench base can look like a good idea to a person who has never worked with one.

Go take a look at the workbenches on the floors of woodworking specialty stores. Vise? Check. Dog holes? Check. Though this might look like a useful workbench, its shortcomings would fill an entire page. For starters: How would you work on the edge of a typical cabinet door? Benches like this give you an instant place to work, but you will also quickly outgrow them. I see a lot of these workbenches pushed into corners of shops, being used as a tool stand. For less than the cost of the top of this bench, you can build a workbench that will stick with you the rest of your life.

Most woodworkers don't ask these questions. So the woodworker buys or builds a bench and starts working on it. And that's when the real education begins, and the shortcomings of the workbench (no workbench is perfect) become apparent. And so the woodworker buys or builds another bench, or he attempts a retrofit of the obvious missing equipment, or he just suffers with what's on hand. It's all frustrating, time-consuming and expensive. And it can be avoided.

All workbenches are designed to do a finite number of things in a woodworking shop. And there are a finite number of vises and devices to choose from. So if you can make a list of all the basic tasks you expect to perform on your bench and then match those tasks to the bench equipment made to accomplish that task, you can come close to getting a good design the first time, even if you are an inexperienced woodworker.

It might not be a perfect process. For example, if you never plan on hand-dovetailing a drawer, I would argue that you shouldn't bother with a shoulder vise. Dovetailing is the task that the shoulder vise excels at. So you might build a bench with a small quick-release face

"You will find something more in woods than in books. Trees and stones will teach you that which you can never learn from masters."

— Saint Bernard, (1090 - 1153), French abbot

THE IRON AGE MEETS THE POST-INDUSTRIAL: I can think of no better way to secure work in the middle of my bench than a holdfast or hold-down. Traditional methods work well in tandem with modern tools.

A 350-POUND FOUR-FOOTED CLAMP: A twin-screw, tail or wagon vise is effective for assembly and disassembly. In early shops, when clamps were less ubiquitous, some benches were designed for clamping.

vise instead. But after a few years of working with wood you might change your mind about dovetailing. So you have to be a bit flexible in choosing the woodworking tasks that will be performed on your bench. Next year, you are going to be a different woodworker.

What follows is the soul of this book. It is a list of the common tasks performed on a bench and the devices that can accomplish those tasks. There also is a fair amount of my opinion about how suitable each device is at accomplishing that task – I think a twin-screw vise is better for dovetailing than a quick-release face vise, for example.

A word of warning: I use both hand tools and power tools in my shop, and so my opinions on workholding devices are colored by my blended approach. I like old techniques (such as holdfasts) to secure modern-style work (for pattern routing).

Once you make a list of all the tasks you'll be doing, you'll see your choice of vises narrow. And then you can see a bench take shape in your mind that makes sense to your pocketbook and prepares you for the future and the skills you will acquire. In fact, the goal of this book is to help you envision and build a workbench that will be difficult to outgrow. So get some paper and a pencil.

ASSEMBLING & DISASSEMBLING JOINTS

First Choice: Tail Vise
Many woodworkers forget that vises are clamps and are effective for assembling and disassembling things. Hands down, if you need to take apart frame assemblies, such as doors, windows or frame chairs, a tail vise is ideal. Raise the dogs up, place the work over the dogs and unscrew the vise. The dogs grip the work and pull it apart gently.

You also can use this function to take apart assemblies that you knocked together without glue but that have joints that are too tight to yank apart. (So you don't need spreader clamps.) It also works well for assembling a joint without glue to test the fit.

Second Choice: Wagon Vise
The wagon vise is good at assembly and disassembly, but it usually has fewer locations for dogs. It's almost a tie for first with the tail vise.

Third Choice: Wonder Dogs
These work OK for assembly and disassembly, but you sometimes have to do a lot more fiddling with them because the Wonder Dog has a small bearing surface that can be difficult to secure on a round chair leg, for example. You can screw a clamping caul to the dog that will solve most problems, but that's an extra headache the above choices won't give you.

Fourth Choice: Face Vise or Twin-screw Vise
You can use a face vise for these functions if it is equipped with a dog that is in line with a row of dog holes. The quick-release varieties of the vise won't help you with disassembly – moving the screw out disengages it and the jaw slides free. So it won't work. If you want to try a twin-screw vise for disassembling things, it's doable if the vise has dogs and the vise is not a quick-release unit.

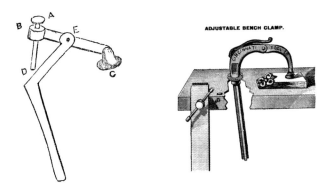

BEFORE THE VERITAS: This hold-down, most often associated with Record, was the hold-down of choice in the early 20th century. You need a metal collar set into the bench to make it work.

ANOTHER HOLD DOWN: Some hold-downs used a screw; this one from the Cincinnati Tool Co. uses a lever. Note that this one also requires a collar that is let into the top of your workbench.

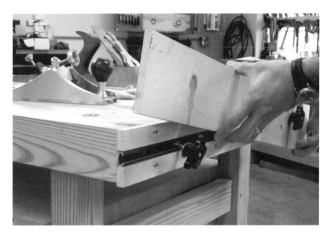

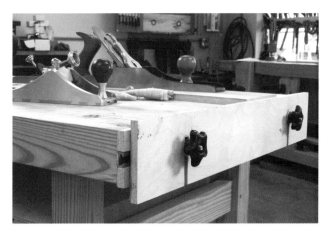

DIRT-SIMPLE SOLUTION: A planing stop can be as simple as a stick mortised into the benchtop. Here are some other ways to set up an adjustable planing stop on your bench: drive a couple screws into your benchtop, screw a deadbolt door lock to the end of the bench, clamp a piece of scrap to the benchtop.

ANY WIDTH, ANY HEIGHT: This is a fancy planing stop on the end of one of my benches at home. It took about an hour to build and attach. The star knobs release the stop so it can move up and down (and even left and right). The secret? The bolts attached to the knobs are riding in a piece of aluminum T-track in the end of the bench (top). Sandpaper is stuck on the inside face of the stop to ensure the stop moves only when you want it to. Turn the knobs and the stop stays put.

FACE PLANING NARROW BOARDS (8" WIDE OR LESS) WITH THE GRAIN

First Choice: Planing Stops

The simplest and best solution for planing the faces of narrow boards is to simply butt one end of the board against a planing stop and go to work. Gravity and the downward force of the tool keep the work flat on the bench. The forward motion of the tool keeps it in place against the planing stop. There's no clamping and unclamping.

Once you start figuring out how to control longer and wider stock against a single-point planing stop, your planing speed will increase. Why? There's no need to clamp and reclamp boards, changing your setup every time you plane a board of a different length. Planing stops, once mastered, are a joy. As you learn to control your stock, you can use the single-point stop with a holdfast and scrap wood batten ($^{1}/_{2}$" x 2" x 18") to keep the tail end of the board from whipping around. You'll also learn to skew the plane during the cut to take advantage of the side support from the batten.

There are many styles of stops. The historical type is a single wooden post that is friction-fit into the benchtop and adjusted up and down with mallet taps. Another type of planing stop is as wide as the benchtop. Those two types of stops are common, but there are plenty of uncommon ones. Some adjust up and down. Some are fixed. Some clamp into a face vise. Some attach to the bench. Some drop into dog holes. Some lurk below the top and can be adjusted up and down with a screwdriver or with some fiddling below the bench.

Need a recommendation? I like the kind that are wide, built into the end of the bench and adjust up and down. These can deal with stock that's thin and thick, narrow and wide, including most panels. (Panels are difficult or impossible to balance against a single narrow stop in my experience.)

My second choice for a stop is a stop that clamps in a face vise and spans the width of the benchtop.

Second Choice: Wagon Vise or Tail Vise

Many woodworkers use a wagon vise or tail vise to secure boards when planing with the grain or sanding. There are some advantages: Clamping the work between dogs requires less skill to keep the stock under control as you work. The dogs keep the work put and you can focus more on the work. But here are the downsides: Every time you

PLANING AT THE OTHER END: One of the odd things about using a wagon or tail vise for planing is that it moves the work to the right end of the bench. Most of the action on a bench occurs at the left end – the right end is typically where assembly takes place. With some practice, you will get used to planing at the right end of your bench.

A SECOND BENCHTOP: A planing board perches on top of your bench (or any bench), allowing you to have a flat surface uninterrupted by a tool tray or the fact that the top of your bench might not be flat enough for precision planing.

DOGS DO ROAM: One of the best things about Wonder Dogs is that you can set them between two holes anywhere on your benchtop.

THE RIGHT AMOUNT OF PRESSURE: When planing or belt-sanding across a panel, you don't want the panel slipping out of the dogs. And you also don't want to bow the stock by using too much pressure. So some woodworkers use metal dogs that have a toothed surface. Be wary when using this setup because your tools can be damaged.

plane a board that's a different length, you need to rearrange the dogs. Plus, add to that the extra step of opening and closing the vise and the minutes accumulate. Also, you do need to be careful about how much pressure you apply with the vise. Too much and your work will bow off the bench. Even a slight bow is bad news. And it doesn't take much pressure to bow ³/₄"-thick stock, especially narrow stuff.

Third Choice: Planing Boards

Planing boards (sometimes called planing trays) are a decent third choice in my book. They allow you to plane narrow stock and wide stock with the grain and (as noted in the next section) they are useful for planing across the grain with panels or assembled door frames. In fact, I find planing trays quite excellent if I'm traveling to a place where I'm not sure what the workbench will be like because they

handle many typical planing situations. However, they do have downsides. The number one disadvantage is you have to make a sizable planing board for it to be useful (24" x 50" is good), and that's quite a thing to store or set aside when not in use.

Fourth Choice: Wonder Dogs

Wonder Dogs have all the advantages and disadvantages of a tail vise, with one additional disadvantage: Planing thin stock requires extra measures to avoid striking the dog or its post with the body of your precious tools.

The supreme advantage of the Wonder Dog is that you can create a tail-vise-like setup anywhere on the bench, and retrofitting a bench with a Wonder Dog is about a thousand times easier than retrofitting it with a tail vise.

BATTEN DOWN THE BENCH: This batten will help me keep my stock under control for working across the grain. Were battens a common part of the traditional woodworking kit? I have no idea. But they are part of mine.

EXTEND YOUR BENCHTOP: A piece or two of scrap that act as an outrigger can support a drawer or an entire cabinet. Note how the face vise works with the outrigger support to immobilize this cabinet while I trim its dovetails. Thicker outriggers are better than thin ones.

FACE PLANING ACROSS OR DIAGONAL TO THE GRAIN

First Choice: Tail Vise or Wagon Vise

When working across or diagonal to the grain, pinching your work between dogs is ideal. These particular vises pinch the work on the end grain as you move the tool across the width of the board, with little chance of the tool striking your bench hardware. Using wooden dogs (instead of metal ones) ensures that your tools are safe from damage. It's easier to replace a wooden dog that has suffered multiple indignities from a fore plane than it is to fix a fore plane that has one brief and fateful encounter with a steel bench dog. As mentioned earlier, the downside to both the tail vise and the wagon vise is that you can apply too much pressure and bow the work. This will make the work behave unpredictably under your tools.

Second Choice: Twin-screw Vise or Quick-release Vise

If you place your twin-screw vise or quick-release vise on the end of your bench, it can be used like a tail vise to pinch the work between dogs. However, be advised that if you go this route, you should place the dog holes in your benchtop close together, let's say 4" apart. If you place them long distances apart you'll end up extending the vise quite a bit for some clamping situations. And that will leave a significant section of your work unsupported from below. So if you set it up correctly, these vise arrangements can work well.

Third Choice: Wonder Dogs

A Wonder Dog and a bench dog will do a fine job of securing your work for cross-grain planing – as long as you are dealing with stock that is thicker than $5/8$" and isn't supposed to end up thinner than $5/8$". If you need to work thin stock, it's fairly simple to rig up a few

BATTENS: This plate, which I stumbled on in a poorly footnoted book, shows battens in use on a bench. This looks like it's a plate from Roubo, perhaps the volume I don't own. The two well-dressed gentlemen are pulling a board through a thicknessing machine (a precursor to the portable surface planer). The tool is wedged between battens that are held down by holdfasts.

GRAVITY IS SIMPLE, CHEAP, GRIPPY: I've thrown away every router pad that's come into our shop. I use a moving blanket, which we need for transporting furniture anyway. When they get dusty, we wash them.

HOLD ANYTHING: Holdfasts and hold-downs are indispensable workshop servants, no matter what sort of work you do. They are like a clamp that has a bar that never gets in the way – it's buried in the benchtop.

wooden shims between the work and the dogs to keep your tools away from the metal dogs in this set-up.

Fourth Choice: Planing Boards

A planing board can be used to work across the grain and diagonally to it. The stops of the planing board restrain the work with little effort from the user. There are some downsides, as mentioned above. A good planing board needs to be large and takes up a fair amount of space. Plus, it's not so good with rough stock, which needs to be shimmed from below to keep it stable while planing it cross-grain, diagonally or even with the grain. If you purchase wood that is already dressed (or if you dress it yourself with machinery, as I do) the planing board is great. Shimming is then infrequent, and the planing board takes care of holding the work in any orientation without bowing the stock as you might with the above solutions.

Fifth Choice: Holdfasts and Battens

Tail vises were innovations in the 18th century. Before the advent of the tail vise, woodworkers would most likely use planing stops with

SOFT AND LOW-TECH: If you have good dust collection on your sander, then you don't need to invest in a downdraft sanding station. You also don't need some fancy "sanding pad" (read: anti-slip pads for area rugs that have been repackaged and repriced). Get a moving blanket, which is great for many workshop tasks.

holdfasts to restrain their wood when working across the grain. While I have only one 18th-century drawing of battens in use, I think it's plausible that they were used when planing as well. Holdfasts were the primary means of holding work. Engravings from Roubo's masterwork show benches with holdfast holes positioned along the far edge of the benches. My own work with holdfasts and battens has shown it's a good way to work – if you don't have an end vise.

FACE PLANING ASSEMBLIES: CABINET SIDES, DRAWER SIDES, ETC.

First Choice: Any Face Vise, Plus Outrigger Support

Many woodworkers are loathe to plane or scrape an assembled cabinet or drawer. Too bad. That's when you really can control the flatness of the sides (for attaching moulding), trim face frames flush and fit drawers. Hands down, the best way to plane the faces of assembled boxes is to support them off the front edge of the benchtop with an outrigger support (usually a thick piece of stock affixed to the bench with clamps or holdfasts). The outrigger supports your work from below and the face vise holds it at the front corner so it stays put as you plane or scrape it. This is a far better strategy than clamping your project up on the benchtop because then your working surface will be too high to work easily.

BELT SANDING NARROW STOCK OR SMALL PANELS

First Choice: Tail Vise or Wagon Vise

Without a doubt, you need to restrain your work when belt sanding small pieces. While large tabletops and the sides of cabinets can be sanded on a blanket or carpet pad alone, smaller door panels or individual boards require restraint. And lots of it. I have seen (and have tried) what might be called a backstop. Essentially it is a wide planing stop that is placed on the outfeed side of a belt sander. From a handplaner's perspective, this seems a good idea at first. The circular

ONE JIG, ONE JOB: One workhorse jig in our shop is designed for routing dados in case sides. You line up the notch in the fence with a mark on your work. Clamp the jig down. Rout your dado. No thinking required. I don't care for Swiss Army-style jigs. I tend to forget all the things they do after a year or so.

BISCUIT JOKE HERE: Holdfasts and hold-downs excel at applying clamping pressure exactly where you need it. This allows you to keep both hands on the tool, which results in far more accurate cuts.

motion of the sanding belt will push the work against the stop. Gravity and the weight of the tool will also help in holding things in place. In practice, however, this is … iffy. It works only if you keep your 1,100 square-feet-per-minute tool aligned directly in line with the grain. Turn it at an angle and small pieces of unsecured work can go flying with astonishing results. So forget the backstop and restrain the work at front and behind when it's small. For that, a tail vise or wagon vise is ideal. As with planing, be sure not to use too much force when securing your work or you will bow it. Adding a pad or blanket under your work can also help your work stick to your benchtop.

Second Choice: Wonder Dogs

These work well with stock thicker than ⁵⁄₈". Thin stock requires some extra jigging to avoid abrading the brass (usually just a couple pieces of scrap do the trick). Sanding a dog won't hurt the sanding belt too much, but it does throw some nice metallic dust everywhere.

RANDOM-ORBIT SANDING

First Choice: A Moving Blanket

My favorite way to restrain and protect my work when sanding with a random-orbit sander (or orbital sander or sanding block) is to place the work on a quilted moving blanket draped over the benchtop. Except for really small pieces of work, which don't lend themselves to power sanding, this is ideal. Downdraft sanding tables work just as well (if you have the cash for a big one), but I have had excellent results with a blanket and collecting the dust through the pad with a shop vacuum. Note that some sanders and vacuums are markedly better than others.

Here are some pointers: The eight-hole paper collects dust better than the five-hole paper. Nothing collects dust better than Mirka's Abranet system; this stuff is basically porous sandpaper and the dust is collected through the paper itself. It seems like alien technology when you use it for the first time.

Finally, you get what you pay for with dust collection. The high-end German sanders and vacuums from Festool and Fein do indeed work better than the consumer big-box stuff. These German tools are used in industry, where dust is not only a nuisance, it's a hazard to the health of the daily user.

ROUTING FACES OF BOARDS

First Choice: Holdfasts or Hold-Downs

This amuses me. When I need to do some pattern routing, rout profiles on an edge or rout dados and rabbets in a case side, I reach for my 18th-century holdfasts whenever possible. These work better than many clamping arrangements, no matter how deep the throats of your clamps are. Holdfasts (and hold-downs) are ideal for routing because you are machining only small areas of your work, so it's easy to place the holdfasts out of the way of the tool. Remember to use a scrap between the holdfast and the work to protect it from bruising.

Second Choice: F-style Clamps

When a holdfast won't do, I secure the work with clamps to the benchtop. This is when a well-designed bench shines. If you have aprons supporting your top, your clamps will not be as useful. If your top is thin with a wide apron banding it, your clamps will sometimes balk at the task. But if you have a thick slab of a benchtop with no obstructions below, you will be rewarded by easy clamping setups for routing. My French-style bench is a workhorse for routing.

Third Choice: Specialized Jigs

There are tool guides and purpose-built jigs for working on faces of boards with a router. A common commercial one is an aluminum fence that grabs the edges of your work. The fence acts as a straight-edge guide for the router's base.

Fourth Choice: Wonder Dogs

If you bore an array of dog holes in your benchtop, you generally can create an environment where the Wonder Dog can thrive. With Wonder Dogs, you might have to do the work in a couple different setups when edge routing – because the Wonder Dog system

A STRAIGHTEDGE MARRIED A CLAMP: I would be grumpy if I had to give up my edge guide with integral clamps. I use a long one to break down plywood with a circular saw and a short one for biscuiting and routing case sides.

NOT GOING ANYWHERE: When chiseling out waste, immobilizing your work is key. And when chiseling out waste between dovetail joints, you want a clamp that is fast and firm. Holdfasts and hold-downs are the answer. They're faster than an F-style clamp.

restrains work on its edges. But you can restrain odd shapes (circles, ovals etc.).

Fifth Choice: Router Mats

Generally, I don't trust router mats. They work with workpieces of a certain size. When the pads are new, they work with pretty small pieces of stock. As the pads become impregnated with dust, they lose their grip. And when they finally give up, that workpiece is going to take wing. If you like router mats, you also should know that they are exactly the same as inexpensive rubber carpet pads, which are used under area rugs on hardwood floors. There's one major difference: The price. Call it a router mat and the price goes up. When routing larger pieces of work, I use my moving blanket below the work. It always has the same amount of grippiness, no matter how dusty it is. And it protects the work from scratches.

BISCUITING FACES

First Choice: Holdfasts

Just like with the router, I reach for my old-style holdfasts when biscuiting the faces of boards. This should come as no surprise. When you biscuit the face of a board, you generally are working against some sort of fence that is secured to the face of the work. Holdfasts and hold-downs excel at applying downward force in a localized area. And if you have a dozen holes in your benchtop, you'll find that you can hold anything almost anywhere with holdfasts.

Second Choice: F-style Clamps

The modern option to holdfasts. They're limited by their throat capacity. However, if you have a bench that's uncluttered by aprons, these clamps work – especially at the corners and ends of your bench.

Third Choice: Specialized Jigs

If you do a lot of biscuiting, you're probably going to purchase a jig that combines a fence with edge clamps. This clever jig (one common brand is the Clamp 'n' Tool Guide) allows you to place the work flat on your bench and move the jig anywhere on the face of the work.

The jig grabs the work. Gravity holds everything down. Most power tool users end up with one of these jigs because it can guide just about any power tool, from a router to a circular saw to a jigsaw.

DRILLING FACES

First Choice: Holdfasts or Clamps

When hand pressure isn't enough to hold the work, I resort to holdfasts or clamps to hold things down. I place a piece of scrap below the exit hole to avoid blowing out the grain, and I work perched off the edge of the benchtop to avoid boring the bench. These devices also excel at holding jigs on the work while boring shelf pin holes in carcase sides.

CHISELING FACES OF BOARDS

First Choice: Holdfasts

Whenever I'm popping out the waste between dovetails I turn to my holdfasts. The same goes when I am roughing out details with a chisel, such as shaping the arm bow of a chair. Holdfasts and hold-downs apply pressure at one point, even in the middle of the bench.

Second Choice: F-style Clamps

This is my number two choice because these clamps are slower than holdfasts, plus I have to stoop to secure the clamps below the bench-

"Economical and rapid production is now a matter of eliminating the human factor as much as possible, a responsibility to be placed upon automatic machines."

— *The Wood Worker* (1921), a magazine for the trade,
in an Advertisement for a Reynolds Automatic
Screw Driving Machine

MAKE ANY MOULDING: Routing or planing small pieces is difficult and (occasionally) dangerous. A sticking board allows you to secure your work so that the tool – a router or plane – can work it. The force of the tool and its cutter help out with clamping here, whereas you are usually fighting the action of the cutter.

top. I think we have only so much stooping in our lives before our backs decide put a stop to it.

Third Choice: Specialized Jigs

There are a number of purpose-built chiseling jigs that both hold the work and guide the chisel at the baseline of a dovetail joint. I have used these, and they work, but they are not a part of my routine because they are slower (for me) than the holdfast.

STICKING MOULDING

First Choice: Sticking Boards

A sticking board is a useful benchtop appliance if you use moulding planes. It's also good for routing small mouldings. What's a sticking board? It's a long piece of scrap that holds your moulding (usually in a rabbet) at the front edge of your bench. The sticking board also has a stop at the end (sometimes both ends) that holds the moulding piece at the ends. You can secure the sticking board to the benchtop with clamps. My sticking board isn't that fancy. It's stopped at its end by my planing stop and braced against side pressure by my bench dogs.

Second Choice: Tail Vise or Wagon Vise

If the stock is wide and thick enough, I'll shape the profile directly on the benchtop between dogs. This works if the fence of the hand plane

SCRAP GUIDES THE TOOL: Does this look familiar? Yup, it's the same setup I use with my biscuit joiner. Holdfasts secure the guides for your tool better than any other clamp.

isn't large (plow planes don't always do well with this approach). If you are moulding the edge of wide base moulding, the tail vise is an excellent solution. Depending on the work and the location of your tail vise you can even hang your work off the front edge of the bench-top, allowing you to use fenced planes.

Third Choice: Wonder Dogs

These work just as well as the tail vise and in a similar manner.

CARVING & INLAY

First Choice: Holdfasts & Vises

I'm unqualified to discuss this topic with authority because I do little carving and inlay. In recent years, I've been doing more carving of furniture components and inlay, but still, I'm an amateur. So take this for what it's worth. For my carving efforts, I tend to work with a combination of holdfasts and dogs. The holdfasts hold the work down on the bench and I brace the work against a dog (two if I can manage) in the direction I'm thrusting with the tool. This works well with irregular shapes as you can wedge the work against a couple dogs and then find a way to secure everything with a holdfast or hold-down. The same goes for inlay, whether it's with a router plane or electric router. For carving legs (cabrioles, ball-and-claw feet) a patternmaker's vise is ideal because you can swing your work around. There also are vises dedicated to carving, especially when doing work in the round.

Second Choice: Wonder Dog

These guys work great for odd-shaped pieces and allow you to clamp objects with ease if you have an array of holes in your benchtop and a couple Wonder Dogs to supplement your regular dogs.

Third Choice: Tail Vise or Wagon Vise

This device works OK in some situations (carving a table apron). But working across the grain can sometimes make the work slip out from between the dogs (especially my beloved wooden dogs). You can use a batten and holdfast to keep the work in place. Or even a batten and an F-style clamp. If you're working on many like-shaped and like-sized pieces, this is a decent way to go.

SUPER DOGS: It's tempting to clamp things more than necessary. When adjusting joinery, usually the force of the tool is all that is required to immobilize the work against some dogs or a stop.

TOO MANY ANGLES: Scraping isn't like planing because it's generally performed in more localized areas. And because of a special feature of a scraper – that it can be used in almost any direction, regardless of grain direction – it gets used that way. And so working against a single planing stop isn't an option. You need to pinch the work or constrain it against more than a single point (unless the piece or assembly has great mass).

Fourth Choice: F-style Clamps

These always seem to be an OK choice with workholding. Use them near the corners of your benchtop and you can get the work done, but you'll work slower because you'll be shifting things around, fiddling with clamps and the like to get things to work.

HAND SAWING FACES OF BOARDS

First Choice: Bench Hooks

Two bench hooks and a backsaw handle most crosscutting applications that need to be precise. Coarse crosscuts with a handsaw are best handled on a sawbench. Why do you need two bench hooks? One holds the work and guides the saw. The other supports long stock on the benchtop during the cut. You can get away with one bench hook if its bed is $^3/_4$" thick and you have lots of $^3/_4$"-thick stock on hand (and who doesn't?). That scrap stock can provide the support you need.

Second Choice: Holdfasts or Hold-downs

Sometimes I need to saw against a guide, such as when hand sawing dados into a case side (sometimes with a stair saw). It's times like that where your bench hooks aren't going to do. You need to clamp the guide to your work and the benchtop. And that's when the holdfast and hold-downs shine. In fact, I turn to these devices first when sawing curved components. These devices can hold the work and your guide firmly enough that you can focus more on sawing and less on keeping your work braced with your off hand.

Third Choice: Tail Vise, Wagon Vise, Wonder Dogs

These are a distant third choice. The force of sawing tends to pull or push the work out of the grip of the dogs, unless you cinch the vise down, perhaps bowing the work.

Fourth Choice: F-style Clamps

And in honorable mention is the F-style clamp. Its reach is limited. It is slower than other solutions. But you can make it work in a pinch.

ADJUSTING JOINERY

First Choice: The Dogs Stand Alone

There are many small adjustments to your joints that need to be made to get things fitted properly. Shoulder planes adjust tenons and rabbets. Bullnose planes adjust assembled casework. Chisels and rasps adjust anything. Before I clamp parts for a super-secure setup, I try to brace the work against two dogs (raised high off the benchtop) and work the tool into the dogs. This works great with shoulder planes and bullnose planes especially. I'll even brace assembled casework or frame assemblies against two dogs to clean out rabbets when I can. If the work is small, I might use a single planing stop. But whenever I reach the limits of my benchtop or my arms, I'll turn to choice number two.

Second Choice: Tail Vise, Wagon Vise or Wonder Dogs

Any of these three devices can pinch your work at the ends, leaving you free to step forward (during a lengthy cut to clean out a rabbet) or apply pressure in a selective area. Generally, the work has to be long or wide before I crank open the tail vise. One caution: I've seen people adjust their joints while gripping the workpiece in a face vise, something I try to avoid. Working with the piece unsupported from below can be problematic. And if you slip your tool may go crashing to the floor because there's no benchtop below to catch it. That said, if I had only a face vise, I would make do.

SCRAPING FACES

First Choice: Tail Vise, Wagon Vise or Wonder Dogs

At first blush it might seem that scraping requires the same workholding strategies as planing. But the two processes are different. When planing, I use the momentum of the tool and gravity to keep the work fixed. That doesn't work with a card scraper, which has less mass and no sole in front of its cutting edge. (If you're using a scraping plane, use the strategies for planing.) You must fix your work to scrape it in most cases. And the tail vise-type devices all work well for this.

ESSENTIAL EDGES: One failing of many workbenches is they don't do enough to help you stabilize a board on edge to work it with hand or power tools. Luckily, a simple design change or a modification can make most benches friendly to edge-work.

BIG BOY: I wondered why old wooden planing stops were so long. My first theory was that they would get chewed up with use. That's true, but a better theory is their length is an asset. Indeed, when you're planing stock that's 4" wide on-edge, you have lots of support from below.

Second Choice: A Planing Board or Stops Plus Battens

Either of these two workbench appliances are superior to a lone planing stop. Planing boards prevent the work from spinning when you begin work at one corner. Planing boards (despite their disadvantages) are likely the best second choice because you can easily move a piece of work to scrape across the grain. Or use battens and planing stops to fence in your boards to work them from any angle.

SCOOPING OUT CHAIR SEATS

First Choice: Scabbing on a Block

You can get fancy with your clamping setups and your seat blanks. Or you can screw a scrap length of 2x4 to the underside of your seat blank and clamp the sucker with whatever you have available: face vise, leg vise, Emmert or tail vise. This gives you complete access to the saddle of the seat and eliminates the risk of splitting the seat blank that comes with holdfasts and F-style clamps. This is the voice of experience here. Don't make it harder than it has to be. No one will care about three screw holes on the underside of a chair seat.

Second Choice: Wonder Dogs

If you have an array of holes in your benchtop, a pair of Wonder Dogs and a pair of regular (wonderless?) dogs, then clamping chair seats is fairly easy. The omni-directional nature of the Wonder Dog makes it great for shield-shaped seats and the like. Although you will occasionally hit a weird patch of grain and pull the blank up out of your clamping setup.

Third Choice: Holdfasts and Clamps

I mention these only to stress that they are slow, get in the way of your tools and are risky. Don't do it.

WORKING ON EDGES OF BOARDS AND ASSEMBLIES

This function of a workbench is often neglected – not only by the woodworker, but also by the commercial bench manufacturer and garden-variety bench designer. You need to work the edges of boards and doors, and sometimes the boards are too long to simply clamp into a face vise effectively (though some woodworkers do this).

This function of a bench isn't just a hand-tool concern. The next time you have to cut some hinge mortises into a door stile or trim solid-wood edging on a long shelf, consider the typical awkward clamping setup. Most traditional workbenches are designed to make it easy to clamp any edge at a comfortable height for sawing, routing, biscuiting, mortising, planing, whatever.

The number one feature in a bench that will make it good for working on edges is having the front legs of the workbench in the same plane as the front edge of the benchtop. Most commercial benches ignore this principle – perhaps because our eyes expect our workbenches to have the graceful overhang of a dining table or side table. Or maybe people have just forgotten how useful this design point really is. Luckily, it's an easy fix with most benches: Re-attach the base to the top so the legs are flush to the benchtop. Or, if you have a fancy bench with trestle ends, you can scab on some pieces to the legs that will create a clamping surface that is in line with the front edge of your benchtop. Or you can build (or retrofit) a sliding deadman into your workbench's design that will give you an adjustable clamping surface that is co-planar with the front of your bench. This is quite handy. All of these solutions can be considered and executed in just a few hours.

The other element missing from many modern workbenches is some way to support long work from below while you are working on the edge of a board. You can, in a pinch, work on the edge of a board with the following clever setup: Clamp one end of the long board

"Everything should be made as simple as possible, but not simpler."
— Albert Einstein (1879 - 1955)
scientist, mathematician, inventor

EASY CONSISTENCY: Need a bunch of spindles all the same size and ready for finishing in a hurry? Plane them as a group. Sometimes I'll clamp them together before I plane away, but usually that's not necessary. This is faster than planing them individually or hand-sanding the edges.

in your face vise. Clamp the trailing edge in a handscrew clamp and clamp the handscrew to the benchtop. I know this works because I've done it many times. Handscrews can hold a tight grip that a big No. 8 bench plane cannot easily break.

But the handscrew support method is slow and is fighting gravity instead of harnessing it. A wooden peg below the work does wonders because you don't have to fiddle with clamps – gravity and your downward pressure do all the work.

But where do you place the holes for your pegs? In the legs? That's good. How about in a wide front apron? That's better. In a sliding deadman? Much better. In fact, a peg in a sliding deadman, a face vise and a bench with the legs flush to the front can help perform a lot of operations quickly that other (sometimes fancier) benches struggle with. And that particular operation is where to begin the list of devices designed for working on edges.

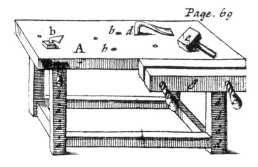

SO WRONG: I think Joseph Moxon got a lot of things right in his book on the early woodworking trade in England, but the twin-screw vise on this bench is just ridiculous. If the rear jaw were in line with the front edge of the benchtop, many clamping operations would be more stable with the assistance of the benchtop.

SOMEWHAT USELESS SLAVE: This is a slave block that's clamped into a tail vise. While it works well with long boards, it's not much help in clamping cabinet doors on edge.

PLANING THE EDGES OF NARROW STOCK

First Choice: Planing Stop

The planing stop and your benchtop are surprisingly effective at supporting and holding work that is 4" wide and narrower. Raise your planing stop up fairly high (mine goes up almost 6" with ease), butt your stock against the stop with the work on edge. Go at it. Gravity and your plane keep the stock immobile as you plane it. This is remarkably fast for dealing with many narrow components of different lengths because there is little (usually no) clamping involved.

Second Choice: Wide Planing Stop

When I need to plane several pieces to the same dimension, I lean heavily on this technique. Clamp a wide planing stop to your benchtop and butt all the boards you need to plane against the wide stop (don't forget to check their grain direction). If you're new to this technique, apply a clamp to the back end of the group of boards so they act like one big board. Now plane away across all the edges, treating them like they are one board. This works wonders and works fast. Keep the pieces clamped together as you flip all the pieces over to plane their other edges. Sometimes you can butt the clamp itself against the planing stop to save time. Sometimes you have to adjust and re-adjust the

NO SHOOTING BOARD REQUIRED: When shooting between dogs, I tend to place the plane on the far side of the work and pull it toward me and along the edge. This feels natural. You can place the plane on the side closest to you if your work and bench placement allow it. A flat and smooth benchtop assists in establishing a square and clean edge.

HELD FOR A HINGE: No matter if you use a router plane or a trim router to cut mortises for your hinges, proper support is critical. A scrap stabilizes the base of the tool.

clamp. Bottom line: If you don't think this procedure is working for you, then keep at it.

Third Choice: Bird's Mouth (Wedging) Jigs

Many woodworkers end up using an old-style wedged-shaped planing stop that allows you to insert your work into the wedged jig and immediately plane away on the edge. I don't find the wedge particularly advantageous compared to simply working against a tall planing stop. But some woodworkers swear by it.

PLANING, SANDING OR SHAPING THE EDGES OF WIDE STOCK

First Choice: Any Face Vise Plus Support from Below

I know this sounds vague, but there are many solutions to this problem. Any face vise, from an Emmert to a leg vise, will pinch and immobilize the work. No matter what vise you choose, there's a critical point you should be aware of: You'll have better support if the rear jaw of the vise is flush with the front edge of the benchtop. The quick, easy and thoughtless way to mount a face vise is to simply bolt it on the benchtop without cutting a recess for the rear jaw. So the rear jaw is proud of the front edge of the benchtop. This makes it difficult to work on long edges with your face vise because it takes the front edge of your top out of the picture. By the way, if you are too lazy to cut a recess in your benchtop (or perhaps you like your benchtop too much to – gasp – cut it) may I suggest scabbing on a piece to the front edge of your benchtop to bring it in line with the rear jaw? The other part of this equation is the support from below for your work.

My number one preference is to have a sliding deadman that has an array of holes bored into it. This is a flexible and reliable way to put a peg right where you want it. There are, of course, other ways to go about this. Holes in the legs. A separate bench slave. A 2x4 clamped to the legs to act as a shelf to support the work. Some people clamp a slave block in the tail vise. The slave block is bored with a variety of

holes. I know this looks like a capital idea at first, but it usually doesn't do jack when you are trying to support shorter boards or doors.

Second Choice: Tail Vise (Or Wagon Vise) With a Bench Plane

I first stumbled on this approach in an old tool catalog that was touting the tail vise as a great device for shooting edges directly on the benchtop. I tried it and it works. Place your work on top of a couple battens. Anything thicker than ¼" will do; it simply has to hold the work high enough to touch the iron. Clamp the work between the dogs. Now turn the hand plane on its sidewall on the benchtop. I like to pull the plane toward me, though you can push in many situations as well. At times, the seemingly vestigial L-shaped outrigger on the tail vise will come in handy to support a long plane as it cantilevers off the benchtop when starting a cut. This shooting method requires a plane with an iron sharpened straight across, a sidewall that is square to the sole and a reasonably flat benchtop. What are the rewards for this extra fuss? It's easier for beginners to control a plane used like this than it is for beginners to master the act of balancing a plane in use on a narrow edge.

Third Choice: Wonder Dogs

Just like with the tail vise and wagon vise, the Wonder Dogs can be used for edge-planing a board on a benchtop.

Fourth Choice: Crochet

The classic old-school way to plane an edge uses no vises. I do it frequently, but it can require a bit more setup than using a face vise. A crochet is a wooden hook-like apparatus located on the front edge of your bench where the face vise goes. When you press the end of the work into the open mouth of the hook, its shape immobilizes the board. Support from below comes from holdfasts, pegs or a 2x4 employed as a shelf. This takes a bit of skill, though not much. If you cannot afford a face vise, you'll find a crochet a great companion. With one clamp, you can even dovetail boards with it.

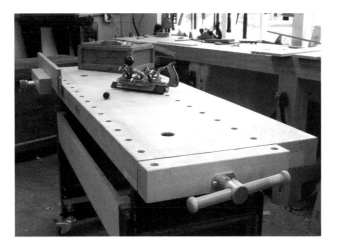

MORTISING FOR HINGE GAINS

First Choice: Face Vise & (Sometimes) Lower Support

The real trick with mortising for a hinge in a door (or face frame) is that you need something additional to balance the tool on as you work. This is true whether you use a router or a router plane. The door's stile alone doesn't offer enough support for the tool to ensure a good mortise. So in addition to securing the door, you need to secure a scrap next to it. Another strategy is to clamp the door stile and face frame stile together and mortise them simultaneously. This ensures accurate alignment between the two hinge gains. With so much going on, clamping can be a challenge. I like a face vise to hold the door and a support scrap at one corner. A clamp (usually a handscrew) holds the scrap to the door. I usually rest one of the wooden jaws of the handscrew on the benchtop if I can. And a peg in the sliding deadman supports the door from below. Another option is to clamp the door so it is 3/4" above the benchtop and to support your router or router plane using a piece of 3/4" scrap on your benchtop.

Second Choice: Face Vise and Clamp

With a small or lightweight door, you can sometimes work directly in a face vise or twin-screw. If the door is long you can clamp the unsupported corner to the front of the benchtop with a long bar clamp.

SAWING EDGES

First Choice: Face Vise

Most of the edge sawing on a workbench involves short cuts. Long cuts on edges and faces are best handled on a low sawbench. These short cuts are usually handled in a face vise. This can be notching the corners of a bottom piece to fit it around some posts. It can be slicing off the little bits of leftover tail scrap when dovetailing drawers. Cutting half-lap joints is another application. For deep notching cuts, I switch gears and use the clamping strategies for letting in hinges.

Second Choice: Bench Hook

A lot of edge sawing involves slicing the edge and face shoulders of tenons. The best way to do this is with a bench hook on the benchtop, as noted in the section above on sawing faces of boards.

Third Choice: Holdfasts

In some of the old engravings in books, it shows woodworkers sawing narrow boards on the benchtop with a holdfast keeping everything in place. I don't find myself drawn to this strategy much, perhaps because of the scale of my work. The engravings I saw (from Roubo's 18th-century texts) were illustrating a joiner's shop, where they were making large doors and sash windows for houses. I can see how a wide door rail wouldn't be easy to mess with on a bench hook.

WORKING ON ENDS OF BOARDS

For the most part, working the ends of boards involves cutting end grain to make joints: dovetails, tenons, rabbets, biscuits. Or it involves trimming that end grain so the finished joint is flush.

The end grain of a board is by far the most difficult to work. It resists planing, sanding, gluing, screwing, nailing and sawing. It, however, can be very accommodating to riving tools, such as a froe, wedge or hatchet, especially when the wood is green and the grain isn't interlocked. However, most operations that are associated with building cabinets bring out the worst behavior of end grain.

As a result of the unyielding nature of end grain, it must be clamped fast and worked with confidence and sharp tools. In general, I find that projects proceed more smoothly when I design and build them in a way that avoids working the end grain as much as possible.

This isn't a new strategy. It is, in fact, quite old. Furniture from the Golden Age of woodworking (the 18th century) shied away from visible joinery – through-dovetails, wedged and proud through-tenons and the like became popular at the beginning of the 20th century. Carcase dovetails were covered in moulding. Mitered joints and what we call breadboard ends also would hide end grain when possible. No

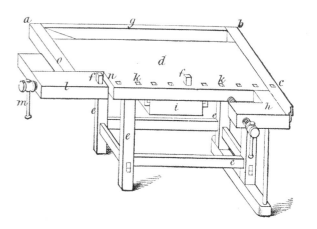

A DOVETAILER'S DELIGHT: If you are fond of cutting dovetails (or think that you will become that way), you would be hard-pressed to find a better vise for this operation than a shoulder vise. It's fast and effective for dovetailing drawer parts, less so for carcase pieces. However, there are always more drawers to dovetail than there are case sides.

AN EFFECTIVE ANGLE: The angled leg vise allows you to clamp parts for dovetailing that are a bit wider and longer than a comparable leg vise that is pointing straight up. It's not as versatile as a shoulder vise, but if you are an occasional dovetailer (as opposed to a religious one) the angled leg vise is a good compromise.

matter what furniture-building strategy you employ, you can't avoid end grain entirely. So here are some strategies.

DOVETAILING DRAWER PARTS

First Choice: Shoulder Vise

The shoulder vise excels at dovetailing parts for drawers. The screw of the vise can be positioned directly on the center of the board's width, which eliminates any chance of the jaws wracking or loosening their grip. There are no bars or screws to interfere with clamping. You can clamp a piece that has one end on the floor just as easily as you can clamp very short work. Are there downsides? When it comes to drawer work, not really. Some woodworkers complain that the dog-leg section of the vise on the front of the bench requires them to lean forward more than they like, but I don't find that to be the case. In fact, I find the dogleg section of the vise an excellent place to brace myself as I work. The shoulder vise isn't perfect, but for dovetailing drawer-scale material, it's the cat's pajamas.

Second Choice: Twin-screw Vise

A close second for dovetailed drawers is the twin-screw vise. For clamping drawer sides it excels in all the same ways that the shoulder vise does. Where it falls short is in the fact that it is a more complex mechanism. And in some designs when the screws operate independently of one another, there is a degree of subtlety required to

Improve the Leg Vise

One of the biggest complaints about leg vises is having to engage some sort of secondary mechanism to keep the jaw parallel as you advance it and to act as a pivot point when squeezing the work. I have a bar in my tail vise that is bored with a series of holes. By moving a steel pin into the correct hole I can control the parallelism of the jaw and set the jaw for different thicknesses. I'm so used to it that I don't think much about it and it has become part of the natural rhythm of my work.

However, if you don't like stooping, you won't like having to do this day after day.

One solution, which is presumably French, is called *Croix de St. Pierre*. I've seen it in action on a commercial leg vise and it is ingenious. It is, essentially, two flat pieces of steel that are joined by a hinge in the center, much like scissors, forming an X shape. At the top of the X, one end is attached to the bench; the other to the jaw of the vise. The two ends at the bottom run in grooves in the jaw and leg of the bench. The scissors action of the X keeps the jaws parallel as you work.

I've always meant to make one of these devices myself for a leg vise, but I've always been satisfied with the occasional stoop to move the steel pin.

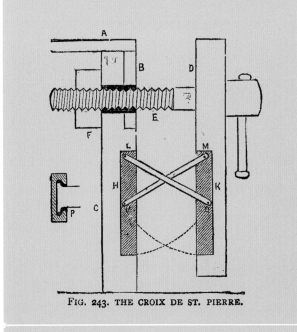

FIG. 243. THE CROIX DE ST. PIERRE.

make the vise work well, much like learning to operate traditional handscrew clamps. You have to learn where the pinch points are on the clamp and how to close everything up so it's clamping the work squarely without stressing the work or the threads of the vise.

DESIGNED FOR DRAWERS: This space between the tail vise block and the benchtop is suitable for dovetailing drawer parts (within reason). The benchtop and vise block secure the work with a Western-style push saw. I've used it with a pullsaw, which seems like something that shouldn't work, but the side-to-side clamping can withstand the pulling action.

Third Choice: Leg Vise

Leg vises can be excellent for dovetailing drawer parts, particularly when the vise is built so it is angled. The angle (mine is at 20° off 90°) allows you to clamp fairly wide drawer sides (mine accommodates up to 8" wide) without the screw of the vise interfering with the work. Leg vises exert enormous pressure on the work (a good thing) but require more stooping to keep the vise's parallel guide in the right place. (Though there are mechanisms that can do this for you, they are uncommon.) Leg vises are good for a shop that doesn't live or die by the dovetailed drawer and requires some more versatility for other clamping operations.

Fourth Choice: Tail Vise

The space between the benchtop and the vise block of a tail vise can be useful. For a year, I used this space anytime I needed to dovetail anything narrow. Drawer sides were the typical customer. The arrangement works rather well with Western push saws and fairly well with pullsaws. Place the work in that open space and tuck it against the corner of the benchtop. Close the vise on it. There. It's now supported on three sides and is automatically at 90° to the floor. Your width capacity is limited by the maximum opening of your tail vise. For an added grip, some woodworkers will line the jaws of the vise block and end grain of the benchtop with felt or leather.

Fifth Choice: Quick-release Face Vise

Sorry, but these vises are a poor choice for dovetailing drawers. The vise's parallel bars crowd out the drawer stock from the center of the vise, which is exactly where the vise has the most power. And when closed down on one side only, the vise's jaws wrack – and badly. You can compensate with a shop-made vise block, which is in essence a stepped wedge. Place the vise block on the outside corner and the drawer side you plan to victimize in the other corner of the vise. Make sure the thickness of the vise block matches that of the workpiece. Close the vise and the work should be clamped more firmly than if you skipped the vise block. This approach is, of course, extra work. And make sure you come up with some trick to keep the vise block

FACE IT: The face vise isn't my first choice for dovetailing drawers that have any significant width. Note the wracking of the jaws without the benefit of a vise block. Even with the vise block, you'll need to add another support mechanism (or two) when dealing with wide pieces.

from swan diving to the floor when you release the tension on the vise. I pierced my vise block with a $^3/_4$"-diameter dowel. When the pressure is released on the vise, the block merely swings at the top of the jaws of the face vise, waiting for its next assignment. With a wide drawer side, you might have to pull out all your tricks: face vise, vise block and a bar clamp across the benchtop to position everything and hold it immobile.

Sixth Choice: Crochet and Holdfast/Clamp

This technique works surprisingly well. The only reason it is at the bottom of this list is that the crochet and leg arrangement necessary for it to work are not common in this age. Here are the basic steps: Wedge one edge of the drawer side into the crochet and then clamp the face of the board near the opposite edge with a holdfast or bar clamp. The holdfast or bar clamp holds the work against the front of the benchtop and the leg, which adds stability. Because there are no bench screws involved, your workpiece can go clear to the floor. You are limited only by the position of your crochet and the holes in your legs for a holdfast. I have found that this setup works well for either Western saws or pullsaws. Its main downside is it's slower than the fancy setups detailed above.

SIMPLE: You can dovetail just about any piece of casework with a crochet plus a clamp or holdfast. It's not as fast as the more complex solutions, but it does require little money to get the bench up and running. This set-up also works when hand-sawing tenons cheeks.

GIVING YOU A LEG DOWN: With the leg flush to the benchtop's front edge, it can be employed to support your work from below. Either a clamp, peg or a holdfast will do the trick. If you use hold-downs in your legs, space the holes so you get complete coverage. This is based on the throat of the hold-down. If your hold-down has an 8" throat, then space the holes 8" or less.

DOVETAILING CARCASE COMPONENTS

First Choice: Twin-screw Vise

If you can get your twin-screw vise to clamp boards 24" wide, then this setup is the bee's knees. It is the simplest one-stop-shopping way to clamp a wide case side that I know of. As mentioned above, there is subtlety required with twin-screws that have independently operated screws. (The Veritas Twin-Screw and some shop-made British examples have screws that work in tandem. Nice.) The downside to any twin-screw vise, as mentioned before, is that once you reach its limit, that's usually all you can do with it. In contrast, other vises can be tricked or tweaked to deal with wider stock. In my opinion, the ideal twin-screw vise for carcase dovetailing is with the vise employed as a face vise. Center the jaws over the left leg (if you are a right-hander). Make sure the leg is flush to the benchtop's front edge. Bore holes in the leg for a holdfast or simple wooden peg to support the work from below. Now go to town with a dovetail saw.

Second Choice: Shoulder Vise – Plus a Clamp

Using the shoulder vise with a bar clamp is the next best way to dovetail a carcase side. The shoulder vise holds one side of the board; the bar clamp holds the other side. All of these setups that involve a vise plus a clamp have some advantages and frustrations. The main advantage is that you can accommodate a board of almost any width. The other advantage is that the approach works with a wide variety of face vises and the shoulder vise. The disadvantage is that clamping and releasing your work can be a bit awkward with large case sides.

If you cannot support the work from below, you can sometimes drop the work to the ground as you release the clamp or the vise. For a typical case side, you can usually use your foot to support the work from below as you release the pressure. The reason the shoulder vise and clamp combination is my second choice (as opposed to my third or fourth) is because you don't have any vise screws that obstruct your work or vise blocks that you have to manage as you apply vise pressure. So things aren't flopping around as much.

TENONS ANYTIME: Most any vise can handle your work when cutting tenons by hand (or when simply undercutting their shoulders).

TWO-DOG DAYS: With the assistance of two dogs (round or square), you can adjust both the shoulders and cheeks of a tenon. You can quickly move the work onto either side of the dogs for pushing or pulling a tool against the dogs.

A CUT BELOW: When undercutting the shoulders of a tenon (as shown above, beneath the side of the chisel), work with the tenon upright so you can see your work clearly.

Third Choice: Leg Vise or Face Vise – Plus a Clamp

The leg vise is my next choice for dovetailing case sides because you can clamp one side of the work all the way down the leg of the workbench. That adds stability during sawing. Once again, you have to worry about keeping your work under control as you release the pressure on the vise or clamp. A wooden peg or your foot can usually keep things in check. You do have to steer your work clear of the vise screw in the leg vise – and sometimes you'll need a vise block to keep the vise from wracking.

If you don't have a leg vise, the quick-release face vise and a clamp can do the same job, but you won't always have the assistance of the workbench's leg (like you will with the leg vise). And I really recommend a vise block when clamping only one end with a quick-release face vise. The wracking isn't good for your vise or your ability to keep your grip.

Fourth Choice: Crochet Plus a Clamp or a Holdfast

As mentioned in the section on dovetailing drawers, this clamping approach works well. However, with case sides, it's unlikely that you'll be able to use a holdfast to clamp the free edge. You're probably going to need a bar clamp. I've also had good luck using my sliding deadman as part of the arrangement: One edge of the board goes into the holdfast, the other gets clamped to the deadman, up near the top of the board is best. This isn't the most stable arrangement for serious sawing – I usually prefer a bar clamp across the benchtop.

Fifth Choice: Holdfasts or Clamps against Benchtop

It's also possible to use two bar clamps across the benchtop to secure the work. I like to do this in front of one leg of the workbench (assuming the leg is flush to the benchtop). If you've bored holes in your leg, you can stick a peg or holdfast in a hole to support the work from below. Once you start supporting from below like this, you'll see the advantage. Promise.

"I will not give away my hard-earned skills to a machine. It's a bit like robbery with violence, for (machines are) not only intended to diminish my bank balance, but also to steal my power."

— John Brown (1932 –), Welsh stick chairmaker and author

SHOOTING THE WORKS: A simple shooting board (plywood ones stay flat for a long time) can help plane the end grain of a board in a predictable fashion. When choosing a plane for shooting, I pick the one with the most mass and a keen iron that's sharpened straight across – no curve.

CUTTING TENONS OR DOVETAIL SOCKETS/TAILS ON ENDS

First Choice: Face Vise, Shoulder Vise or Leg Vise

Securing your work for cutting tenons is much less trying than for dovetailing. When I cut tenons by hand, I use the traditional technique: I clamp the work at an angle so I can see two faces of the work at the same time and advance on both lines. Then I turn the work around, place it upright, and finish the cut.

This technique makes sawing tenons easier and clamping is easy, too. That's because you don't have to worry as much about the vise's screws because you are clamping the workpiece at an angle. Ditto for the vise blocks; you generally don't need them. Clamping the work at an angle spreads the work out over more of the vise's jaws, reducing the urge of the vise to wrack. Add to that the fact that the stock for your tenon is generally narrow and you'll see that there are many good ways to get this done. Any face vise, shoulder vise or leg vise is up to the job.

As you get into tenoning wider stock you have two choices. You can work with a vise that has wide jaws (such as a leg vise or shoulder vise) or you can treat the joint more like a big rabbet and do it flat on the benchtop using planes and chisels to remove the bulk of the waste. Sometimes the approach you use is dictated by the width of the work and sometimes by the length (think breadboard tenons on a tabletop). When you start working flat on the benchtop for tenoning, clamps and holdfasts are generally the order of the day.

Second Choice: Tail Vise (Between the Vise Block and Benchtop)

I mention this technique only so that you'll think about that clamping surface between the tail vise and your benchtop. It's useful, though not so much for tenoning. You can indeed clamp narrow bits of wood at an angle appropriate for tenoning: Tip the top of the stock away from you and the bottom of the stock will stick out between your legs. But you'll quickly run out of clamping power as the stock gets wider.

ADJUSTING TENON SHOULDERS

First Choice: Against Dogs or a Planing Stop

I prefer to adjust the shoulders (and cheeks) of tenons with the work flat on the bench, except when the work involves a chisel or other two-handed tool (a rasp, chisel or file). In general, try to work with the stock braced against something stout: two dogs, a planing stop, a bench hook. This way, the progress of your shoulder plane is clearly visible when the work is flat, as is your knife line or pencil line. Working this way prevents you from stooping to see your line, which is what happens when you secure the work upright in a vise. It's also faster to rely on gravity and the force of the tool to hold it in place than of a vise's screws.

Second Choice: Face Vise, Shoulder Vise or Twin-screw Vise

When chiseling shoulders, a vise is best. You are generally working with the tool in a vertical position and you are generally undercutting your shoulders to get a tight fit at the shoulder (you dirty cheater). Having the work upright in a vise allows you to see the cut as it progresses and allows you to use two hands to control your chisel.

Third Choice: Tail Vise

Again, the opening between your tail vise's jaw and the benchtop can be put to good use. And clamping your work for paring the shoulders is an ideal use for this part of your bench.

Fourth Choice: Holdfasts or Clamps

If your work is very wide, then it usually has to be humped up onto the benchtop, secured with holdfasts or clamps and then worked with a shoulder plane or chisels.

BISCUITING ENDS (AND FACES)

First Choice: Benchtop and Stops

A good bench can be an asset to your biscuit joiner. One of the hardest cuts to make with this useful tool is to cut biscuit slots into end grain. When this cut is made using the tool's fence alone, there is a common tendency to tip the tool a bit and produce a cut that is not angled just right. The same problem occurs (and is even worse) when biscuiting face grain at the ends of boards. There just isn't much meat there to balance your tool on. When I biscuit end grain (typically a shelf side), I'll lay it flat on my benchtop and butt one end against my wide planing stop. Then I lay the biscuit joiner flat on my benchtop and lower the fence so it touches the face of the work. Some people skip this step, which is fine. I don't. I'd rather have the extra layer

"It is a curious and sad fact that although most machines are developed not to cheapen quality but to lessen cost, this is precisely what usually happens."

— Graham Blackburn, *Traditional Woodworking Handtools*

SHOOTING WITHOUT A SHOOTING BOARD: You can clamp your work between your bench dogs to shoot the ends – as long as your benchtop is flat. Be sure to work the outfeed side a bit before working the full edge. This will help prevent the end grain from breaking out on one edge of the board.

HANGING OUT: By using a scrap clamped to the benchtop, you can plane end grain at a comfortable height. Secure one corner of the assembly in a face vise so you can work the end grain on the assembly in a quick and aggressive manner.

of aluminum between me and that spinning carbide blade. Then I push the tool against the other end of the board and cut my slots. No clamps whatsoever. I'll use the same approach on the benchtop when biscuiting faces. I remove or retract the biscuit joiner's fence and work with it upright on the benchtop. I'll clamp a fence to the work to position the tool (using holdfasts) and then use a piece of scrap that is the same thickness as my stock to support the cantilevered part of the tool. This works well and involves a minimum of clamping.

PLANING END GRAIN OF BOARDS NARROW AND WIDE

First Choice: Shooting Boards

In general, planing end grain is even harder than sawing it. You need sharp tools, and moistening the end grain with alcohol also helps the job. The most accurate way to plane end grain so it is square to the faces is to use a shooting board. This simple workshop appliance (usually three pieces of wood) holds the work as you plane the ends. It takes a little practice to master the shooting board, but the rewards are substantial. Even if you are a die-hard power-tool user, a shooting board can do things that no power tool can. Exhibit A: Reduce boards in length in .001" increments. When I'm fitting muntins and mullions in a divided-light door, or fitting a shelf in dados, shooting boards are quite useful. Shooting boards generally hook over the front edge of your benchtop, so you don't really have to worry much about securing them. Some woodworkers clamp the hook in their face vise.

I consider a shooting board essential bench equipment for every home shop woodworker. It beats the snot out of trying to plane long stretches of end grain freehand. There are also a wide variety of shooting boards for miters, bevels and moulding. They are good for specialty work. Make a simple shooting board first and you'll probably end up making a few more in short order.

Second Choice: Bench Hook

If you won't build a shooting board, you can use a bench hook to do the same job on small bits of wood. If your work is long, you'll also need something to support the work that hangs over your bench, otherwise, say goodbye to that square cut you were trying to get.

Third Choice: Tail Vise

If the stock isn't too long, you can lay it down on a thin bit of scrap and pinch it between the dogs of your tail vise. Then you can shoot the ends of the board with a plane that you slide on its side on the benchtop. Again, don't forget that you need a flat benchtop for this to work. This works quite well for wide boards that aren't too long. You can even shoot the end of the case side for a base cabinet this way if you pull your bench away from the wall.

Fourth Choice: Face Vise, Shoulder Vise or Twin-screw Vise

Yes, you can plane end grain freehand, and sometimes it's the only way to accomplish a task. The traditional vises (sometimes accompanied by a bar clamp) can secure your work for most of these jobs. If you can, support your work from below; planing end grain generally requires a lot of downward pressure.

PLANING END GRAIN OF ASSEMBLED CORNER JOINTS OR ASSEMBLED CASEWORK

First Choice: Cantilevered Platform Plus a Vise

Working on assembled furniture projects with planes, chisels or sanders seems daunting at first because of the size of the work. But there are tricks that can help. When working on assembled pieces (just like when you're working on individual boards) there are three goals:

"To the very last, he [Napoleon] had a kind of idea; that, namely, of 'La carrière ouverte aux talents,' The tools to him that can handle them."

— Thomas Carlyle (1795-1881) Scottish-born historian and essayist Source: "Sir Walter Scott" *London and Westminster Review*, 1838)

Do You Need a Massive Old-School Workbench?

In 2006 I taught a class in handwork at a school where Thomas Stangeland, a maestro at Greene & Greene-inspired work, was also teaching a class. Though we both strive for the same result in craftsmanship, the process we each use couldn't be more different. He builds furniture for a living, and he enjoys it. I build furniture because I enjoy it, and I sell an occasional piece.

One evening we each gave a presentation to the students about our work. One of the pieces I showed was an image of my French workbench. I discussed its unusual workholding devices and how the bench was a bit of a Thor Heyerdahl experience.

Thomas then got up and said he wished he had a picture to show of his workbench for the last decade: a door on a couple horses. He said that a commercial shop had no time to waste on building a traditional bench. And with his power-tool approach, he just needed a flat surface and some clamps to work.

It's hard to argue with the end result. His furniture is beautiful.

But what's important to note here is that you can get by with the door-off-the-floor approach, but there are many commercial woodworkers who still see the utility of a traditional workbench. Chairmaker and furnituremaker Brian Boggs uses more newfangled routers and shop-made devices with aluminum extrusions than I have ever seen in a shop. And he still has two enormous traditional workbenches that see constant use.

The point here is that a good bench won't make you a better woodworker. And a not-quite-a-bench won't doom you to failure. But a good bench in any shop will make many power-tool operations easier and open the door to permit you to try many hand-tool operations. The bench is simply another tool. It's the biggest wooden clamp in the shop.

As Thomas was wrapping up his part of the show he showed an interesting slide of an enormous and thick slab of an exotic wood he had been stashing for years and years in his shop.

"I just need to find the right project for it," he said. "Hey Thomas," I heckled, "that slab sure would make a great benchtop."
He laughed. Next slide, please.

BIG WOODEN CLAMP: After seeing the work of hundreds of professional woodworkers, I know that you don't need a good bench to do good work. Why build one then? It makes all work easier and makes handwork possible.

Get the surface you want to work on to a height that is comfortable for you. Two: Support the surface from below so it doesn't flex under pressure from the tool. Three: Prevent the assembly from wracking and self-destructing because of the pressure from the tool. Lots of woodworkers try to adjust themselves more than they adjust the work. They work over their heads. They stand on stools. They work on the floor or on their knees.

There are other options (usually). Because of the open-frame nature of casework, you can use this to your advantage with some assemblies. This requires a strategy and some cleverness. First, the strategy: Build the outside of the carcase. Work that shell until it's ready to finish. Then the open carcase can be supported on a cantile-vered platform off the workbench and clamped to the bench in some manner. This allows you to plane, scrape or sand the sides of the case (and even perhaps the top and bottom – though those might not need much attention in a cabinet). Then you can prepare the interior components as flat boards and fit them into the carcase. In the end, this allows you to easily work surfaces that will become difficult to work later on.

Note that this strategy might need to be altered for the scale of the piece. Really large cabinets might require their interior pieces fitted before you work the outside because you are going to have to lay the carcase on its sides on your shop floor (or on planks) to work them. And the interior pieces will stiffen the case. Drawers are one assembly that is best worked as a shell without the bottom in place: You can work them easily from all sides with the work on a cantilevered platform. If you have the bottom in the drawer already, use the strategy outlined below.

Second Choice: Face Vise Plus a Sliding Deadman

For narrow assemblies, drawers and doors mostly, you can work the ends (and faces) by clamping one corner in a vise and supporting the work from below with a sliding deadman alone. If you really need to stiffen things up for your work, you can clamp the assembly across the benchtop as well.

How to Design Your Bench

Boards (and flat assemblies – such as doors) have three kinds of surfaces: faces, edges and ends. So when you design your workbench, you should begin with the goal of building one that will accomplish at least those tasks with the tools you now use – or plan to use.

You also will be working on the end grain, face grain and edge grain of assembled boxes, so you need to make sure that you can accommodate some of this activity as well.

So you are sitting there with a blank sheet of paper, or a blank computer screen, as you design your bench. It's tough to make a first sketch, a first design. So let's do a warm-up exercise. I highly recommend it because it points out why building your own workbench – instead of purchasing one – is worthwhile. Let's pick apart some typical commercial workbenches, plus a 19th century craftsman-built bench and a couple other designs, using our guidelines and see how these benches measure up.

The 1882 Workbench from *Carpentry and Building* Magazine

This bench is a complete success, though it's more complex than necessary. The plan was submitted to *Carpentry and Building* magazine by W.A.Y. of Pierce's Landing, Pennsylvania, and was published in the August 1882 edition. Here are its vitals: 10' 3" long, 33" high, 18" deep (plus a 9"-wide tool tray at the rear). The 4"-thick top is made of alternating strips of walnut and ash (flashy!). The legs are thick: The vise leg is 4" x 5". The other legs are 3" x 5". All the legs are mortised into the top.

Carpenters' and Cabinet-makers' Bench.—Sketch Accompanying the Communication From W. A. Y.

1882 BENCH: This bench was featured in the August 1882 edition of *Carpentry and Building* magazine. Note the offset and jack-legged leg vise. This bench is more than 10' long, 33" high and 18" deep (with a 9"-wide tool tray at the back). The top is 4" thick. This bench is capable of all common workshop tasks.

EVERYTHING YOU NEED (EXCEPT A PLACE TO WORK): The H.S. & Co. No. 25A is highly prized by tool collectors, but it shouldn't be the bench of your dreams. Look past the included shiny objects to see that inside this bench beats the heart of a kitchen cabinet.

The leg vise and sliding deadman allow you to work on edges of boards or panels. The tail vise and dogs allow you to work on faces. The jack-leg leg vise (and the sliding deadman) allow you to work on ends of boards with ease. There are no aprons to impede clamping. The bench is quite long and not too deep. I am hard-pressed to find anything to criticize except for the tool tray (a personal preference).

Hammacher, Schlemmer's Workbench

Now let's pick on a classic from Hammacher, Schlemmer & Co. – it's actually a more difficult assignment. While this company is still in business, the closest thing it sells to a workbench these days is a portable air hockey game. So a little criticism of its offerings of last century are unlikely to hurt sales of its laser-guided pool cue (item 72641, $59.95).

The Manual Training Outfit 25A looks like a swanky setup for $65. In addition to the maple workbench with a face vise and tail vise, you get 26 high-quality tools, including a Stanley No. 3 smoothing plane, a Disston 22" panel saw and a Millers Falls No. 323 bit brace with an 8" sweep. Sweet. Sign me up.

Or perhaps not. Let's talk about the length of that benchtop. Though the catalog doesn't call it out, it's easy to figure by using the Disston 22" saw for scale. My guess puts the benchtop at 56" long.

NOT QUITE ROMAN; NOT QUITE RIGHT: This is one of the assembly benches in our workshop, but it's almost identical to my first workbench in our shop. This is basically what Roman workbenches looked like – except the legs were tenoned into the top.

MAKESHIFT AND SHIFTY: This is Senior Editor Glen Huey's temporary bench until he builds a nice big Shaker-style one. It looks a lot like my first bench, without the fancy roll-around drawers below. This bench is tricky to use with hand tools.

That's too short for traditional casework. Though most individual parts in a cabinet will be 48" long and shorter, mouldings and assembled projects would quickly get out of hand for this bench.

On the plus side, the legs appear flush with the front edge of the top. Score one for the Hammacher. But the bail pulls on the three overlay drawers look like they might interfere with clamping things on edge. Speaking of that, where will you clamp a cabinet door when mortising its edge? There's a big storage cabinet below the benchtop – with no system of pegs or a deadman to support items from below.

In a pinch, you could pull out the drawers partially and hope they would be situated to lend a hand. And for many assemblies, you would be able to make do. But it wouldn't be ideal. And speaking of the cabinets below this bench, the storage is welcome, but be aware of what you are giving up: Room to clamp. The bench has a nice little cubby below the benchtop and cabinet box, but trust me, you ain't getting an F-style clamp there unless you stick the clamp's bar up in the air as you cinch it down. That cubby was designed to allow the benchdogs to slip fully into their holes, and perhaps to allow a few more tools to be stored under there.

If this were my bench, I'd make a slave block that would clamp in the tail vise and run it to the floor. I'd bore it with ³/₄" holes every couple inches and make a peg that could be used to support longer stock. Plus, I'd work on the edges of narrow boards on the benchtop, between dogs. Those strategies would cover most of the problems.

So all in all, the bench isn't designed for working on edges of boards and assemblies. I've seen worse than this, however, and the workbench could be made to work with shorter pieces.

Let's look at working on the faces of boards. Again, the top isn't long enough and will interfere with what should be routine tasks. (This bench needs to be almost twice as long in my book.)

There's a nice-looking face vise mounted in the end vise position on the right side of the bench. There's a dog that lines up with a row of dog holes (I count nine) located no more than 2" in from the front edge of the benchtop. This row of dogs is a bit too close to the front edge in my opinion. The bench is easier to laminate this way in a factory, but a bit of a pain to use. If you moved the dog holes so they were 4" in from the front edge that would be much better. It would put the dog in the vise in line with the vise's screw, producing less racking

pressure on the vise, and it would allow you to grip the centerpoint of an 8"-wide board, which is nice. As the vise is now, it would wrack a bit and you'd have to add pressure to keep the work secure, and that added pressure could cause you some bowing in your stock.

Other issues for dealing with faces of boards: There is no planing stop listed or shown. You'd need to add one or make one (or get out the random-orbit sander – always an option). There are no holdfast holes. And just drilling some would be no good because of the kitchen cabinet that lurks below. There are some commercial plastic holdfasts that might work with this bench, but there is no guarantee. In fact, securing things using downward clamp pressure would be limited with this bench setup. You could apply a clamp at the ends of the bench, and you could get an F-style clamp on that front edge if you used it with the bar of the clamp sticking up in the air (never fun) and put the clamp head in the cubby space.

For working on the ends of boards (planing, sanding, tenoning and dovetailing) the iron quick-release face vise is a pretty good choice for a commercial bench. You would need to make a simple vise block to keep the vise from wracking. And you'd want a bar clamp to work in conjunction with the vise when sawing on wide boards.

So what is this bench good for? It has a good deal of tool storage: the drawers and door below, a tool tray and a tool rack on the back edge. It's OK for working on edges of boards, somewhat limited for working on faces and OK for working on ends. All in all, the bench is a bit of a compromise and is really just too small for most work.

But in a power-tool workshop this bench would be fine. You'd be a bit miffed when trying to clamp some things to the bench for routing and the like, but all-in-all you wouldn't complain too much. I should know. This bench is much like a workbench I built for *Popular Woodworking* magazine that was designed to work as an outfeed table to a table saw, offer tool storage and handle the occasional handwork task. At that, the bench performed (and still performs) quite well.

An Unintentional Roman-style Workbench

Admittedly, I do a fair amount of handwork in conjunction with my machinery and hand-held power tools. And my power-tool-only friends tend to roll their eyes when I start waxing on about workbench designs. Their contention is I'm too fussy, that all most North

POWER-TOOL WORKBENCH: This design, which we still use in our shop, is compact, stores a bunch of stuff, but is miserable for working on edges of long boards. My original plan was to use the dog holes on the front edge of the top plus the drawers. That was lame.

Americans really need is a flat-panel door, a couple sawhorses and some kind of vise. Then you can take the money you saved by not building a traditional bench and buy another plunge router.

My first workbench at the magazine was just such a workbench. The benchtop was a solid-core veneered walnut door that was almost 2' thick. These 1920s-era doors were the cafeteria doors to our Art Deco building, which had begun its life as a Coca-Cola bottling plant. The slabs were heavy and stable and pretty to look at – we still use them 12 years after we saved them from the junk pile.

The base was a set of sawhorses made from poplar 2x4s and a plastic kit that allowed you to make the sawhorses without many angle cuts. The vise was a nice Wilton quick-release vise that I had installed in the tail vise position. Its placement was a tough choice – I had only one vise and no other vise hardware.

I screwed the door to the sawhorses and bolted the vise to the door. I built it before lunch and was working on it that afternoon. Years after building that bench, I was struck by how much it resembled early Roman workbenches shown in frescos. The only differences between

my bench and the Roman version were that I screwed the base and top together and the Romans tenoned the legs into the top. Also, they didn't have a quick-release Wilton vise. Of that, I am sure.

So let's take this workbench and see how it would do in a workshop that required little handwork.

First, the good points. This bench was fantastic as a clamping surface. Its wide open area under the benchtop allowed me to clamp anything anywhere. I clamped a lot of router templates to that bench, plus stuff that needed biscuiting and drilling. I could assemble things directly on the benchtop because I could clamp pieces and assemblies to the benchtop, giving me extra support.

The quick-release vise (in the end-vise position) was good for a little bit of handwork. I could hold things for block planing and sawing. And because the bench was up against the shop wall, all the forces involved kept the bench stable during these operations.

The benchtop was long (more than 6') and wide enough (about 24") for woodworking. With a moving blanket spread out on the benchtop, it was an excellent place to sand. The top was a laminated structure and never went much out of true. I would flatten it up mostly to remove the glue and stain that had absorbed into the thick walnut veneer. And it was inexpensive, an excellent bonus for a young journalist with a family. All-in-all, I had no complaints until I started incorporating more handwork into my projects and couldn't always use the benches of the other editors.

That was the beginning of the end for that bench.

For planing faces of boards, I bored some holes in the benchtop in line with the dog on the vise that was in the tail vise position. This allowed me to clamp long boards between dogs, but the bench was too lightweight for heavy planing forces. While planing along the length of a board, the bench would creep left toward the drill press table. So working on faces by hand was difficult with that bench.

Because of the open nature of the top, I had no problems clamping stuff for chiseling and sawing. My real problems came when trying to work on edges of boards.

Except for the narrow stock I could clamp between dogs or in the vise, the bench was worthless for working on edges. When I had to mortise a door stile for a hinge or a mortise lock, I was out of luck. I had to move to someone else's bench. This was enough of a pain in the neck that I started using non-mortise hinges. That's a workaround, but not always a good one. Changing your furniture designs based on your bench isn't fun.

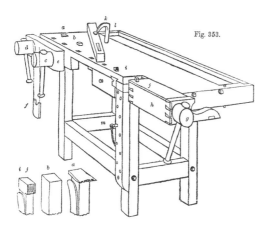

Fig. 353.

HOLTZAPFFEL'S BENCH: This is one of my favorite bench designs and is from Charles Holtzapffel's *Construction, Action and Application of Cutting Tools*. It has demerits (of course), but is a fair design.

"Work thou for pleasure — paint or sing or carve The thing thou lovest, though the body starve — Who works for glory misses oft the goal; Who works for money coins his very soul. Work for the work's sake, then, and it may be That these things shall be added unto thee."

— Kenyon Cox (1856 - 1919)
American academic, painter

ALSO APPEALING: Shaker-style workbenches, such as this one built by Stephen Fee, have an indescribable appeal. Unlike some benches with cabinets below, this one will allow you to work on the edges of boards with ease. Clamps and holdfasts aren't going to work as well, however.

Working on ends of boards was quite difficult. I could cut tenons in the vise and plane and sand small pieces, but dovetailing almost anything was an exercise in frustration. I tried everything.

It quickly became apparent that the bench that was perfect for me when I was a power-tool woodworker was holding me back as I introduced hand tools into my work. As a bench for any significant amount of handwork, it was a disaster.

So this raises a question: Are there benches just for handwork and benches just for power-tool work? I don't think that's how it works. While a Spartan bench will be fine for power-tool-only woodworking, a good hand-tool workbench will be excellent for both hand- and power-tool tasks. All of the attributes that go into a good traditional workbench also make the bench ideally suited for power-tool activity.

So even if you are a menace to the power-tool grid in your town, there is a good reason to build a traditional bench. It will handle power-tool tasks with great aplomb, and it will wait patiently as you decide if you want to incorporate more hand tools into your work. When you do (most home woodworkers make this move if they stick with the craft), then you will find your bench is ready to help you jump-start into handtools.

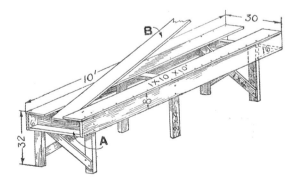

CARPENTER'S WORKBENCH: This bench from *Audels Carpenters and Builders Guide* (the 1947 edition) is designed to be knocked together on a home construction site. Note its resemblance to the English Workbench in this book and how it manages to sneak in tool storage.

A Power-tool Workbench

Several years ago I built a bench that attempted to bridge the gap between a traditional hand-tool bench and a power-tool slab on horses. It's a decent bench, but has some flaws.

On the good side, it works magnificently as an outfeed table for a cabinet saw. It stores a shop's worth of hand tools and is great for dovetailing and basic planing chores. The twin-screw tail vise is capable of a great many tasks and I've clamped some odd objects with that setup.

But the bench has its limits, and by now you should be able to pick these out with your eyes barely open. The bench is too short for working long stock. It doesn't handle planing the edges of boards well once they reach a certain width and length. The drawers below do help lend some support below the stock, but there's only so much they can do. Plus, there's just barely enough clearance under the top to put in an F-style clamp.

In the end, I give my own effort a *B*. We still use this bench, however, so don't write it off entirely.

Charles Holtzapffel's Bench

Though I like a functional bench more than a flashy one, I'm not immune to the wiles of a well-proportioned piece of work. One of the workbenches shown in Charles Holtzapffel's *Construction, Action and Application of Cutting Tools* (1875) has always charmed me with its stout looks and flashy features.

In some ways it looks like a typical 18th-century woodworking bench. The twin-screw vise in the face vise position is an excellent choice. The legs are flush to the front of the bench. There's a tail vise in the end vise position (with a sinuous outrigger support arm).

But the design has some things I'd change. Though one of the legs is bored for a peg to support long stock, I think this bench would be a pain for working on the long edges of doors. The twin-screw vise would probably help you hold most drawer parts and assembled drawers, but assembled doors would be a challenge. Plus there's the drawer, which impedes clamping to the benchtop. And the tool tray, which will attract a mess. I'm not too crazy about either of those features on a workbench.

But there is something about this bench that calls to me to modify it a bit and make one for my own. Perhaps in the next book.

So as you stare at that blank sheet of paper, don't be afraid to dream about the kind of woodworker you might become. Dissect a few commercial workbenches that you find in the catalogs. Decide for yourself what sort of features appeal to your budget, your mechanical inclination and your patience. Then let the pencil (and eraser) loose on your page.

"A boat is not a boat unless it's in the water."

— John Gardner, founder
of Mystic Seaport's boatbuilding program

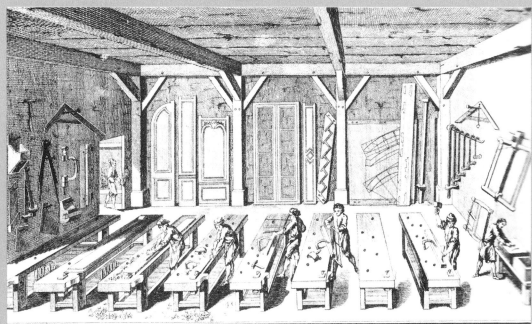

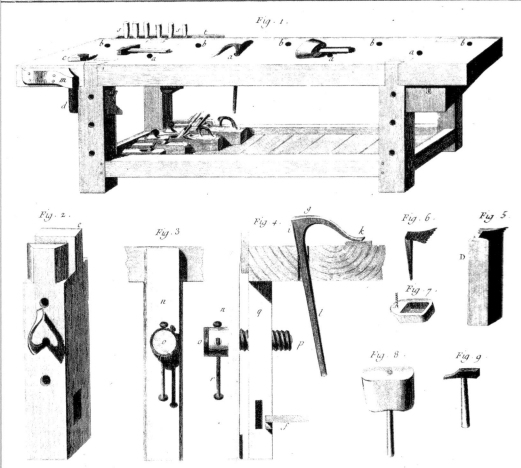

A FRENCH BENCH AT WORK: This plate, from one of Jaques-Andre Roubo's volumes, illustrates the basic French bench during the 18th century, which changed little up into the 20th century.

Chapter Four

About the Benches in this Book

In this book, there are plans for two benches that (as drawn) are good for both power- and hand-tool work. What I like about these two workbenches is that they take different paths to arrive at the same result: a bench that can accommodate a full range of woodworking operations.

Each bench can be fitted to take a variety of workholding devices. If you don't like a wagon vise, then use a tail vise or a Wonder Dog system. If the leg vise looks too archaic to your modern eyes, then you can use just about any other face vise in that spot, from a Far East quick-release vise to a vintage Emmert.

I refer to these benches as English and French, but those names are imprecise. The heritage of each bench is pretty mongrel, which is true of most workbenches, methods of work and woodworkers. The French bench is drawn from Jacques-Andre Roubo's enormous *L'art du Menuisier* (*The Art of the Woodworker*, 1769-1775). However, some of the bits and pieces of this bench show up on so-called German workbenches.

The English bench is adapted from Peter Nicholson's *Mechanic's Companion* (1831). This style of bench pokes its head up in a number of books during the next 100 years in Great Britain and the United States, and then the design all but disappears.

The Dominant Continent

Both the English and French bench are now hardly a blip on the radar screen compared to what most woodworking catalogs call the continental bench, shown on the next page. The continental style of workbench shows up everywhere and seems to have a German and Scandinavian pedigree. It was popularized in the 20th century in the United States by the Ulmia workbench, a company that has a rich past of supplying woodworking equipment but an uncertain future.

The anatomy of a continental workbench is important to know so you can see why the French and English versions are different.

- The continental bench is generally built on a trestle-style frame with sled feet. The benchtop frequently has a skirt that encloses it on all four sides — and these skirt pieces can be bolted on, finger-jointed or dovetailed at the corners. This detail makes construction more complicated than a simple slab top.
- The benchtop is usually pierced by a row of square holes for bench dogs. And these holes are angled and shaped to conceal the bench dogs when not in use. Sometimes there is a round hole or two in

the top to accept a holdfast. The bench can have a tool tray at the rear, though that's not a given.
- The face vise on the left corner of the workbench is typically a face vise with a single vise screw or there's a shoulder vise at that location, for those woodworkers who do a lot of dovetailing. The shoulder vise (as mentioned in earlier chapters) is a tricky bit of engineering and requires another leg be added to the trestle base to support the dogleg section of the shoulder vise.
- On the right side of the bench is typically a traditional tail-vise setup with an L-shaped jaw. The jaw is pierced with angled and square dog holes. If there's not a tail vise, there will usually be a wooden-jawed vise on the end of the bench that will act as a stand-in for the traditional tail vise. A few benches will put a twin-screw vise or single-screw vise on the end of the bench and rig it up with a couple dog holes in its wooden jaw to act as a tail vise.

This continental workbench is visually appealing, appears massive and seems — at first glance — to have everything you need to work wood. And if you do a limited amount of handwork, you'd be mostly right. I've worked on a fair number of these benches during the last 13 years, and they have their merits. But let's look at the bench from the wood's perspective for a minute. These benches can be great, but they can be frustrating at times, too.

In 2000, we brought a commercial continental workbench into our shop that was made in Eastern Europe. (The brand of the bench is meaningless because you cannot purchase it anymore.) From a distance, the bench was quite sexy. It had a wooden-jawed face vise on the left side of the bench and a tail vise on the right that was married to a line of dog holes on the top. The fit and finish of the bench was pretty good for the price.

"By all means read what the experts have to say. Just don't let it get in the way of your woodworking"

— John Brown (1932 –)

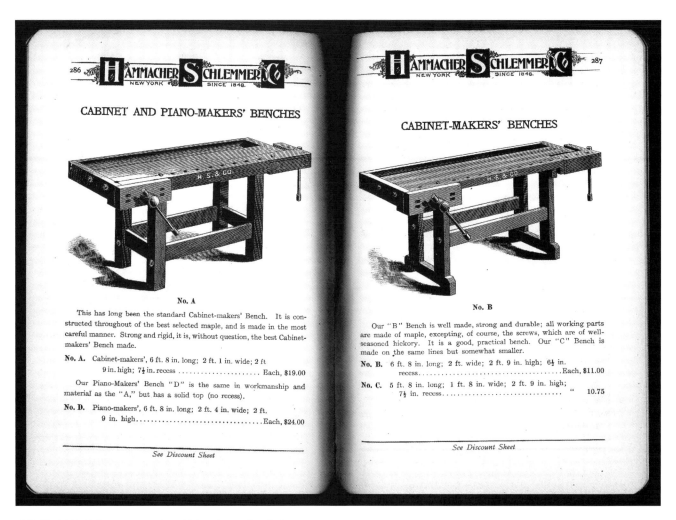

HAMMACHER SCHLEMMER & CO.
NEW YORK SINCE 1848.

CABINET AND PIANO-MAKERS' BENCHES

No. A

This has long been the standard Cabinet-makers' Bench. It is constructed throughout of the best selected maple, and is made in the most careful manner. Strong and rigid, it is, without question, the best Cabinet-makers' Bench made.

No. A. Cabinet-makers', 6 ft. 8 in. long; 2 ft. 1 in. wide; 2 ft
9 in. high; 7½ in. recess .... Each, $19.00

Our Piano-Makers' Bench "D" is the same in workmanship and material as the "A," but has a solid top (no recess).

No. D. Piano-makers', 6 ft. 8 in. long; 2 ft. 4 in. wide; 2 ft.
9 in. high...................................Each, $24.00

See Discount Sheet

CABINET-MAKERS' BENCHES

No. B

Our "B" Bench is well made, strong and durable; all working parts are made of maple, excepting, of course, the screws, which are of well-seasoned hickory. It is a good, practical bench. Our "C" Bench is made on the same lines but somewhat smaller.

No. B. 6 ft. 8 in. long; 2 ft. wide; 2 ft. 9 in. high; 6½ in.
recess....................................Each, $11.00

No. C. 5 ft. 8 in. long; 1 ft. 8 in. wide; 2 ft. 9 in. high;
7½ in. recess............................... " 10.75

See Discount Sheet

THE CONTINENTAL PERSUASION: This bench, usually called a European or continental workbench, is a popular style. When made properly, it's both massive and capable of most workholding chores. If you build one you might want to think about also building a bench slave to help support the ends of long boards.

So what was the problem? Like many continental workbenches, this one was not well-suited for working on the edges of wide boards or assemblies, such as doors or panels. Any time I needed to work on the edge of a wide board I would clamp one end in the face vise and then I'd clamp the other end to the front edge of the benchtop. And then the fun would begin. No matter how firmly I'd clamp the piece, it would slip when I applied significant pressure to the work. Why? The beautiful and too-slick film finish on the bench.

I was reluctant to judge the bench harshly on this alone. After all, many woodworkers use a bench slave with their workbenches to prop up long pieces of work. But then I tried clamping things to the benchtop for pattern routing, and that's when I got my feathers ruffled. The benchtop looked massive, but it wasn't. The top was quite thin and was merely banded by a wide skirt board. So when I went to clamp stuff to the top with an F-style clamp, the pad of the clamp couldn't touch the underside of the top because of the skirt. So I would clamp stuff to the skirt; but that's not always ideal because sometimes you want to apply pressure in toward the center of the benchtop. I could sometimes use a parallel-jaw bar clamp to increase my reach, but other times I needed to reach more deeply into the benchtop.

The face vise wracked considerably, though that's not the fault of the design of the bench, merely the execution. So I made a vise block for the face vise. When I went to cut dovetails on this bench, I would clamp narrow boards using the jaw of the tail vise on the right (this works well for drawer sides). But wider boards had to go into the face vise and required both a vise block and a hefty clamp across the top to make the work behave for the saw.

There is typically no planing stop on a continental workbench, especially the commercial ones. Some woodworkers, such as Frank Klausz, have added a planing stop to their designs. But other woodworkers either have to build a stop that clamps into the face vise, or they work between dogs using the tail vise. This dog-clamp-dog style of working gets time-consuming with the screw-in, screw-out action, especially if you have a fair number of boards that are different lengths. And I wish the bench were longer. The typical 6'-long bench has some limitations.

I gave the bench a pretty favorable write-up in *Popular Woodworking* magazine. That was before I had gotten frustrated with the way the top was made, the slick finish and the fact that the handy drawer blocked access to one key dog hole. A few months after the review

MY ROUBO BENCH: I don't have a drop of French blood in my veins, but I am quite attached to this bench. Note the wide planing stop across the width of the benchtop and the sliding deadman. Those are non-French accessories, but they are effective for my work.

L'Encyclopedie, a collection of 71,181 articles on the state of the arts, sciences and trades in France between 1751 and 1772.

Let's look at this style of bench from the original Roubo illustration, and then look at how I modified it. The French bench is – above everything – the most excellent three-dimensional clamping surface I ever worked on. With a couple clamps, you can secure almost any size board or assembly for working on the faces, edges and ends. For working on the faces of boards and the edges of boards (up to a point), you can work against the planing stop. Working on panels with hand tools can be tricky, however. You can use holdfasts in conjunction with the planing stop or – if you have to work the entire face of the board – wedge the board against the planing stop and some battens secured by the holdfasts. I did this for a year. It got old.

As shown in the illustration at the beginning of this chapter, you work on the edges of panels and wide boards by using the crochet – the hook at the end of the bench. You wedge the board into the hook and secure the board to the legs or stretchers using a variety of methods. Holdfasts in the legs work sometimes. Or you can create a ledge for the work to perch on. The ledge can be a scrap of 2x4 that's clamped to the legs with holdfasts or modern clamps. Again, this works, but it involves some fiddling about that you might not want to do. There is, however, no cheaper substitute for a face vise than the crochet. Mine is made using scrap ash and two big carriage bolts.

How about working on the ends of boards? In the stock configuration, you wedge the edge of the work into the crochet and secure the other end with a clamp or (if you are lucky) with a well-placed holdfast. You also can support your work from below with a holdfast or clamp that presses the work to the gloriously wide leg.

So even in this simple form, the French bench can do a lot of things fairly well. I added a few details that make it quite a bit faster to use, as shown in the photo at right.

- Leg vise: Roubo shows leg vises in his book, so it's not a stretch of historical fact to add one to the left leg of the bench. The leg vise makes it faster to secure boards for working on their edges and ends. You can then omit the crochet or (as I did) keep it because it's still useful, it's cheap to make and it's fun to use.

- Sliding deadman: This is not in Roubo's book, but I love a sliding deadman. This device, which is flush to the front surface of the bench and pierced with holes, can support long boards and wide panels when working on edges. A deadman can also support your work from below when working on ends.

appeared I wished that I could review the bench again to point out its flaws, but woodworking magazines typically don't do that. Perhaps we should.

After that review, I resolved to design workbenches that were more useful, less expensive and easy to build. I attempted a number of strategies: a $175 workbench, a workbench for power-tool woodworkers, and a workbench that could be built in 24 hours (I built four of those). All these forms had their merits and are still in use today. And each bench inched me a little closer to the ideal. I turned away from the continental workbench, but I stayed on the same continent and dusted off my wife's high school French-to-English dictionary.

The French Workbench

The French workbench appears to be a simple design – almost too simple – for cabinetwork. One criticism of the design is that it is shown being used in a joiner's shop in Roubo's first volume – workmen are building doors and sash windows in the engraving. And so it must be designed to build only frame-like assemblies, oui? Non.

If you page through the other volumes of Roubo, you will see the same style of workbench being used for marquetry, carriage-building and garden-related woodwork. Other French books of the same era show a similarly massive workbench, particularly Denis Diderot's

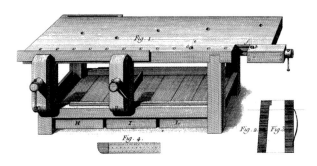

ANOTHER ROUBO BENCH: In a later volume, Roubo shows off this so-called German workbench. It has two leg vises (one slides!), plus a tail vise and tool storage.

- Wide planing stop: Again, this is not from Roubo. I much prefer a wide planing stop to a narrow single-point one. It allows me to work boards and panels with the grain that are as wide as my benchtop. It's faster and simpler than working against holdfasts or battens. I also think that this English device must appeal to my English genes from my mother's side. Roubo and other early sources show a toothed metal stop that embedded in a wooden stop that moves up and down.

I tried using a few metal stops, including a beautiful reproduction of an 18th-century one, a couple stops made from railroad spikes and the commercial aluminum stops that you embed in your benchtop and raise and lower with a thumbscrew.

These stops can mark your work, especially when you use them properly, which is to push a board securely up against the metal teeth. They do help keep your stock under control, and they can be good if you build period reproductions, which generally hide the end grain with mouldings. The risk with a metal stop is that your planes will strike the metal if you make an error, and your iron or the sole of your hand plane will get damaged. Because my furniture frequently exhibits the end grain, I don't use the toothed stop much at all. Let your work and your proclivity for living dangerously be your guide.

- Wagon vise: I added this gizmo in the end vise position mostly to allow me to work across the grain of boards and assemblies without the hassle of moving around battens. Roubo shows a variant of a wagon vise with detailed drawings. Mine is different because of my commercial metal screw. Because my wagon vise was a retrofit, I used the round brass dogs from Veritas. These dogs can also faintly mark your work and be a hazard to cutting edges. I've had pretty good luck with them over the years and have yet to strike them with a plane. The dogs have gotten sanded on occasion.
- Holdfast holes: I refrain from pockmarking my bench and legs with holes for holdfasts unless I absolutely need the hole and have considered its position carefully. I have one hole that I should have moved $1/2$" closer to the center of the benchtop.

As the Roubo stands today, I am well-pleased with its ability to handle a wide variety of work. I'm to the point where I never say about the bench: "If only...."

The English Efficiency

When most people think of an English-style workbench, they usually think of what some people call the *strong table* workbench. It's an apronless table with four stout legs. Or it has a small apron as shown in the illustration at left. Some people call this bench an Ian Kirby bench, after the modern English craftsman and author.

The bench's built-in workholding is generally quite simple – a face vise that is not at the far corner of the bench but is between the legs. Some benches even center the vise on the front edge of the benchtop.

A lot of workholding is done with accessories that clamp into the face vise, including the planing stop and a wide variety of gizmos (the English call them *appliances*) for shooting edges and ends of boards. I've worked on this style of workbench and find it lacking for working on edges as is. There are, of course, appliances for this. But it begins to feel a bit like a food processor as you are rummaging under the bench for the appliance that makes julienne fries.

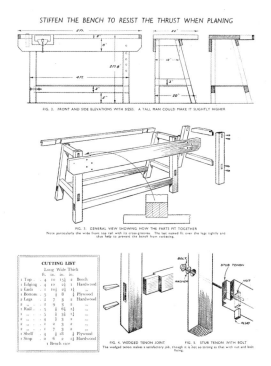

MIDDLE ENGLISH: This bench is drawn by English cabinetmaker Charles Hayward and bridges the gap between the old English bench designs (with an apron) and the new ones (which eschew the apron).

An Older English Bench

The English-style workbench I'm partial to was drawn in Peter Nicholson's book on carpentry and joinery. This is the bench you'll find the interpreters working on at Colonial Williamsburg, and it's a form that shows up even into the 20th century, especially in books on house carpentry. You'll never find anything like it for sale in the woodworking catalogs.

So let's look at this bench as Nicholson drew it and then as I built it. The most eye-catching aspect of Nicholson's bench is the wide front apron that is pierced with holes for pegs or holdfasts. This makes the bench ideal for working on the edges of boards and offers support anywhere along the bench's front.

The apron also turns the top into an effective torsion box, which allows you to use far less material to build your workbench (less than half, actually) than you would with a same-sized French bench. The top is thin (mine is $2^{1}/4$"-thick in the center) and gains rigidity from the aprons, the leg assemblies and three ribs under the top.

The aprons also allowed the joiner or carpenter to transform the space under the top into a tool crib. They would make one of the top slabs removable and build a box between the aprons that would hold the bench tools. Not only is this handy storage, but the tools add weight to the bench.

There's a face vise with a wooden jaw and a wooden screw. These vises are notorious for racking in use (just ask the interpreters the next time you are at Colonial Williamsburg), and so you'll need a vise block. The holes in the apron work with the face vise for working on both edges and ends when used in conjunction with a holdfast.

On the benchtop, there is a single planing stop, but other than that, the top is a wide expanse of nothing but wood. Like the so-called strong table workbench described above, you'll need appliances to

MODERN ENGLISH: Nothing says *English* like a wide front apron. This bench is similar to 19th-century English workbenches, but it has some modern adaptations, most notably a wagon vise in the end vise position.

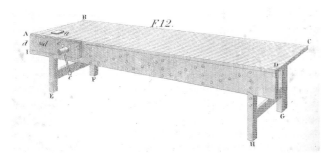

OLD ENGLISH: You don't see this bench much in shops or modern woodworking texts. It disappeared during the 20th century and was replaced by the continental bench as the bench of choice.

make this bench effective for working on wide panels – that is the bench's biggest weakness in my book.

The Modern English Bench

My English workbench has probably been corrupted so much by other forms that the English would likely disavow it. Most notably, I angled the legs at 20°. This isn't to resist planing or wracking forces, but to allow the leg vise to clamp wider boards. Is it traditional and appropriate? I think so. Early English accounts show some benches with angled legs and benches with leg vises, though there is little doubt in my mind that the face vise Nicholson drew is the dominant form.

I kept the single planing stop and have made a wide planing stop that clamps into my leg vise. However, my biggest historical transgression was the addition of the wagon vise. This is to get around building a planing tray for working on panels. In hindsight, building a planing tray is far simpler than adding a wagon vise, but the bench is what it is. I've also added some round holes to the benchtop for hold-downs or holdfasts.

So for working on boards' faces, I use the planing stop, the wide planing stop, the wagon vise and a hold-down. For working on long edges, I use the leg vise and the system of holes in the apron with a holdfast. For working on ends both wide and narrow, I use the leg vise in conjunction with a holdfast or hold-down in the apron.

All in all, this somewhat-English bench minimizes the amount of bar clamps you must use, keeps the appliances you need to build to a minimum and is inexpensive to build. There are some tricky bits to consider, however, which is the topic of the next chapter.

"Well, my standard formula was the better work you do, the more chance that you'll starve."

— James Krenov on teaching at the College of the Redwoods in an interview conducted by Oscar Fitzgerald in Fort Bragg, Calif., Aug. 12 and 13, 2004

ONCE COMMON: The wide front apron, angled legs and jack-legged leg vise are all unfamiliar to most modern woodworkers. However, about 200 years ago, each of these features could be found on benches for carpenters and joiners. These features disappeared as the continental bench became the preferred form.

Chapter Five

The English Workbench

The Ghost of a Bench: This workbench may not have been designed with the cabinetmaker in mind. It shows up in Peter Nicholson's *Mechanic's Companion* (1831). Accompanying this drawing is a short description of the bench in the section titled "Joinery." While modern woodworkers consider joinery to be a part of what we do to build furniture, joinery had a different meaning in the 18th and 19th centuries.

While carpenters built the framework of the house, it was the joiner who supplied the decorative surfaces inside: the windows, doors and mouldings that distinguish a simple barn from a home. It would be easy to think of joiners as the latter-day equivalent of the modern finish carpenter, but it's not quite that simple. Though modern-day finish carpenters are among the most highly skilled workers on a jobsite, joiners were called upon to do even more.

They typically would build sash windows, passageway doors and the wide variety of mouldings and fitments that would go into a house of that day. The tool kit of a joiner looked much like the toolkit of a cabinetmaker, with backsaws, joinery planes and moulding planes in strong evidence. But the tools had profiles that were intended to do house-scale work instead of furniture-scale.

So it should come as little surprise that Nicholson wrote that the typical bench for a joiner should be 10' to 12' in length, which is longer than most modern workbenches. This makes sense when you consider that long runs of mouldings had to be prepared for a house.

Other than that detail, much of the work that occurred on a joiner's bench would resemble work performed on the bench of a furniture maker. There are lots of mortise-and-tenon joints, rabbets, grooves and mouldings. Among the differences: The furniture maker would be cutting dovetails more often, though Nicholson discusses the dovetail saw as an essential tool for joiners in making drawers. The joiner would be making more mouldings than a furniture maker.

For the modern woodworker, I think that the distinction between the two benches and methods of work are insignificant. The joints and workholding challenges are similar. The tools are quite similar. And the wood is the same.

This bench shows up repeatedly in the 19th and early 20th centuries. In G. Forster's 1816 painting of an English woodworking shop and in manuals for carpentry, such as *The Amateur Carpenter and Builder* (1904), in plans offered by Stanley tools, in *Audels Carpenters and Builders Guide* (1947), and in Charles Hayward's *How to Make*

Woodwork Tools. But I have never seen this style of bench in an early woodworking catalog as a bench you can purchase. Instead, it is shown as a bench that you can build yourself.

Then, one day in the 20th century, it falls from favor.

After the middle of the 20th century, the joinery profession disappears. After World War II, houses are built differently. Windows and doors are manufactured. House carpenters work with small handheld electrical tools, so the need for a jobsite workbench dissipates. The continental-style workbench, which has always been around, becomes ascendant.

Why Build This Bench?

When I stumbled upon this bench in an old book, it looked to me like the spiritual father of the plastic Black & Decker Workmate. The English bench seemed serviceable, but not serious. It seemed designed to be built quickly out of inexpensive materials — not something for a lifetime of service. But it was a dominant form among workbenches for more than a century. And the more I examined its particulars the more I was determined to build one and put it to work.

As I sat down to sketch a construction drawing, I had my laptop's CAD software at my left hand and Nicholson's book at the right. As I read Nicholson's description of the innards of the bench and tried to translate it into pixels, it became apparent that inside this old bench beats the heart of something modern: a torsion box.

"That's another thing the rural Welshman in me likes — that the tools and technology of the blacksmith aren't, or don't need to be anyway, terribly sophisticated. As with any craft or hobby, you can spend a fortune just getting set up, or you can spend next to nothing and get on with it."

— Don Weber, bodger, blacksmith, writer and teacher, from the article "The Magic of Iron & Fire," in *Popular Woodworking* magazine

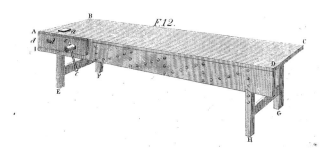

HALF-ENGLISH: My English bench (top) is based on a bench from Peter Nicholson's *Mechanic's Companion*. And though the design is old, what's under those aprons is considered quite modern: a torsion box.

ONE LOAD, ONE BENCH: This trunk load of yellow pine is all I needed to build the English workbench. Once you get the materials, the next critical step is to treat it like you would any furniture-making wood.

Many pieces of contemporary furniture use a torsion-box construction to create an assembly that's rigid and lightweight. Essentially, the torsion box is like the wing of an old airplane or our own body cavities. The torsion box is made up of a number of stiff but thin ribs that are joined together and then covered in a lightweight, flexible and thin skin.

The ribs stiffen the exterior skins. And because the construction is mostly air, it's lightweight. When you see shelving units that are cantilevered off a wall and covered with heavy books, you're likely looking at a torsion-box construction.

"Between each pair of coupled legs, the length of the bench is generally divided into three or four equal parts," Nicholson wrote, "and transverse bearers fixed at the divisions to the side boards... for the purpose of supporting the top firmly, and keeping it from bending."

Yup, that's a torsion box. The beauty of the torsion-box construction is that it requires far less wood to create than the massive slab top of the French workbench. From a modern woodworking perspective, this is a big deal. While it was simpler in the 18th and 19th centuries to get a single slab top of massive proportions, today we are likely to make up our tops from some (sometimes many) narrower boards. The top for the French bench in this book required me to glue up 25 layers of boards. The English bench? Three boards and four edge joints (and a lot less glue, time and clamps).

Still another good reasons to build this bench: the wide aprons. This sounds counter-intuitive, but the wide aprons are an asset. Even though they restrict you from clamping stuff to the benchtop (to the point of being a fault) they make up for this defect in assisting when-

ever you want to work the edges of boards – which is a function that's sorely lacking on many modern and commercial benches. Once you use a bench that helps you work on edges, you'll wonder why other forms of benches have to make it so hard.

Begin With the Wood

This bench wants to be made out of construction-grade lumber. It was designed for carpenters and joiners, so making the bench out of purpleheart is a bit of a disconnect – like building a Shaker-style party barge. When you go to pick your lumber for this project, do not buy any 2x4s. It seems tempting to make the legs out of that size stock and "save" time with ripping. Resist the urge. All 2x4s are twisty, knotty lessons in frustration. They will work against you.

I've built a lot of benches out of dimensional stock, and I always get letters and phone calls from readers that go something like this: "Where did you get that primo pine?" I'll tell you: the home center. People don't believe me, but it's true. In fact, I don't even look that hard when I go to the home center. I usually pick off the top of the stack and cull enough material in about 40 minutes to make a bench.

In fact, the only time I've had trouble was when I was at the Home Depot near our office and there were only a couple boards in the lower rack. Naturally, I scaled the orange metal racks to open a new bunk of pine to pick through. They don't like it when you do this. They call the manager and yell at you.

So here's the trick: Stroll by the 2x4s and head directly for the 2x12s. If you have a full-size pickup, go to the 16-foot 2x12s. The widest and longest stuff will be the clearest and straightest. And usually

A MODERN CARPENTRY BENCH: This sawhorse setup is part of what doomed the English bench to obsolescence. With a circular saw, miter saw or crosscut handsaw, you can quickly get your boards to length. Then take them to the table saw for ripping.

STICKERED FOR DRYING: Try to stack up your wood to allow air to flow around the end grain of your boards and through the face grain as well. This means you should separate the layers of your woodpile with stickers – thin strips of scrap.

it is also the driest. You want to use a species that contractors use to frame out a floor or a ceiling in your area. In the South, this can be Southern yellow pine. In the East, this can be fir. Out West, look for hemlock, fir or hem/fir (which can be either species). Don't use white pine or sugar pine – it's not stiff enough for a benchtop, though it could be used to construct a workbench's base.

Pick out the boards carefully and use a moisture meter if you have one. You can use boards that are 17 percent moisture, but you will have to wait for them to come into equilibrium with your shop. Having some material that is wet (12 percent) and drier (9 percent) can be used to your advantage when building a bench. However, the really wet stuff takes its time in drying and delays your workbench – sometimes by a month or more.

When you get the stuff – and the old books called the wood *stuff* – the first order of business is to crosscut and rip the boards to slightly oversized chunks that will then sit until they get close to equilibrium in your shop.

Here's the funny thing about softwood. It has a reputation for warping, so we assume that it's one of those woods that moves a lot with the seasonal changes in humidity, such as red oak – a real mover and a shaker. This is not quite true. Softwoods such as yellow pine and fir move around and warp and twist as they reach equilibrium with their environment, but then they are fairly stable, much more like cherry and maple than red oak. But because softwoods come into our hands when wetter (fir is the soggiest in my experience), we think they are prone to considerable seasonal movement.

Because moisture moves in and out of wood through the end grain faster than it does through the face grain, your wood will achieve equilibrium much faster if you first crosscut it into smaller chunks. You still want pieces that are safe to pass through your machines, so try to shoot for chunks that are about 1" or 2" longer than your finished dimension.

As you choose your pieces, use your moisture meter (if you have one) to its best advantage. Choose the wetter boards to make the bench's legs. Choose the driest stock for the rails between the legs.

The stock of middling wetness is fine for the aprons and the top. By segregating your boards, you can use their moisture content to assist your joinery. The mortise in the slightly wet leg will shrink onto the dry tenon on the rail. This will result in a tighter joint. With this approach, you'll be able to start working with your lumber as soon as the rails arrive at equilibrium with your workshop.

Now rip your stock so it is close to finished width. I usually shoot for $^3/_4$" oversized on the width. Why is this step important? While it won't significantly speed up the drying of your stock, it will allow you to squeeze a bit more thickness out of your boards. A 2x12 will cup considerably more when drying than a 4"-wide board. The smaller cup on the narrower board will be easier to machine flat.

Most dimensional lumber comes with at least one good straight edge, which you can use against your rip fence. If you don't have an edge that looks straight, it's safer to joint one long edge on your jointer before ripping it to size. This is, of course, easier after you've crosscut most of the pieces.

Now wait. Check your pile every week and mark the moisture content on each board so you can chart its progress. If you don't have a moisture meter, I'd wait three weeks and then use your sense of touch to guess how wet your boards are. The end grain of your wetter boards will feel cooler than the face grain. When the end grain and face grain feel similar in temperature, your boards are fairly dry. But usually, three to four weeks is enough time.

JOINTING FOR PRECISION: I am fastidious about keeping my power jointer and planer in tune. Even so, I find that a jointer plane can make a flatter surface that is easier to glue up. Here's how: You want to first plane a slight hollow in the middle of the length of the board. Begin planing about 3" from the end and stop your plane 3" from the other end. Make three or four passes like this. Then make a pass along the entire length. Try it. It works.

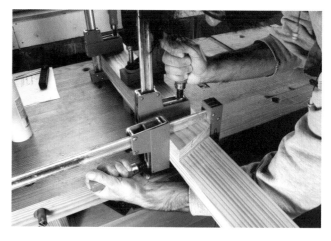

CLAMP BOTH WAYS: By clamping each leg assembly across its width you'll line up the two layers, making for much less cleanup. You don't need to apply a lot of pressure, just enough to line up the two layers.

I know this sounds like a long time to wait, but you will be punished if you don't give the wood an opportunity to dry out a bit. It will warp after you machine it flat – I guarantee it.

Laminate the Legs

While you could build the legs for this bench using 4x4 posts, I wouldn't recommend it. I tried that with one bench years ago. If you think 2x4s are gnarly, wait until you try the 4x4s. Instead, laminate the legs from two pieces. This has myriad advantages. One: Your wood will be clearer. Two: Making the giant notch for the front and rear apron of the bench is easy. You simply cut one layer shorter (and at a 20° angle) and then glue them up. Voilà: Instant notch.

So cut your leg stock close to finished size, perhaps ¹/₂" more than the finished length. You want a little extra left to trim at the feet and at the top. The dimensions provided are to make a bench that is about 35" high. So this is the time to scale things up or down.

Cut the 20° angle at the top of the shorter layer, but leave the rest of the ends square. You'll trim them at 20° after glue-up. Now straighten out your stock as best you can with your powered jointer, planer or your jointer plane.

If you glue up the legs with care you'll save headaches later in fitting them to the apron. Spread a consistent but thin layer of yellow glue on the surface of the short layer, line up the two ends of your two layers and clamp things up. If you are using a resinous wood such as Southern yellow pine, leave it in the clamps for five hours. The resins in this wood resist penetration by the water in the glue. As the glue dries, turn your attention to cutting the tenons on the rails.

Beefy Tenons; Deep Mortises

The traditional way to cut a mortise-and-tenon joint is to cut the mortises and then cut the tenons. If you cut your joints by machine, as I do, you can use the consistency of the machine cutters to reverse that process. Why would you do this? To reduce your layout chores. If you can use the actual tenons to lay out the mortises on your legs, you reduce the math in subtracting out the tenon's shoulders for each piece.

The price of this process is you have to first make one test mortise using your tooling so you can use that to test-fit your tenoning setup. The tenons are ⁵/₈" thick on this bench. That's a bit thick by traditional standards. The rule of thirds would insist they be more like ⁷/₁₆" or so. But because these rails go into very large legs, there is no chance that the legs will be weakened by these joints. Plus, quite honestly, my

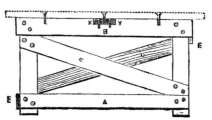

FIG. 217. ELEVATION OF BACK OF BENCH.

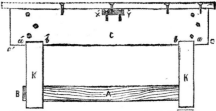

FIG. 218. ELEVATION OF FRONT OF BENCH.

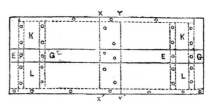

FIG. 219. PLAN OF TOP OF BENCH.

GETTING CROSS: Many English bench designs use diagonal cross braces to add support.

TENONS WITH A DADO STACK: One nice thing about making tenons with a dado stack is you cut the shoulder and the cheek with one setup. You do need to keep firm downward pressure on the work, however. Note that I've raised my basket guard for this photo and the saw is off.

A STAND-IN FOR THE APRON: You don't want to lay out the top of the legs using a measurement – it can trip you up. Use a scrap that is cut to the same width as your aprons and use that to mark a line at the top of the leg. This will ensure you won't miss.

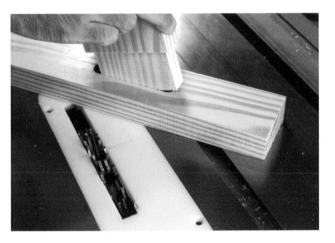

TEST-FITTING IN A TEST MORTISE: If your face cheeks need to be trimmed back you can raise the blades slightly, or use a rasp or shoulder plane to fit the tenon. I try to get as close as possible with the machines.

A TRICK FOR DEALING WITH THE ODD LEGS: Because of the shape of the laminated legs, they are a challenge to work on, whether that's planing, sanding or boring them. To remedy that problem, I took a piece of scrap from the project, cut a 20° angle on one end and applied some PSA sandpaper to the end. This little scrap supports the leg and holds on to the angled end grain of the leg. It's quite handy.

$5/8$"-diameter Forstner bit is sharper than my $1/2$" (I don't own a $7/16$" Forstner bit). So decide how big you want your joints and then bore a test mortise in some scrap using a Forstner bit and a drill press. Make a series of overlapping holes, then bore out the waste between the overlapping holes. Keep repeating this until the mortise is complete.

There is a variety of good ways to make tenons. If you are comfortable with your method, stick with it. I generally prefer a dado stack when working with large-scale stock such as this for two good reasons: the table saw has more guts than a router table for this operation. And the dado stack allows me to work with these long pieces flat on the table saw, which is easier than balancing a long heavy piece on end, as with other table saw methods.

I'll set up my dado stack with the maximum number of chippers my table saw will accommodate. I set the height of the blades to match the desired depth of my tenon's face shoulders. In this case, $5/16$". To set the length of the tenons, I use a fence on my saw's sliding table

(a wooden fence attached to a miter gauge also suffices) with a stop to set the length of the tenons. Cut your face cheeks.

Then raise the dado blade to $5/8$" and cut the edge shoulders on all the tenons except for the edge shoulder at the top of the top rail. It needs to be larger: $1^1/2$". Raise the dado blade to this height and trim the remaining edge shoulders of the top rails. The large shoulder ensures that the vulnerable end grain wall of your mortise will not self-destruct during fitting or assembly.

Dressing and Boring the Legs

Clean up the legs so they are straight and square and prepare to cut the 20° angle at the top and bottom of the legs. First you need to lay out the angle at the top of the legs. Take a scrap that is the same width as your apron piece and place it on the legs, up against the short layer. Trace the shape of the apron onto the legs and cut the top angled edge of each leg.

REDUCING YOUR ERRORS: Remember: There are right legs and left legs. It's best to bundle them and mark their orientation in the finished bench to prevent mistakes. Here I'm lining up the angled laminations on a group of legs to confirm my marks line up before trimming the leg's mate.

THE TENON RULER: By using your tenons as a ruler you don't have to measure out the offset of the tenon's shoulder. Simply mark the location of the rail on your leg, then show the rail to that mark. Trace the shape on the leg. Bore a mortise there.

VERY BORING: When making mortises on the drill press, I never pare the mortise's walls with a chisel. That can introduce error. The only chisel work I do is with a corner chisel to square the rounded corners. To avoid paring walls, I bore the mortise over and over, removing waste all long its length until the Forstner bit can slide freely in the mortise left-to-right.

With the top edges trimmed, bundle your legs in pairs: one left pair, one right. Mark out the 20° angle on the foot of one of your legs and cut that to shape. Then use that first leg as a template to mark out the second. Trim the second leg identical to the first. Repeat this process with the other pair of legs.

Now you can use the actual tenons to lay out the mortises on the legs. Bundle your leg assemblies and mark out the locations of the mortises on one leg and carry those marks over to the mating leg using a try square.

Boring the mortises is efficient on the drill press. Chuck a $^5/_8$" Forstner bit in your drill press and set the fence on your machine to bore along the center of your leg. The mortises are of two different depths, and these require two separate strategies.

The mortises for the lower rail are 2" deep and won't require any special consideration. They are just deep and blind mortises. Simply set the drill press to make the mortises $2^1/_8$" deep and go to town. However, the mortises for the top stretcher are a different story. They are through-mortises because you want to achieve the maximum length possible for the tenons on the top aprons. Remember: The leg is thinner up at the top than it is at the bottom.

You have two choices with these through-mortises at the top of the legs. You can bore them with your support block below (which is what I did) or you can turn the leg over and bore through the leg and into a larger piece of scrap. Either works.

There are other drill press chores at this point that you should tend to. If you are going to add a leg vise to the workbench, you need to bore a mortise and a hole in the front left leg. The $1^3/_8$"-diameter hole is for the vise screw. The mortise is for the parallel guide that assists the leg vise in applying tremendous force without racking.

Boring the hole for the vise screw is, of course, simple work. The through-mortise for the parallel guide takes a bit more layout to do correctly. This through-mortise is $^3/_4$" wide and 3" long. Mark it out on the face side of your leg using the construction drawing as a guide. Then transfer that same layout to the backside of the same leg.

Bore the mortise halfway through on the drill press, then flip the leg over (flip it end over end to keep the same reference surface against

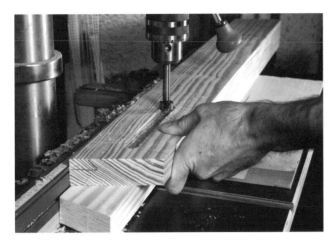

A BLOCK BELOW: Rather than chewing up a piece of plywood to bore these through-mortises, I used my handy support block to keep the leg stable while boring the joint.

LESS MEASURING, MORE ACCURACY: If you tried to measure exactly where the bevel should be on the top of the top rails, you'd probably be off by a little. That's why it's best to mark out the angle when you get each end assembled, then rip the rails to their proper shape.

SQUARING HOLES: When using a corner chisel, resist the urge to make the cut with one big bite. There is more chance that the chisel will go off course or get stuck. Take two or three bites to get accurate results. Begin at the inside and work your way back into the corner with the last pass being right on your layout lines.

your drill press's fence). Then bore out the other side of the mortise so the two meet in the middle.

With all the boring at an end, you should clean out the corners of the joints, squaring them to fit the tenons. A corner chisel makes quick work of this operation. A stout firmer chisel can also do the job, but with more fiddling, layout and cutting.

Fit all your joints. Examine the shoulders of your tenons for gaps and ensure that the tenons fit snug in their mortises. With the ends dry-assembled, letter all your joints so you can assemble them correctly with glue. Now mark out the angle on the top rails, using the top of the leg as the guide. Disassemble all the pieces, bevel your table saw's blade to 20° and rip the top rail to proper width at the saw. Assembly is next. Clean up all your rails and prepare them for finishing. Clean up the legs, too, though they'll require some more work after assembly as well.

Boring and the Drawboring

Whenever I build a project that requires an extra measure of stoutness (chairs and workbenches are prime examples) or use wood that is a little bit wet, I drawbore the joints for extra strength.

Drawboring is an old process that has fallen out of favor thanks to modern glues, modern kilns and piston-fit joints. But it's still a good trick to know and use. In essence, you bore a hole for a peg through your mortise. Then you assemble the joint and mark the hole's location on the tenon. Disassemble the joint and drill a hole through the tenon that is about $1/16$" closer to the shoulder of the tenon than the mark. This $1/16$" offset (or a bit stronger) is appropriate for heavy work such as this. Use a smaller offset for smaller work.

Then assemble the joint. If you own a drawbore pin — a tapered metal pin with a wooden handle that looks like a machinist's drift pin — you can test your assembly by twisting the pin into the assembled joints. The pin also slightly deforms the mortise and the tenon to ease the path of the peg. Glue up the joint (if desired) and drive an oak peg into the holes. If the joint is made correctly, no clamps are necessary.

Begin by boring $3/8$"-diameter holes through your mortises. You can drill these holes through the leg or stop them before they emerge

PREPARE FOR PEGS: Drill your initial bores with a brad-point bit. You can do this on a drill press, but a handheld drill is accurate for this job.

A BIT OFF: When you begin drawboring, you want to carefully measure everything out. After you do a couple dozen drawbores, you'll develop a feel for it and do it by eye. No measuring offsets or precision boring apparatus. These holes are through-holes, which is why I have the work-piece propped up on scrap.

ASSEMBLY: This is what assembly looks like. In the leg that's flat on the benchtop, I put glue in the mortises. Then I pushed the rails into their mortises. For the other leg that I'm positioning, I painted the mortise walls with glue, flipped the board over quickly and pushed it onto its tenons. A couple raps with a mallet and a block of scrap wood seats everything quickly before driving the pegs.

on the other side. Drilling them through is the safer approach (more on this later). The centers of the holes are $^5/_8$" in from the edge of the leg. I used two pegs in each joint for the top rail; and one peg in each joint for the bottom rail.

With all the holes bored in the mortises, assemble the joints and use your $^3/_8$" brad-point bit to transfer the locations of the centerpoints of each hole onto the tenons. Disassemble the joints and drill holes through the tenons that are $^1/_{16}$" closer to the shoulder than your layout lines indicate.

Reassemble everything and test your fits with a metal drawbore pin (if you own one). Then take some $^3/_8$"-diameter oak dowel stock and cut a bunch of pegs about 4" long. Whittle one end of each peg with a taper that resembles a sharpened pencil, but without the sharp writing tip. A strong (but fairly short) taper is the key to assembling this joint without disaster.

The taper allows the oak to snake through the offset holes without self-destructing as it slams into the tenon or far wall of the mortise. Using oak – as opposed to maple – ensures that the peg is more likely to bend rather than break when stressed by the structure of this joint.

One detail: The joinery purists will rive out their pegs from straight stock and create the pegs using a dowel plate. I've done this hundreds of times myself. It's gratifying and produces nearly inde-structible pegs. But cutting the pegs from straight-cut, straight-grained oak dowels is also a good option. These dowels are cheap ($1 for 36") and really work with drawboring.

I glue my joints. If I'm using a yellow glue, I'll put a single clamp across the joint I'm drawboring. Because yellow glue can set up

quickly (too quickly in a hot or dry shop) you want the shoulders of the tenon tight against the mortises before you drive the pegs. The clamp helps this. If I'm using liquid hide glue (another favorite of mine) I don't bother with a clamp because I have an open time with the glue that's as long as an hour.

Drive the pegs. Use a hammer or a mallet. When the peg starts to resist as it bends into the curve, keep tapping it firmly, even as your progress slows. As the peg passes through both components of the joint the peg will give up on its fight and eventually dive to the bottom of the hole. Or, if it is a short-grain, obstinate and brittle peg, it will bust apart no matter what coaxing you give it.

When this occurs, you have a couple options. If you drilled your holes through the mortises so they passed all the way through the legs, you're in luck. Simply get another peg and start driving it behind the first broken one. Usually the new one will push the old one out the

BENCHES ARE BORING: I'm always struck by how much accurate boring is required when building workbenches. This gizmo for my handheld drill helps keep my tool at 90° when making holes for dogs and the like. Typically, I'd drill these freehand, so don't feel compelled to rush out and buy one of these jigs. They're a bit flimsier than you want, and the depth stop for the plunging mechanism slips easily.

FAST FLUSHING: You could cut your tenon a little short so that you don't have to flush it up after assembling the legs. But because this is a critical joint, I decided to get the maximum amount of joinery surface, even if it added an extra step. Use mineral spirits or denatured alcohol to moisten the end grain before you trim it.

CLAMPING CORRECTLY: You don't need a lot of clamps for assembly. But you do need to place them strategically and apply pressure in a gradual fashion. First use the smaller clamps to snug up the apron to the wide flat surface of the leg assembly. But don't apply the death grip yet. Then clamp across the leg and the top of the apron as shown and apply steady pressure to bring the apron into place in the corner. Now snug things up.

exit hole. If the peg has splintered badly, you might have to resort to plan B: drilling out the hole through the assembled joint. This will remove the offset hole in the tenon, clear the hole of waste and allow you to reassemble the joint with a new peg. It won't be a drawbored, mechanical joint, but it also won't be firewood.

With the pegs driven in place, you can saw or pare them flush with the legs and clean up your assemblies.

Aprons, and Getting the Bench on its Feet

The aprons are an essential part of the skeleton of this workbench. You want them as flat as can be so they'll attach easily to the leg assemblies. Working on 8'-long pieces of wood is a challenge. Add to the fact that these aprons are 11" wide, and you'll see that there's a challenge ahead.

Most importantly, make the inside face of the apron boards, which will attach to the legs, as flat as you can. It's actually easier to work on the exterior faces of the aprons after assembly. If you are having real difficulties with getting the inside faces flat, you can resort to working on just the two sections of each apron that will attach to the legs. When taken too far, this approach can introduce problems at assembly. But if you have a cup or bow of $\frac{1}{8}$" or less, you'll be OK.

With the inside of the aprons flat, you also can clip the corners of the aprons as shown in the construction drawings. And then drill the

UNDER THE HOOD: Here's what to look for as you glue the apron down. You want the wide surface of the apron to contact the leg assembly as well as possible. Wipe away any squeeze-out as you apply pressure so you can see if you have any gaps in the joints that need to be closed up.

CLAMP THE BACK: Once you have the first apron placed properly, the second one is easy. Check your joints for gaps as before and allow the glue to dry overnight before you begin pushing it around a lot.

BRING IN THE REINFORCEMENTS: Three screws through each leg will give you an extra measure of security. Though they are not mentioned in the old books, I decided to vote my own conscience here.

FAST FLUSH: While some woodworkers might choose a flush-cutting saw for this task, I think you'll find it too slow and too likely to wander in the cut – they are designed to trim dowels, not workbench legs. A cross-cut backsaw makes quick work of this task. Use your off hand to press the blade against the apron as you cut.

$3/4$"-diameter holes in the front apron, again using the pattern in the construction drawings as a guide. While you can change this pattern of holes to suit you, be sure to watch where these holes make their exit inside the workbench. You can make some holes useless if they exit the apron and hit the leg assemblies.

With the aprons ready for assembly, turn your attention to the leg assemblies. Use a square or wooden straightedge to examine the legs, particularly where the through-tenon on the top rail emerges from the leg. You want the tenon flush. Trim it with a block plane if necessary.

Assembly isn't difficult if you use gravity as an assistant. Clamp your leg assemblies to some low sawhorses so the apron lays on top of the leg assemblies, as shown in the photos. Position the leg assemblies so the apron drops exactly where you want it. The apron will require clamping in two directions. Use a few clamps to squeeze the apron onto the legs and one long clamp to pull the apron tight against the corner you formed by laminating the two leg pieces.

When the glue sets up after an hour, flip the bench onto its feet and glue the other apron in place using the same clamping setup. This time, gravity helps hold the apron in place. After you clamp up the second apron, check the assembly to ensure it is square. I use a length of twine to check the diagonals from corner to corner. If the assembly is out of square, brace one of the two corners of the bench that is on the longer diagonal against a wall or something else stout. Shove a bit on the other corner on that diagonal. Check your work again.

Remove the clamps and then prepare to reinforce the joints with #10 x 2" screws. The apron and the legs are bonded in a cross-grain orientation. So there's a chance that the expansion and contraction of the apron could weaken the glue joint. Hence, the screws. First drill your pilot holes, then drill your clearance holes and the countersink. As you drill the clearance hole, rock the drill up and down a bit to make the hole oval shaped. This shape of clearance hole allows the screws to pivot a bit as the apron expands and contracts.

PARALLELOGRAMS: The cleats are easy to install and clamp if both long edges are 20°. To do this, rip one long edge of a wide board to 20°, then move the fence toward the blade to rip free a parallelogram cleat.

WATCH THE GRAIN: Though this is shop furniture, you should compose the top so that the grain runs in the same direction throughout all the pieces. It's easy to do and is good practice for a dining table.

SAFE AND EASY: When you work with large stock, there are some operations that are best for hand tools because it would be tough to move the piece over your machines. This is one instance. A few well-placed strokes with a backsaw define the width of the notch for the vise.

With the workbench's base assembled, you can flush up the top surfaces of the base to prepare it for the benchtop. My legs came out a tad taller than the aprons, as did the top rail. Luckily, it's easy to fix. Saw the tops of the legs flush to the apron, then waste away any excess material on the top rails with a rank-set jack plane.

Building the Top

Before you begin gluing up the top, glue in the cleats that will attach the end assemblies to the benchtop. I took some fall-off scrap pieces and ripped both long edges at 20°. Then I crosscut them to fit snugly between the legs and tight against the top rail. You can drill holes for the screws now, or you can wait. I waited.

The top is comprised of three 2x12s, though you can substitute other dimensions to get to the desired 27" width. Compose the top based on appearance and getting the grain of the three boards all aligned so that you can plane the entire top in one direction.

When you have the boards aligned to your liking, mark a large triangle across the joints that will guide you as you glue up the top.

Now comes a decision: Do you want a wagon vise? If you do, now is the time to start making space in the top for the mechanism. If you have chosen to forego any sort of integral end vise, then you can proceed with gluing up the top and getting it flat.

If I were building this bench and was either intimidated by the wagon vise, or I thought it would be too much trouble, I'd definitely purchase a quick-release vise and mount it in the end-vise position. Then I would add a thick (a 2½"-thick) wooden jaw to the movable jaw of the vise. This would give you many of the advantages of a tail vise and remove about 10 hours of work for you. If you decide to build the wagon vise, then congratulations. You are as determined as I.

Build the Wagon Vise

The first important step in building the wagon vise is to rip the benchtop board that goes at the front of your top into two pieces. With the required edge jointing and the saw kerf in this equation, try to get the front part of the board at 5" wide and the rear at 4" wide, perhaps a little more. Let's call this board the *dog board*.

With the dog board ripped in two, you can cut the notches on the ends that will create the opening for the movable wooden jaw of the vise. The notch on the rear dog board is 1⅝" wide; the one on the front dog board is 2⅜" wide. Both are 17" long. Cut the width of the notches with a handsaw and cut the length using your band saw.

To add a row of bench dogs to the bench, you need to beef up the thin top along the row of dogs. Then you'll cut the notches for all the dogs and re-assemble the two dog block sections into one unit. To double up the thickness, I used 2"-wide scraps that I cut to length so they would fit between the two leg assemblies of the bench. If you make the doubling any longer, you'll end up notching out your leg assemblies, which would be a pain.

Take each of these two strips of doubling and glue them to the dog blocks along the edge where these two pieces will eventually be glued together. Allow the glue to dry, then joint each of these surfaces and prepare to cut your dogs.

BALANCING ACT: Because you are working with a piece that is 8' long, it's a challenge to balance it on the saw and hold it in place during the cut. You are better served to have some sort of outboard support for your work. I used a portable stand.

ONE PIECE AT A TIME: The vise block is made by laminating several short pieces. First glue up two that will be milled with dog holes. Then glue up two more that will enclose the dog holes. After you cut the dogs, glue the two laminations together and then cut the block to final size – making sure that the dog holes in the vise block line up with the dog holes in the dog block.

CHECK YOUR WORK: After you rout the slight recess for the dog's head, place the dog in the hole and make sure there's enough space for it.

A bit of canine philosophy here: You will probably be able to squeeze about 6" to 7" of throw out of your vise screw for the wagon vise. However, it would be a mistake to space your dogs every 6" or so. That's too far a distance. While it seems to save time in the construction, it will drive you nuts for years in the future. Space your dogs with 3" between each hole. That will reduce the amount of turning you'll be doing to secure your work.

You want to size your holes to fit your dogs snugly. I purchased my wooden dogs from Lie-Nielsen Toolworks, and I based all of my holes off them. Wooden dogs hold most work quite well and won't damage your tools (you can add a thin layer of leather to a wooden dog to improve its grip). Metal dogs have tiny teeth on the faces (they look like a meat tenderizer). They grip the work particularly well when working cross-grain, but they do pose a hazard to cutting edges.

What's important about the dog holes is that they be angled by 2°. The holes in the dog block are angled toward the vise block. The holes in the vise block are tipped toward those in the dog block. Size your dog holes so that your dogs won't tip back significantly under

pressure, and that a dog will stay in position (up or down) without coaxing. You don't want your dogs dropping into their holes (like prairie dogs) when left unattended.

You can mill these holes in a variety of ways. The best way I've ever seen is an aluminum routing template that is used with a big router equipped with a template guide and straight bit. If you are going to build benches for a living, you can visit a machinist and get a template made or make your own with plywood.

I took a different route (or rout). I milled out the majority of the waste with a dado stack in a table saw and then finished up shaping the dog hole – adding the extra room for its head – with a routing template.

There are probably other good ways to do it, so you don't have to copy my method. It's based only on the tools I have in my shop. I own a small plunge router that doesn't have a template-guide adapter. And I have a gutsy table saw with a nice dado stack.

Lay out all the cuts for the dogs on your dog block. I used two pairs of dividers to do this. One was set for the size of the dog hole and the other was set for the spacing between each hole. Shade in your waste areas so you don't get confused at the saw.

Load up your table saw's arbor with as many wings and chippers as your saw can spin. Angle your miter gauge (or sliding table) to 2° and cut your dog holes. I merely lined up each cut by eye because each hole required two passes to make. Setting stops would be a pain.

With all the holes cut, angle your miter gauge 2° the other way and cut the two dog holes in the movable vise block.

Now make a router template that will cut the extra space for the head of the dogs. I made my template from some plywood scraps and used the dog itself as a pattern to trace around. I cut the shape on the band saw and refined the pattern with a rasp and sandpaper. Finally, I glued a small block onto the template that acted as a fence so I could clamp the pattern to my dog block.

The shape is routed out using a straight bit with a bearing on the top. My 1¹/₂ hp router wouldn't do this cut all in one pass. So I set the depth stop on my plunge router to cut at two depths: one where the bearing ran on the pattern, and the second where the bearing actually

CAUTIOUS EDGE WORK: You want this joint to be strong because it will be regularly stressed. Take your time fitting the two pieces. Here I'm balancing one dog block on another and examining the seam for light.

Every pass you make with your jointer or jointer plane will tighten up the dog holes. This can be good or bad, depending on how tight or loose your dog holes are.

I jointed this dog block once, and then I simply worked its mate until I got the fit I wanted. When satisfied, glue up the two dog blocks by putting glue only on the edge with the dog holes. Don't overdo it or you'll have lots of unpleasant squeeze-out in your holes. Once the dog block is glued up, joint the edges of your other top boards and glue up the reminder of the top.

The top is essentially complete; now turn your attention to the bench and the guts that will make the vise work. The vise screw needs to be fastened to something that is stout – it will bear a good deal of the pressure from the vise when it is engaged. Although a properly used wagon vise shouldn't see extreme pressure, you can bet that it will be misused during its lifetime. It's better to make it stronger.

The end cap piece is the key to the vise. The vise screw mounts to it. And the end cap is attached to the workbench's aprons with dados, steel corner brackets and bolts. The first step to installing the end cap is to mill two dados across the aprons to accept the end cap. Whenever I want to mill dados in wide pieces, I turn to a straightedge guide and a router. The straightedge guide is essentially two pieces of wood attached at right angles. One piece sits tight against the apron; the other guides the router.

You'll need to make these 1¼"-wide x ½"-deep dados using a couple of overlapping passes. It's simple work. Simply mark out the location

DADO AFTER ASSEMBLY: Don't try to do this process before assembly. You want the dados to be exactly in line with each other. The only way to ensure that is to rout them after the base is assembled.

ran on what was cut before to make the final pass. It's a bit of a tricky setup that I boxed myself into. If I had to do it again, I would simply use a template guide and a straight bit.

Clamp the pattern and rout the shape. Then place a dog in the recess you have completed and make sure there's enough clearance. It's easier to fix now than when everything is assembled.

Now you can glue the two dog blocks back together and then glue the completed unit to the other two boards for the top. As you are creating this edge joint between two dog blocks you need to be careful. Jointing the dog block that has the dog holes in it has consequences.

BIG-BOY BRACKETS: With the vise flange in place, clamp the L-brackets where you want them and mark the locations for the bolts. Here's how I drilled these holes: From the inside of the bench, drill a ³⁄₃₂"-diameter hole through the center of each hole and through the wood. From the outside of the bench, drill a countersink using a bit that has more diameter than your washers. Place the center spur of the Forstner in the through-hole you just drilled. Drill a recess that's deep enough for the bolt head. Stop, then drill a hole for the bolt through the center of the recess you just drilled. The ³⁄₃₂"" hole will guide you throughout.

BOLTS ALL AROUND: Tighten up the bolts firmly on the end cap first, then tighten up the bolts to the apron. Note that I didn't bolt through the holes nearest the corner of the bracket. It didn't seem necessary. But check back with me in about 10 years for the real answer.

FIRST WORK ON THE BENCH: Flattening the underside of the top is fairly straightforward once you have the base constructed and leveled.

PRIMITIVE PLANING STOP: To hold the top while planing across its grain, I pushed it up against two screw heads that I had sticking out of the cleats that will be used to attach the top.

of the dados on each apron, place your guide in place and make the cut. Move the guide again and repeat.

Cut the end cap for the workbench and slide it into the dados in the aprons. It should stick out a bit at the bottom. It's best to cut it flush. So transfer the shape of the aprons at that point to the end grain of the end cap. This should be a 45° angle. Rip that edge to shape with a saw and clean up the work with a hand plane.

Before installing the end cap permanently, drill the hole through the end cap for the vise screw hardware. The vise hardware comes with a threaded flange that the screw travels through. You want to attach this piece correctly, and this is where I struggled like the dickens to make everything work. Here's the problem: You want the vise screw to be as close to your benchtop as possible because that arrangement will apply clamping force right where you want it. But you also want to put the vise screw in a place that is heavily reinforced so everything is stout.

In the name of stout, I schemed to reinforce the end cap with steel L-brackets. But the L-brackets forced me to move the vise screw hardware down lower than I liked. As I wrestled with this problem, I started searching the U.S. Patent Office's web site and found several plans for patented wagon vises that would be so simple (if they still existed). They all involved a metal frame that bolted to the underside of the benchtop and – in theory – would be stout and smooth. So if anybody out there is interested in manufacturing some vise hardware from expired patents, drop me a line.

So I drilled the hole in the end cap in the location shown in the construction drawings and then glued the end cap in place. Then I attached four L-brackets to the inside corners of the workbench with nuts, bolts and washers. It was stout all right, but would it work?

To find out, I had to get the top onto the base and complete the fiddly guts for the wagon vise. The top was still in two pieces. I needed to get each piece reasonably flat, get their edges jointed and glued up and then fixed onto the base itself.

When I get into a risky bit of work, my thoughts drift to the antique tool chest by my bench at home that has a tricky, sticky and

ALL THE CLAMPS: When you clamp the top to the base you want the top's edge to be flush or slightly proud of the front apron. The top is ½" wider than necessary, and I'll trim that off at the back later on.

RIBS MAKE IT STIFFER: The three transverse supports prevent the top from flexing. I attached these with screws (as shown). Then I got wise and replaced the screws with Miller Dowels.

unpredictable lock. Most days, I can open the chest with ease. I rotate the key. The cylinders turn. The lid lifts.

But every so often, the lock refuses to work. I rotate the key. The cylinders turn. The lid sticks. I curse and then repeat the process until the lid opens. However, a couple times during the last decade, no amount of fiddling would open the chest. And instead of reaching for a wrecking bar, I'd just walk away and come back to the chest later.

Some days, I get that same uncertain feeling in my chest whenever I get ready to flatten and join boards that are long, wide or wild. Today was one of those days as I set out to flatten the top. The section of benchtop on deck this afternoon was 22" wide and 8' long. It was pretty flat, but it needed to be really flat to sit tight onto the base of the bench. Some days, it doesn't matter how skilled you are. Or how many times you've trued up a slab of wonky wood. Some days the wood wins and you exit the shop with your tail between your legs.

The first challenge when dealing with wide and long panels is finding a place to work on them. With this section of the top, the answer was simple. I placed it on the base itself and pushed it against the heads of a couple screws that I placed into the holes in the cleats that eventually will join the base to the top.

The ends were out of true and some quick work with a fore plane across the grain brought them into line with the center section of the top. A couple passes diagonally across the top with the fore plane got the surface flat enough to push it against the fence of our powered jointer.

Senior Editor Glen Huey looked over as I was working the top and offered (sincerely, but with a twinkle in his eye) to put the top in his truck and run it through his wide-belt sander in his home shop.

I declined, saying that the exercise with the fore plane would allow me to justify drinking a second beer tonight after work. Glen smiled and nodded his head. All was going well, but edge-jointing the top piece was another tricky piece of work. It's another part of a project that can go wrong for no good reason. I jointed the edge. I jointed its mate and showed them to one another. I was shooting for a spring joint and I got one, but it was a little strong on one end of the top.

Undeterred, I straightened out the end with a few passes of a block plane. Within a few minutes the whole top was glued up and clamped with a tight seam all along the 8' top.

I had earned an extra beer, and the tool chest didn't win this round.

Glue it, Screw it and Hope

Attaching the top to the base is a challenge to do well. Here's the brief write up: Glue the front edge of the top to the front apron. Then attach the remainder of the top to the base using screws driven through the cleats. The screws nearest the front of the bench are in a simple, straight hole. The remainder of the screws are in holes that have been slightly reamed out to an oblong shape. Note that for all the screws I also used a washer to limit how far the screw's head plunged into the work. This ensured that none of the screw tips would poke through the top when I planed it flat.

The net effect of this is to keep the front edge of the top fixed in relation to the apron and forces any seasonal expansion and contraction of the top to the back edge of the top, where it's not a nuisance.

What's difficult is getting that front edge seamlessly tight, especially if there's any bow or twist to the top (as there was with mine – it was cupped a bit). So before you attach the top, spend some time with a straightedge and a plane checking out the base and trying to level things up all around. Then lay the glue down on the front edge and clamp things up.

Once the glue is dry, flip the bench over onto a couple sawhorses. To complete the structural skeleton of the workbench, you should screw in three transverse supports to the underside of the top. These stiffen the top in lieu of a benchtop with great mass.

"Today's woodworking is left-brained. It is focused on machining wood like it was plastic or metal. Many woodworkers actually believe that a micrometer is a woodworking tool. Because of dust and noise, they dress up like they were going to work in a toxic waste dump."

— Michael Dunbar, *The Windsor Chronicles*, Spring 2004

WEST MEETS EAST: We tend to push our hand planes, but sometimes it's best to take a cue from the Japanese and pull them through the work. Here I've attached my vintage Stanley No. 386 jointer fence to my jointer plane and am pulling the whole rig toward me. This allowed great control, especially at this work height.

FIND THE BOTTOM: You want the dowels in your vise block to pierce the block right below the benchtop. Hold the vise block in position and scribe a line where the benchtop and vise block meet (top). Now you can drill a ⅝" hole through the block that's tangent to this line (bottom). Then drill a second stopped hole that's about 2" back of the first hole.

These transverse supports are spaced equally along the underside and are positioned so they don't cover up a dog hole. Notch each support to fit over the dog block on the underside of the top. Screw each to the top in a manner similar to attaching the base to the top. Drill a clearance hole for a screw at the front of the bench that's straight. The remaining three on each transverse support are slightly reamed out. You also can attach these supports with Miller Dowels. I know this because I later pulled out the screws and drove in Miller Dowels. This step will ensure no metal ever protrudes through the top.

Now you can flip the bench on its aprons and trim the top flush to the aprons. I didn't have a lot to trim so I used a jointer plane with a fence. If you have more than ⅛" to remove, think about using a router that's armed with a straight bit and a pattern-cutting bearing. If you have a gross excess to remove, think circular saw and then router.

Finish up the Wagon Vise

I trimmed up the vise block to fit the slot in the benchtop and screwed the pad on the vise's hardware to the vise block. The way the wagon vise works is by having the vise block run in a couple tracks on the underside of the benchtop. The tracks are made by gluing up some scrap pieces to create two slots on either side of the vise block. Then

you need something to run in these slots. I used a couple of ⅝"-diameter dowels that are friction-fit into the vise block and are removable.

The dowels captured in the track serve two functions: They keep the vise block from drooping when the vise is not engaged. And they prevent the vise block from riding up above the benchtop when you clamp something using the dogs. As a result, you want the dowels to be right below the top. So position the vise block in its slot and mark out where the underside of the benchtop touches the vise block.

The next steps are easier to do with the bench upside down, so flip the sucker over. Push the dowels into the holes you just drilled in the vise block. Don't glue them in; when the vise requires adjustment or repair, you can just pull the dowels out and the vise block will lift out of the top of the bench.

The dowel that passes through the vise block only needs to protrude about 1" or so on the other side. And depending on how your brackets are bolted in you want to position the dowel so it doesn't bump into the bolts and nuts.

Now build the track for the dowels to run in. First you have to know how much open space to leave for the dowels. So with the dowels in position, close the vise all the way and mark the position of the forward dowel. Now unscrew the vise all the way and mark the

OPEN AND SHUT: The buildup blocks are just a hair thicker than the dowels. The less slop you have in the mechanism the better. These build-up blocks are just about to be glued and nailed in place.

READY TO WORK: Fit the strips that connect the build-up blocks. Don't attach them with glue because they might have to be removed someday. I tacked them down with a brad nail, then drove a single screw in at each attachment point. This construction allows you to disassemble things later if need be.

position of the rear dowel. Now you know where to place the build-up blocks for the track.

The size of the build-up blocks is critical. Too thick and your vise will wobble and ride up and down. Too thin and your vise won't move. Shoot for a thickness that is a bit stronger than your dowels' diameter. Glue and nail the four build-up blocks in place and then dig up some scrap for the pieces that will connect the build-up blocks.

The Leg Vise

After using a leg vise for a couple years on my French-style workbench, I was a convert. When it comes to choosing a face vise, I prefer it to an iron quick-release vise. The quick-release function of that vise is hype because most of your work with a vise on the front of your bench will be with a narrow range of thicknesses. (When a quick-release vise is in the end-vise position, however, that's another story.)

Making a leg vise is straightforward work and takes as much time as to install an iron quick-release vise. The first step is to drill a 1³⁄₈"-diameter hole in your leg for the vise's screw, and to hog out a through-

Measuring Shop Time

When I build furniture, I log the time I spend at each step in construction: 60 minutes on the top, 75 minutes to cut the mortises and tenons, 30 minutes to remake a munged-up apron.

The reason I keep this record is a bit of a mystery to me. I pitch it when I purge the shop of the shavings, scraps and screw-ups at the end of a project. But before I cast the log into the burn pile, I add up the minutes I've marked there and marvel at how few hours in my life are spent actually woodworking.

Now I don't like to get too philosophical about something so physical, but the hours I spend at woodworking are some of the best waking moments I have. And recently an acquaintance named Brian Welch passed on to me a passage from chapter 18 Henry David Thoreau's *Walden* that shook me good. Here it is:

"There was an artist in the city of Kouroo who was disposed to strive after perfection. One day it came into his mind to make a staff. Having considered that in an imperfect work time is an ingredient, but into a perfect work time does not enter, he said to himself, 'It shall be perfect in all respects, though I should do nothing else in my life.'

"He proceeded instantly to the forest for wood, being resolved that it should not be made of unsuitable material; and as he searched for and rejected stick after stick, his friends gradually deserted him, for they grew old in their works and died, but he grew not older by a moment. His singleness of purpose and resolution, and his elevated piety, endowed him, without his knowledge, with perennial youth. As he made no compromise with Time, Time kept out of his way, and only sighed at a distance because he could not overcome him. Before he had found a stock in all respects suitable the city of Kouroo was a hoary ruin, and he sat on one of its mounds to peel the stick. Before he had given it the proper shape the dynasty of the Candahars was at an end, and with the point of the stick he wrote the name of the last of that race in the sand, and then resumed his work.

"By the time he had smoothed and polished the staff Kalpa was no longer the pole-star; and ere he had put on the ferule and the head adorned with precious stones, Brahma had awoke and slumbered many times. But why do I stay to mention these things? When the finishing stroke was put to his work, it suddenly expanded before the eyes of the astonished artist into the fairest of all the creations of Brahma. He had made a new system in making a staff, a world with full and fair proportions; in which, though the old cities and dynasties had passed away, fairer and more glorious ones had taken their places. And now he saw by the heap of shavings still fresh at his feet, that, for him and his work, the former lapse of time had been an illusion, and that no more time had elapsed than is required for a single scintillation from the brain of Brahma to fall on and inflame the tinder of a mortal brain. The material was pure, and his art was pure; how could the result be other than wonderful?"

After reading this passage I got in my truck on my day off and braved the Christmas traffic to go to the office to do a little work on the leg vise for the English workbench. I logged only 75 minutes, but it was the best month of the entire day.

TRACE YOUR BENCH: Put the vise jaw on the leg and shift it around until it's right where it should be. Then trace around the leg, apron and top. Then trace the hole and the mortise in the leg. These marks will guide you as you shape the jaw.

WEIRD PLACE FOR A FLANGE: From looking at the vise hardware, the manufacturers want you to install the flange the opposite of the way I'm doing it – the screw holes are nicely countersunk for that set-up. But you have to drill a much larger hole to install the flange that way, and that will weaken the leg. Install it the other way. It works just as well.

WALK THE DOG: Use dividers to step off the locations of the holes in the parallel guide. I'd give up all of my digital measuring equipment before I gave up my dividers.

mortise below that hole (mine was ³/₄"-wide and 3" long) for the vise's parallel guide. Position the vise's jaw on the leg and transfer the position of the hole and mortise to the jaw. Now install the threaded iron flange that comes with the vise screw. Install it on the inside face of the leg.

Drill the matching 1³/₈" hole in the vise's jaw and bore out a through-mortise in the jaw. However, make this mortise a little narrower than the mortise in the leg: Mine was ¹/₂" wide and 2" long. I bored out the mortise on the drill press and squared up the corners with a chisel. Now you can shape the jaw as you see fit. I made mine resemble the shapes of leg vises from the 18th century (skinny at the floor; chunky at top). Do what you will, but I recommend the jaw be no narrower than the leg and that you keep the jaw as wide as possible near the workbench's apron.

Now work on the parallel guide. You will tenon and wedge it into the jaw – after you bore it with an array of ³/₈"-diameter holes. The holes are for a metal pin that when positioned in a hole will pivot the vise's jaw against your work. Different holes are for different thicknesses. If this doesn't make sense to you at first, don't fret. It seemed

odd to me at first glance as well. Once you get the thing together the light bulb will come on.

The holes are in two long rows and are spaced 1" apart. On the top row the holes begin 1" from the shoulder of the tenon. On the bottom row the holes start 1¹/₂" from the shoulder. Then I added one more hole: It's centered between the two long rows and is ¹/₂" from the shoulder. This is the hole you'll be using the most – it's for clamping ³/₄" material. Once you drill out the holes, countersink them to make the metal pin easier to insert. On the end of the parallel guide that isn't tenoned, I clipped the corners at 45°, just for looks.

The parallel guide should fit snugly but smoothly in the mortise you bored into the leg. The closer the fit, the smoother the action of the jaw. If you make it too tight, however, the jaw will hang up. This requires judgment on your part. Consider the expansion and contraction of the species of wood you choose for the parallel guide and what season it is when you are building. Then size the parallel guide so you will always have ¹/₃₂" of clearance above and below the guide. If you make it too tight, you can always adjust it later with a card scraper or some coarse sandpaper.

TIGHT, THEN LOOSE: When fitting a through-tenon, you first want the fit to be snug. Then you'll widen the mortise on the exit-wound side into a trumpet-shape. That way when you wedge the tenon, it also will deform into a trumpet shape – locking it in for good.

USE THE CHISEL GEOMETRY: You can make this harder than it is. Here's the easy way: Strike a line that's $^1/_{16}$" beyond each end of the mortise. Then take a ½"-wide chisel and score the mortise wall up to the line (top). Then stand your chisel on end and drive it down (below). The geometry of the chisel's edge allows it to cut down a bit and then the chisel will be driven into the open mortise (where there's less resistance). This simple whack creates the perfect trumpet-shaped mortise for wedging.

Now cut the tenon on the end of the parallel guide. You want the tenon to be longer than necessary so it protrudes about $^1/_{16}$" from the jaw when the two are mated. As with the other tenons for this workbench, I cut this one using a dado stack on my table saw. Then I fit the tenon into the through-mortise using a shoulder plane.

Now you can shape the mortise to prepare it for the wedges. You want the mortise to be slightly longer on the exit side than it is on the side where the tenon is inserted. How much longer? That depends on the joint's size and how much abuse the tenon can take. For this joint, both components are durable (an ash jaw; a white oak parallel guide) but the joint itself is small. So I added $^1/_8$" total – $^1/_{16}$" of length on each end of the mortise.

To wedge the mortise you need wedges. I cut mine on the band saw by angling the tool's miter gauge to 7° and then ripping wedges from some white oak that was $^1/_2$" thick, 1" long and as wide as I could find. Here's the trick: Trim one end of your wedge stock on the saw. Then flip the work over and slice off a wedge. This gives you a perfect wedge with a 14° angle.

Now you need to make cuts in the tenon for the wedges. Some books would have you saw kerfs down the tenon, perhaps even ending them with a little hole. Do not bother. I once tried all these techniques, which sounded smart at the time. Then I sawed apart the joints to see what happened inside.

I was shocked.

The little kerfs and little holes don't help close the inside of the joint. The tightest joints had tenons that had been split with a chisel – an old chairmaking trick I picked up at a Canadian class. So glue up the joint, then make two splits in the tenon using a $^1/_2$"-wide chisel. Put a little glue in each split and drive in your wedges.

After your glue dries, trim the tenon flush with the jaw and install the assembled jaw into your leg. I like to glue a piece of leather to the jaw and the workbench itself to assist in clamping my work. You can do this now or wait until after you finish the bench (or until you've recovered from building this very large project).

Oh, and the pin that goes into the holes in the parallel guide? You can use a $^3/_8$"-diameter dowel (use something stout). No matter how stout, there is a risk of snapping the sucker after some use. If you get

TAP, TAP AND WALK AWAY: Drive the wedges in with a hammer and listen to how the sound changes with each tap. The wedges will come to resist you. That's about the time you should stop driving them. OK, a couple more taps will be fine in this joint. It's solid.

WAX PAPER AND LEATHER: Real leather (not pleather) glues well to wood with simple yellow glue. Coat each skin with a thin but consistent film. Put them in place (one on the apron; the other on the vise jaw) with a sheet of wax paper between the pieces of leather and close the vise.

CUTTING IN: Mark the depth of each section of your mortise using tape, a permanent marker or both. When chopping with a mortise chisel, it's best to keep the bevel across the grain. If you mortise deeply with the bevel running along the grain, you likely will split your work. You can pare the long-grain walls of your mortise with the chisel after the mortise has been excavated, but chopping along the long grain is generally a no-no.

MESSY, BUT CORRECT: The mortise for the planing stop doesn't have to be pretty, but it should support the stop all around. Once you excavate the mortise, fit the stop and screw it down. If you did it correctly, the body of the stop should be a bit below the benchtop when the stop is all the way in the down position.

tired of replacing the dowel, try using a $^3/_8$"-diameter steel rod (a $^5/_{16}$"-diameter O-ring keeps the rod in place in the angled piece.) That has worked great for me with other leg vises.

Planing Stops

I don't much care for the metal planing stops that rise up and down out of a recess in your workbench's top. The metal can damage your tools. And the manufacturing quality of these stops fits their price: The stops are cheap and so is their construction.

Nevertheless, I decided to install a couple metal stops in this bench in the interests of getting to know them better. They are not difficult to install, but it is a time-consuming process. Whoever designed the castings for these stops should have his or her head examined. The underside is quite complex, and it doesn't have to be.

The best way to install these is with a mortise chisel and a $^3/_4$" auger bit. First decide where you want the stops to go. I placed one directly in line with the square dog holes that go with my wagon vise. That

SHELF SUPPORTS: This is the heart of the shelf below the apron. I glued the cleat to the long shelf support. Then I cut the ends at a 20° angle to match the angle on the legs. (Ah symmetry!) Then I attached the shelf supports to the legs with glue and Miller Dowels. (Screws would be fine here, but I like wood more than metal.)

way I can actually clamp some really long work between the vise's dog and the stop.

The second stop should be installed about 7" away from the first stop. Why? This allows you to work with a wide variety of materials. When you work against a single planing stop, there's a limit to how wide a board you can work until you end up flinging the work across the bench. For me, that limit is about a 6"-wide board. So a second planing stop that's 7" away from the first will allow me to plane wide boards without resorting to some other way to affix them for work.

Plus, I own an 8" powered jointer, so the 7" spacing makes sense.

After choosing where to put them, place the stops upside down on your benchtop and trace around each with a marking knife. Go slow and use light pressure, especially when cutting with the grain. With both locations marked, use a ruler to determine where to put the ¾"-diameter hole that will house the spring-loaded basket of the stop. I drilled this hole with an auger bit and bit brace.

Now cut the remainder of the recess for the stop. Work from the center out to the edges. The center is the deepest point of your recess, plus, the hole you drilled allows the chips to escape the mortise.

The two critical points of the mortise are at the front (where the stop is screwed to the benchtop) and at the back, which has to resist typical planing forces. Here are a couple details about these stops to be aware of. One: The hinge of the stop is eccentric. You need to give a little more clearance at the rear for the hinge than you probably think. You'll know if you need more clearance; the stop won't open.

Also, the little pins that hold the basket that holds the spring are weak. Even a slight stress breaks them. You can replace those stops, or you can ensure that your ¾" hole is drilled to the correct depth to support the basket from below, making the pins vestigial.

With your mind on workholding, it's a good time to drill holes for holdfasts. It's easy to overdo and drill holes that you'll never use or (even worse) are in the wrong place. My recommendation: Start with four and ponder additional holes like you would a new body piercing.

Here's my philosophy on the four holes: The first hole is on the end of the bench where the two metal planing stops are and is 6" in from the back edge of the workbench. This hole does a lot of things, but its most important job is reinforcing a shop-made planing stop

that clamps into your face vise. To drill the hole, position your stop in your vise so it's clamped where you want it. Then drill a hole that's tangent to the stop and 6" from the bench's back edge.

The remainder of the holes are based on the reach of the holdfast. You want your holdfasts to reach all along the back edge of your bench with no dead spots. This allows you to clamp battens down anywhere along the back edge of the bench, which will support your work from the side.

The Veritas Hold Down has a reach of about 9", so I subtracted a bit from that reach and drilled my holes on 16" centers. All of the holes are 6" in from the back edge of the benchtop.

Adding a Shelf

At this point you can call it quits or build the shelf. Some woodworkers would be tempted to take a third course: adding a few drawers below to store essential shop equipment. Turning this bench into a cabinet could make it less useful. Drawers could interfere with your feet if placed low to the floor.

At the least, adding a bank of drawers will make it difficult – nay, impossible – for you to reach up under the top and push a dog up. A shelf, on the other hand, will allow you to keep your most-used tools at hand during a project. Your bench planes, for example, should camp out on the shelf as you work. Do this and you will find that you work a little more efficiently.

The shelf can be simpler than the one I show. You could screw a couple 2x4s on edge to a long piece of plywood that fits between the legs and let that assembly rest on the rails on the ends.

I opted for something more complex, stronger and interesting. All told, it requires you to buy three more 2x12 x 8' boards. For me, that cost was less than $35 – a bargain. First I created two L-shaped stretchers by gluing a 1¼" x 1¼" x 84" cleat to each long shelf support. This created a rabbet for the shelf boards.

With the cleat and shelf support assembled, attach these assemblies to the workbench. Rest the assemblies on the lower rails and glue them to the legs. I reinforced each joint with large Miller Dowels. Now turn your attention to the eight shelf pieces.

After surfacing your lumber, rip it to the maximum width possible and then make the tongue-and-groove joints on the board's edges. The tongue is ⅜" x ⅜". I made this joint on my table saw using a dado stack. First I cut the groove on one long edge of each board. Then I cut a matching tongue on each board's other edge.

After the boards have their joints cut, crosscut them to fit on the shelf supports. You want the fit to be snug.

"(T)hrough most of this age, the thinkers still made and the makers still thought."

— William Bryant Logan on 17th and 18th century shipbuilding; from *Oak: The Frame of Civilization* (Norton)

SLIDING INTO HOME: The shelves won't be glued, but you want the tongue-and-groove joints to fit closely but easily. Slide the shelf pieces in. Then remove them and number them so you can be sure to get them back in easily.

BEADS MAKE IT BURLY: My ³⁄₁₆" beading plane makes a tasteful bead. Remember that beading planes work like grooving planes: You start the cut on the far end of the work and work back toward the end vise, taking longer and longer strokes.

If you are following the plans correctly, you should have more shelf than you need — the ends of the two outside pieces should stick out over the shelf supports. This is good. Center the eight shelves on the shelf supports and space them so there is a ¹⁄₈" gap between each shelf piece. I used a ruler snitched from a 12" combination square to offset the shelf pieces as I placed them.

With the shelves in place, mark a cutline on the two outside shelf pieces so they will be inset 1¹⁄₄" from the ends of the shelf supports. Then rip the end pieces so they have a 20° bevel on one long edge.

Then prepare the shelf pieces for finishing. I cleaned them up with a jointer plane and then cut a ³⁄₁₆" bead on one long edge of each board on the grooved edge. This is both decorative and functional. The bead strengthens the corner and makes it look good.

Install the shelf pieces with Miller Dowels (one in the center of each end) or with a similarly placed screw. No need for glue. I used the Miller Dowels so that I could pop them loose if I ever needed to modify or repair something up in the body cavity of this bench.

Finishing

Break all the edges with sandpaper and then finish the bench. Please don't put a furniture-grade finish on your bench. A slick finish will allow your wood to scoot all over the place as you work. But I don't like letting the bench go nude either. It's too likely to absorb nastiness (glue stains, etc.) that could transfer to or scratch future workpieces.

There are a lot of fussy workbench finishes that ask you to heat stuff up, rub it in and work way too hard. Instead, buy some Danish oil (typically a mixture of boiled linseed oil and a little varnish). Rag on a couple coats and then go to work.

This finish is easy to apply and doesn't leave a film that can be cracked by beating on it. And the finish allows just enough protection against spills and stains to be helpful. When finishing furniture, I avoid these so-called Danish oils for projects that will see a lot of use, but a workbench is different. You are going to flatten the top regularly and refresh the finish, so an oil/varnish blend is ideal.

And Then to Work

I had a girlfriend in high school who had two unusual characteristics. Lynette was a drama major (not a recommended trait in girlfriends) and her father owned a sweet MG convertible. Whenever I would go to her house for dinner, her father would be under the hood of the vehicle, wrench in hand, until the fried okra hit the dinner table.

The MG was always in need of something, and Lynette's dad had to do it himself. This was, after all, Arkansas. And anything that wasn't built in Detroit elicited stares from the townsfolk.

As I completed the English-style workbench I found that — like its British four-banger brethren — the bench needed tuning.

For example, I flattened the top one week, but it went a bit out of true the next. So I flattened it again. I also began wondering if the top was stiff enough to withstand heavy planing. The top has an almost imperceptible springy feel that gave me pause.

Perhaps the problem was that I was comparing this bench to the Roubo-style French bench. The top to that bench is almost 4" thick and is unyielding to all punishment. But that bench took twice as long to build and required three times the material. Clearly, I needed to take the English bench for more of a test drive.

As I began breaking in the bench, I found things about it that were nice. The angled leg vise is fantastic. The large front apron is excellent for supporting long and wide work. And I've been clamping stuff to the benchtop without trouble by using the wagon vise.

Bottom line: I go through this process with all my projects. I start with great optimism. After a series of highs and lows, I complete the project. I stand back, take a look and focus on its flaws. Then, after I put the project into use, I mellow. The flaws fade and I can see the project for what it is — somewhere between optimism and despair.

After some use, I found this to be true with this bench. The springiness I felt in the top was mostly a product of the fact that I was using a softwood. The top wasn't really deforming under pressure.

It was a happier ending than my relationship with Lynette (and her dad's MG). He sold the green convertible and Lynette dumped me for an officer of the drama club. But this bench stays in the picture.

English Workbench

	NO.	PART	SIZES (INCHES)			MATERIAL	NOTES
			T	W	L		
❏	4	Legs, inside	1¼	4	38 *	Yellow pine	20° angle at ends
❏	4	Legs, outside	1¼	4	25 *	Yellow pine	CTF, 20°
❏	2	Top end rails	1¼	9	24½	Yellow pine	1¼" TBE
❏	2	Bottom end rails	1¼	4	26	Yellow pine	2" TBE
❏	3	Transverse supports	1¼	2	24½	Yellow pine	Notch over dog doubling
❏	1	End cap	1¼	9¼	25½	Yellow pine	in ½" d. dado
❏	2	Aprons	1¼	11	96	Yellow pine	
❏	2	Top boards	1¼	9¼	96	Yellow pine	Trim the finished top to 27"
❏	1	Top board (dog block)	1¼	4	96	Yellow pine	
❏	1	Top board (dog block)	1¼	5	96	Yellow pine	
❏	2	Dog doubling	1¼	2	56½	Yellow pine	
❏	2	Attachment cleats	1¼	1½	22	Yellow pine	Attaches top to ends

Shelf

	NO.	PART	SIZES (INCHES)			MATERIAL	NOTES
			T	W	L		
❏	2	Long shelf supports	1¼	3½	84	Yellow pine	Trim ends at 20°
❏	2	Cleats	1¼	1¼	84	Yellow pine	Trim ends at 20°
❏	8	Shelf slats	1¼	11⅛ *	19½	Yellow pine	⅜" x ⅜" tongue on edge

Leg Vise

	NO.	PART	SIZES (INCHES)			MATERIAL	NOTES
			T	W	L		
❏	1	Leg vise jaw	2	8	38 *	Ash	Cut long, trim to fit
❏	1	Parallel guide	⅝	3	16	Oak	½" x 2¾" x 2⅛" TOE
❏	1	Vise handle	1	1	15	Ash	

Wagon Vise

	NO.	PART	SIZES (INCHES)			MATERIAL	NOTES
			T	W	L		
❏	1	Wagon vise block	4	5¼	7	Yellow pine	Laminated from 4 pieces
❏	1	Through dowel	⅝ dia.		9	Yellow pine	Pierces vise block
❏	1	Stopped dowel	⅝ dia.		4¼	Yellow pine	Stops in vise block
❏	3	Build-up blocks	⅝	1¼	2	Yellow pine	Trim to clear brackets
❏	1	Long build-up block	⅝	1¼	3½	Yellow pine	
❏	2	Dowel track strips	⅝	1¼	14½	Yellow pine	Nail to build-up blocks
❏	1	Vise handle	1¹⁄₁₆	1¹⁄₁₆	15	Ash	

KEY: TOE = tenon on one end; TBE = tenon, both ends; * = oversized, cut to fit

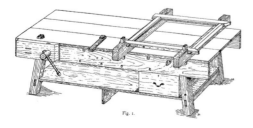

Fig. 1.

A Joiner's Bench from George Ellis's *Modern Practical Joinery*.

"Yup, in my humble opinion, workbenches are like lasagna; you don't buy them, you make them."

— James Mittlefehldt, on the Sawmill Creek forum on the Internet

THE NICHOLSON

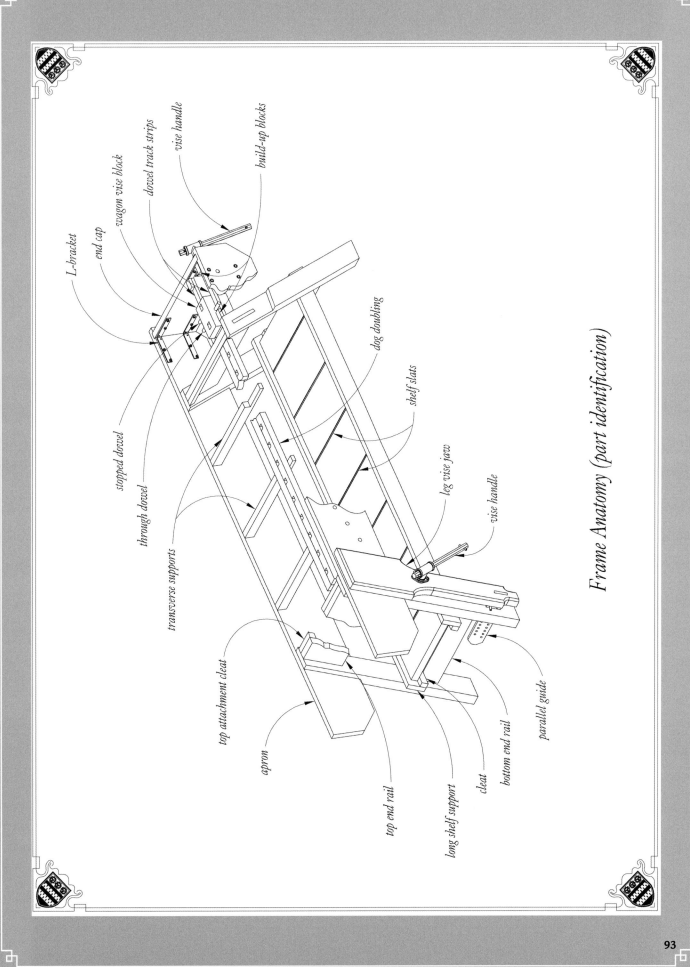

Frame Anatomy (part identification)

L-bracket

end cap

wagon vise block

dowel track strips

vise handle

build-up blocks

stopped dowel

through dowel

transverse supports

dog doubling

shelf slats

leg vise jaw

vise handle

top attachment cleat

apron

top end rail

long shelf support

cleat

bottom end rail

parallel guide

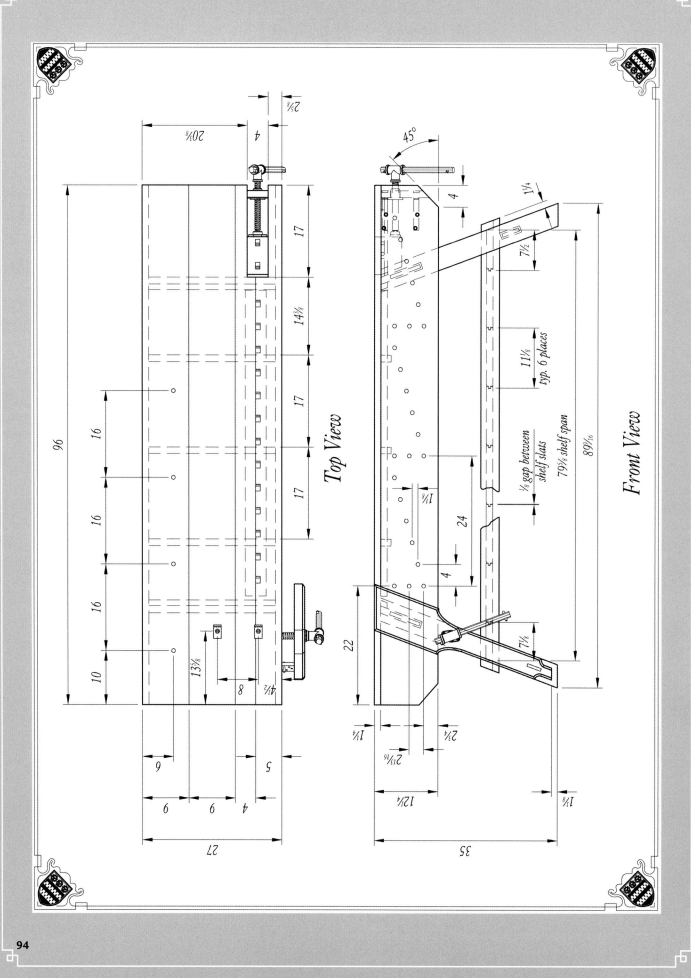

Top View

Front View

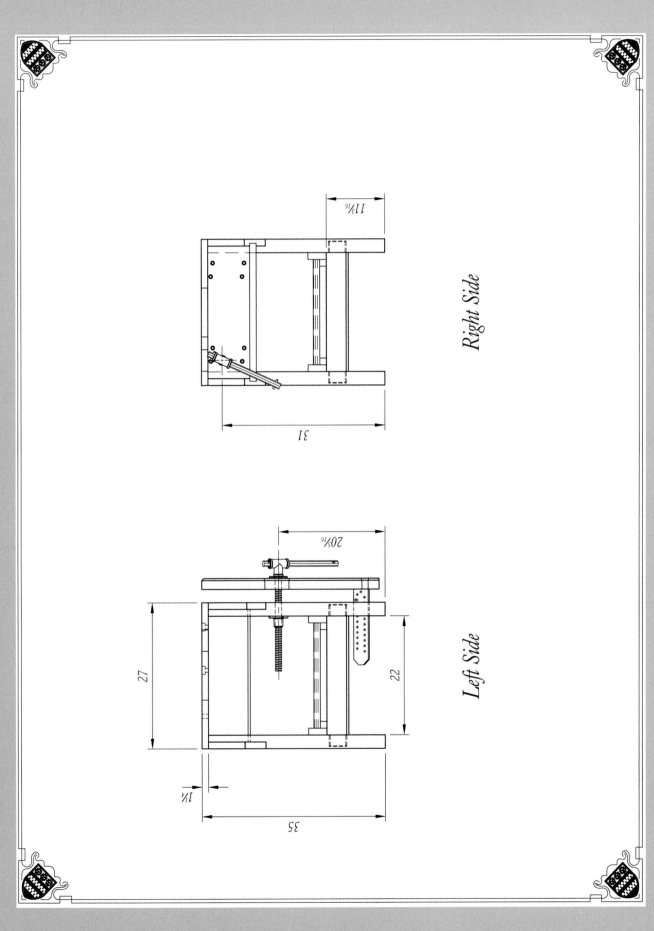

Right Side

Left Side

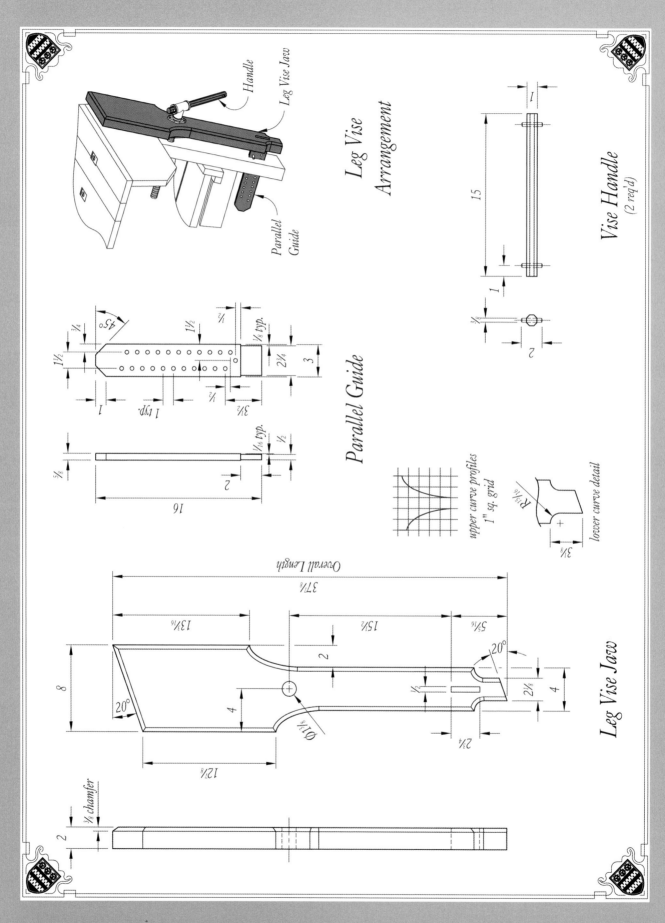

Handle

Leg Vise Jaw

Leg Vise Arrangement

Parallel Guide

Vise Handle
(2 req'd)

15

1

1

⅜

2

Parallel Guide

¾

45°

1½

1½

1½

½

⅛ typ.

2¼

3

3¾

1

½

1 typ.

⅛

2

16

⅟₁₆ typ.

½

upper curve profiles
1" sq. grid

lower curve detail

R1⁵⁄₁₆

3¼

Leg Vise Jaw

Overall Length

37⅛

13¾₆

15½

5⁵⁄₁₆

2

20°

½

20°

8

4

Ø1½

12⅞

2¼

2⅛

4

2

⅜ chamfer

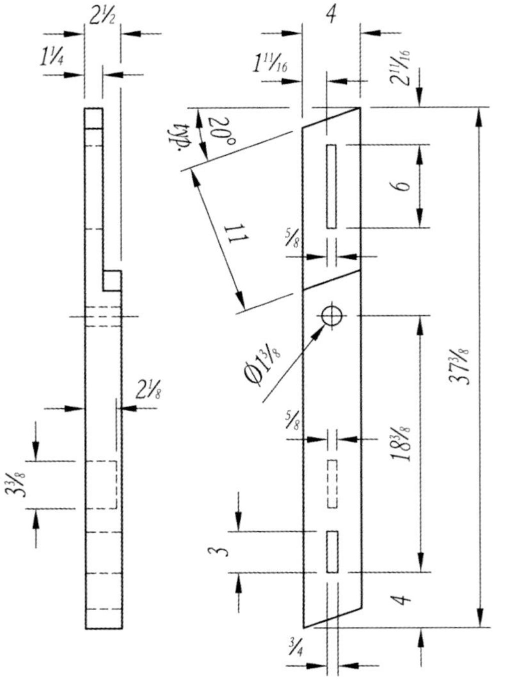
2½
1¼
4
1 11/16
2 11/16
20°
typ.
11
6
5/8
Ø1 3/8
2⅛
5/8
18⅞
37⅜
3⅜
3
4
¾

Front Left Leg

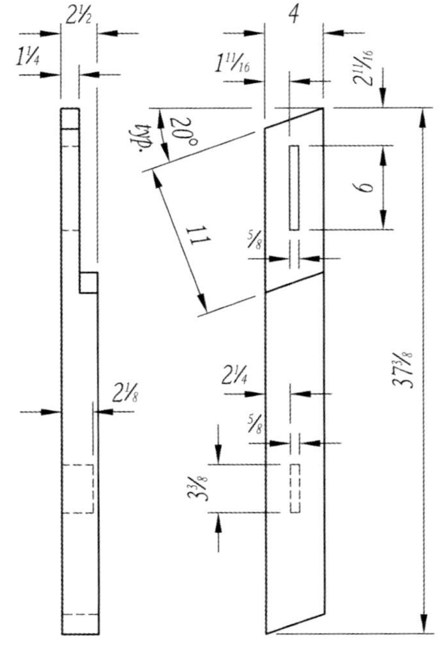
2½
1¼
4
1 11/16
2 11/16
20°
typ.
11
6
5/8
2⅛
2¼
5/8
37⅜
3⅜

Front Right Leg (opposite of shown)
Back Left Leg (opposite of shown)
Back Right Leg (as shown)

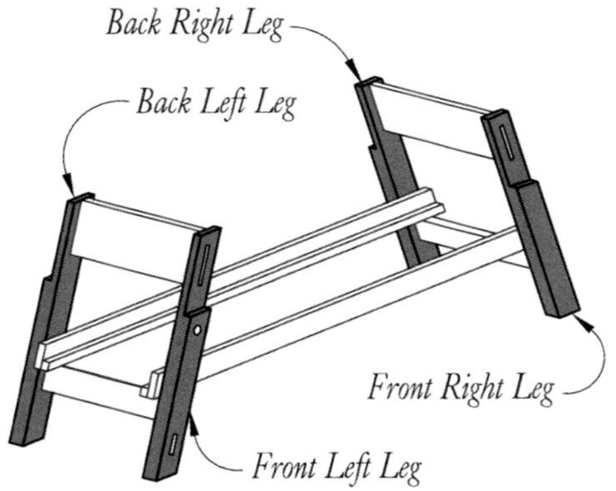
Back Right Leg
Back Left Leg
Front Right Leg
Front Left Leg

Leg Arrangement

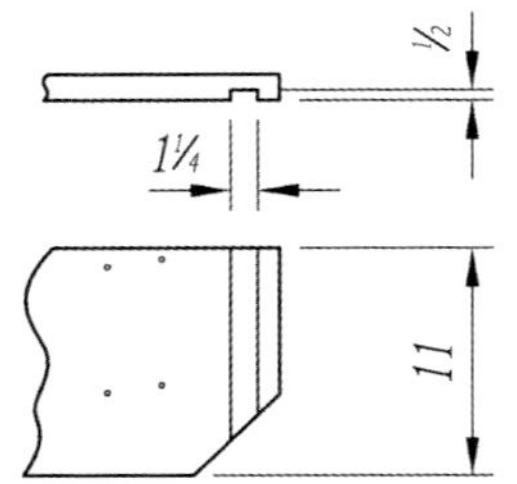
½
1¼
11

Apron to End Cap
Groove Detail

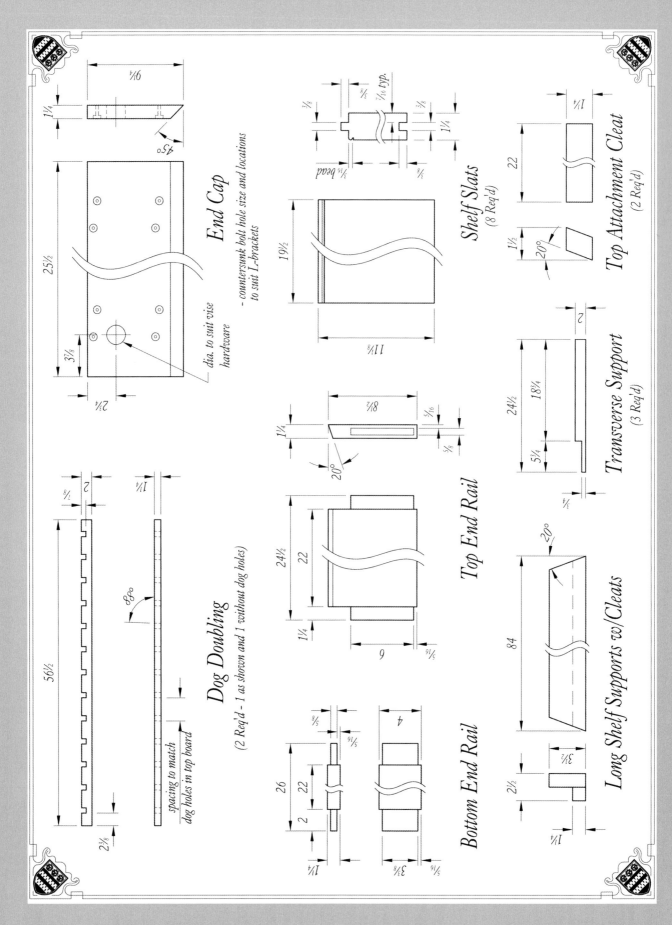

End Cap

- countersunk bolt hole size and locations to suit L-brackets

dia. to suit vise hardware

Shelf Slats
(8 Req'd)

Top Attachment Cleat
(2 Req'd)

Transverse Support
(3 Req'd)

Top End Rail

Dog Doubling
(2 Req'd - 1 as shown and 1 without dog holes)

spacing to match dog holes in top board

Bottom End Rail

Long Shelf Supports w/Cleats

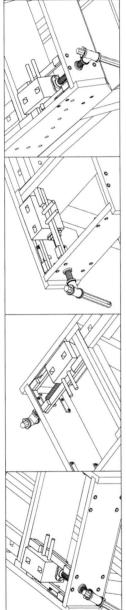

Views of Wagon Vise with Top Boards Removed

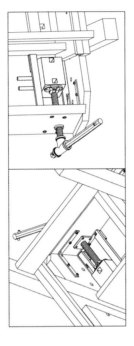

Views of Wagon Vise From Underside of Bench

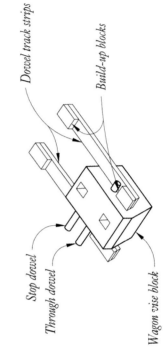

Dowel track strips

Build-up blocks

Stop dowel

Through dowel

Wagon vise block

Wagon Vise Arrangement

1⅜

7

4

3

2¼

5¼

1⁹⁄₁₆

88°

Ø⅝

5⁹⁄₁₆

1¼

20°

Wagon Vise Block

A NOUVEAU ROUBO: A few nights ago my 6-year-old asked me what my favorite *thing* was in the whole wide world. What one thing would I want to keep if the rest of my things were taken away? My answer: This bench. Her answer: The family bank account.

Chapter Six

The French Workbench

While the English workbench might be a fascinating evolutionary dead end, the so-called French bench is something that has survived in many forms. It has evolved. It has been corrupted. Gaze at the workbench drawings in Jacques-Andre Roubo's enormous *L'art du Menuisier* (*The Art of the Woodworker*, 1769-1775) and compare them to the workbench drawings in the 20th-century tool catalog by La Forge Royale. Some details have changed in the 150 years between the printings of those two books, but the same DNA courses through both illustrations.

This form of bench shows up in the famous reconstruction of the Dominy family workshop at Winterthur, which was in operation in the 18th and 19th centuries. And whenever I get to lay my own hands on an old workbench, either in a collection or in the shop of a craftsman, I can see many ways that Roubo's book echoed in the benches built in the Colonies.

You can see it in the massive and thick tops that are free of aprons or other supporting mechanisms. You can see it in the simple workholding devices. These benches will typically have a vise (perhaps two), a planing stop and some device for propping up the edges of a long piece of work so you can work on an edge.

Other than that, it is only a massive three-dimensional clamping surface. It is pure overbuilt function, and that is its charm. It will hold any board for building furniture, and it doesn't care if you use power tools, hand tools or some blend of the two.

In the more than two years since I built this bench, I've made a few modifications to the original French form, but the bottom line is this: I have yet to find a workholding task that challenges this bench. I've built Windsor chairs, Shaker cabinets, Creole tables, boxes big and small, contemporary shelves, router jigs and who knows what else. Curved stuff, straight stuff, small pieces, large panels and even some 8'-long 2x4s all stayed put without putting me out. In other words, I wouldn't trade this bench for anyone else's.

There's a price to pay to build the French bench. You need to devote some more labor, wood and lifting to the task. Oh, and a gallon of glue, if you build the bench using construction materials.

There are other ways to build this bench which you could consider that involve less laminating. You could build it exactly like Roubo specified and use a single massive slab for the top. Find someone who owns a band saw mill (the Wood-Mizer sawmill company keeps a data base of people who do custom cutting). Then you have to dry the slab, or find someone with a kiln. And you have to be able to process it (and that is some heavy lifting).

Another option I've investigated (but not yet tried) includes using laminated construction beams for the bench. You can get these construction beams in enormous thicknesses, widths and lengths. And they are already glued up and fairly square. Of course, they aren't something you will find at the home center, so you're going to have to find someone who supplies them to the trades and then find a way for them to be delivered to your shop.

And if you look around, you might find other ways to build this bench. When I was in Germany in 2006 I visited the Residenz in Wurzburg, an enormous palace built for the bishop princes that ruled that area. While the building was impressive, I was most smitten by some of the materials being used by the artisans who were restoring one of the building's painted ceilings. The scaffolding was all supported by some impressive-looking laminations that were stacked up like children's building blocks. The laminated blocks looked like white pine 2x6s that had been glued up into slabs that were as wide as 16" and 6' long.

They were all perfectly dressed and finished with a film finish to boot. And I know they were a commercial product because many of them still had bar codes and labels (in German, dang it) stapled to the end grain. They looked like perfect bench-building materials for a French workbench — a fact that I didn't feel compelled to tell to my German tour guide.

"Simpler is better (except when complicated looks really cool)."

— Daiku-Dojo web site, daikudojo.org

Understanding the French Bench

I first encountered this style of bench while paging through a copy of volume one of Roubo's *L'art du Menuisier* during a business trip to New York City. Roubo was a professional 18th-century woodworker and well-educated man, and his four-volume work on the craft is one of the seminal works in the field.

I was actually looking at the book with its owner, Joel Moskowitz, to settle a fine (read: meaningless) point of disagreement about historical workbench heights. As we were yammering and flipping pages we hit plate 11, which shows this workbench for joiners. A light went on in my head. This bench had a lot of details that resembled my workbench back in our shop in Cincinnati. The front edge of Roubo's workbench was flush with the legs, a change I had made a few months earlier. The Roubo bench lacked any apron or other awkward supporting structure below the length of the top. I had just reworked the sliding deadman on my bench to remove clamping obstructions. But Roubo's bench was different than mine in other ways. Mostly, it was simpler and more massive than my bench, which was sturdy enough (I thought at the time) and had been cluttered by clamping gizmos.

When I returned to the office after my trip to New York City, my head was buzzing with ideas about this French bench. And so I sat down and started looking at every image of old workbenches I could find in my books at home and work. It quickly became evident that there are some important differences between the Roubo bench and some modern benches:

Size and mass: In his text, Roubo specified that a proper workbench's top should be thick and long – as much as 6" thick and between 6' and 12' long. The thickness adds weight, provides strength to the workbench's base (more on that point later) and makes the top stiff so you don't need an apron below for support. Why is this an important detail? Aprons obstruct your clamps when you secure anything to your bench. If you've ever used a bench without an apron, you know how liberating this feature is. As to the length, make your bench as long as your shop will permit with at least a couple feet of clearance at each end. A long bench allows you to assemble projects at one end and continue to cut, plane, rout and sand at the other. A large workbench actually saves space because you don't have to build an assembly bench. As to the bench's width, you want to be able to clamp across the width of your bench; and tops that are wider than 27" will start to interfere with using a common 30" clamp. Similarly, a bench narrower than 18" will be tippy unless braced against a wall.

Placement of the top: The workbench's top is placed on the base of the bench so that the legs and stretchers are flush to the front edge of the benchtop – there's no overhang at the front or at the back. This design feature allows you to use your bench's legs and stretchers as a clamping surface. When you are working on anything wide – such as mortising a door's edge – you can secure it easily to the legs or stretchers with a clamp.

Simple workholding: To work on the edge of a board, Roubo shows a hook (it's called a *crochet* – French for *hook*) at the location where most benches have a metal face vise. The shape of the crochet allows it to grab one end of the work and immobilize it when you

work from right to left, such as with a plane. You can use a wide variety of methods to support your work from below: holdfasts in the legs, a sliding deadman (if you have one) or even a 2x4 clamped to the legs. For working on the faces of boards, you work against the single planing stop (metal teeth are optional) or you can use the holdfasts in the top in a variety of manners. The holdfasts can be used directly on the work (such as when you are drilling or mortising) or you can use the holdfasts to secure thin scraps of wood to your benchtop to work against.

Unusual joinery: The legs of the Roubo workbench are joined to the top with a double through-tenon. For any woodworker with a passing knowledge of the properties of wood, this looks like disaster. After all, the top will expand and contract while the stretchers below will not. Will this bench self-destruct? No. This bench is not a dining room table, where the strength of the structure comes from the joinery between the legs and aprons. The vast majority of the strength of this workbench comes from the top. There are no aprons (hurrah!) and the stretchers are quite small. So when the top shrinks and expands, the only thing that really happens is that the joints at the stretchers open up a little and the bench gets a little bit of an A-frame shape. After a year of work, I measured the distortion of the workbench's base. It was indeed an A-frame shape, but barely. At the front of the bench, the top of the bench was $^1/_8$" narrower that it was at the floor. This distortion did not in any way interfere with clamping or securing my work.

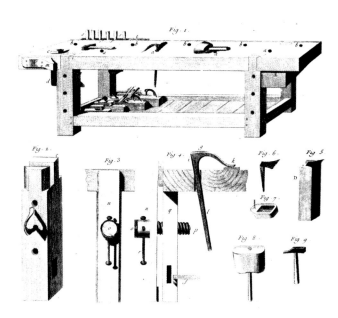

EVERYTHING YOU NEED TO KNOW: When I built this French workbench, all I had in the way of instruction was this plate and a few rough dimensions passed to me by a French-Canadian woodworker. The lack of detail wasn't a big deal because there aren't too many details to attend to.

NAVIGATE THE WATER: Get a moisture meter if you want to avoid surprises. When working with softwoods, you can use the moisture meter to separate the wet boards from the dry ones. You'll know when the wood reaches equilibrium with your shop, and you'll be able to work with boards that aren't at equilibrium with confidence.

A leg vise: In later volumes of his work, Roubo suggests adding a leg vise to the front of the workbench, though it is not shown on the bench in the initial drawing. I was a bit torn as to what to do. I was interested in the crochet (because I'd never tried one), but the leg vise seemed a bit more familiar to me. I decided to build both. Getting the crochet and vise jaws positioned correctly took some care, but it was the right decision to add both. In fact, I have found that I use them in tandem quite frequently.

Use the Wood's Moisture to Your Advantage

Like my English bench, I built the French one using Southern yellow pine, a construction material typically used as joists or (when treated with preservatives) for decks. I purchased all of the wood for this bench (with a bit of stock left over) for $250 at my local home center. You should be aware that softwoods such as Southern yellow pine, hemlock and fir will not be as dry as your typical kiln-dried hardwood. The moisture content of yellow pine – sometimes called longleaf pine – is at equilibrium in our shop at about 10 percent. The stuff straight from the store usually is wetter. With this batch of pine some of the boards were as wet as 17 percent. (I have worked with fir from a home center that was so wet that it sprayed a stream of water when I ripped it on the table saw.)

Don't be alarmed by the high moisture content. You can use it to your advantage when building this bench. You need a moisture meter to do this, however. Mark every board with its moisture content and then segregate the boards. Choose the wettest boards for the top and legs, those parts will shrink on the stretchers of the bench, which should have a lower moisture content than the other parts. This approach will keep the joints tight and will slightly distort the base's shape, which is going to happen anyway.

At the lumberyard, take your time when picking your boards, and use your eyes and your moisture meter to guide your choices. Pull the boards from the rack that are as clear of knots, splits, shakes and bark as possible. Don't be afraid to ask the people at the home center to open a new bunk of material for you – it typically is stored in the racks above the open bunk. Use your moisture meter to find the driest ones and make a pile of possible boards. If you pull more boards than you need for the bench, examine them all closely for twist and wind.

If you don't have a moisture meter, a good way to judge wetness is by roughly gauging the weight of the board in question. Wetter boards weigh quite a bit more. Sometimes the extra weight is resin – yellow pine is sticky stuff. But you are still better off by choosing the lighter-weight boards.

As noted in the chapter on the English bench: the wider the softwood stock, the clearer and straighter it will be. Don't buy 2x4s for this project. Please. They are the worst when it comes to knots, bow, twist and wind. You might think, "I am saving time because I won't have to rip anything." That is a fool's paradise. Stick to 2x12s and 2x10s and rip out the boards you need for each component.

ARROWS GUIDE THE GLUE-UP: Mark the direction the grain is running on each edge as you pick your boards for each top section. This also will make life easier when (or if) you true up the top with a handplane.

A PAIN IN THE PINE: In this assembly you can see how the board on the left is bowed. I positioned the concave side of the bow toward the inside of the assembly. Clamp pressure in the middle of this assembly will flatten the entire board against its neighbor.

DON'T SKIMP ON GLUE: You want a thin, consistent film of glue on the board. I pour a line of glue down the board and spread it (quickly now!) with cardboard and then stack it on its neighbor. This trick gives you a little more time to get the clamps on.

EXTEND-A-BED: Dealing with 8'-long stock on any power jointer is difficult. The beds are not really designed to handle this size stock. And because the boards weigh a lot, even keeping them under control is difficult. That's why I recommend you set up some sort of infeed and outfeed support system. It will help hold the board so you can focus on moving it steadily across the cutterhead.

Basic Joinery Made Easier

This bench can be built by a beginner. I know several people who built this bench as their first-ever woodworking project. (Before even building the obligatory set of bookshelves.) All told, there are 12 housed joints in this bench and nothing is complex or angled. And here's a bonus: You don't have to cut any tenons when building this bench – though it is entirely mortise-and-tenon construction. All of the tenons on the legs and stretchers are created when laminating the boards together. The longer boards in the lamination become the tenons. The shorter boards act as the tenons' shoulders.

All of the joints in this bench are drawbored. This early and nearly forgotten technique will make all of your joints stouter. But most of the work in this bench is in gluing up the boards to create the top, legs and stretchers. I'd start by buying a gallon of a slow-setting glue,

such as Titebond Extend, and making sure your powered planer and powered jointer are tuned up.

Good Stock Preparation

This project can be built with a 6" power jointer and 13" portable planer – you don't need industrial equipment. Begin by ripping all your boards down to the sizes you'll need for your laminations. I ripped them ¼" oversize to allow for trimming after everything was glued up. Remember that dimensional lumberyard stock is sold undersized. A 2x12 is actually about 11" wide; a 2x10 is typically 9" wide in the real world.

Then plane and joint all your boards to a finished thickness of 1¼". If your stock can finish out a little thicker, then let it. Embrace the extra weight and thickness. I recommend beginning gluing up the top

ON THE COLLECTING OF CLAMPS: How many clamps does it take to make a workbench top? Answer: As many as you have. No matter how many clamps we own, I always dig deep into our collection for big glue-ups.

EDGE PATROL: When you start assembling your four top sections you want the joints to be tight. Because these assemblies are so big, you won't be able to use clamp pressure to remove any gaps. Take your time and do it right.

in sections, four boards to a section. This allows you to then run the completed section over a 6" jointer and through your planer to true it.

Because you're going to machine or handplane these sections after assembly, you want to make sure all the grain is running in the same direction in the boards.

The other thing to watch for is which way the boards bow. No matter how carefully you prepare your stock, some of the boards are likely to have a small bow. Plan your sections so the bow faces the inside of the assembly.

Here's another tip about surfacing your lumber. Ignore this paragraph if you are using a well-seasoned hardwood. It doesn't apply. When you work with softwoods, especially yellow pine, you are better off surfacing whatever wood you are going to be working with for the next day only. Do your business with that batch, then surface the next batch for the next day's work.

I know that this seems like it's a pain. It is. But it's good advice. Softwoods tend to shift around after you surface them. And if you leave them overnight they will do circus tricks for you. ("Roll over!") This will happen even if the boards appear to be at equilibrium with your shop. Once you get them glued up into a top section, they might still move around a bit, but they will settle down soon enough. And then they become quite stable. I'm sure there is a tree scientist somewhere who could confirm, explain or mock this assertion. But I've found it to be true after surfacing thousands of board feet of the stuff for furniture-grade work.

So work in stages. It will save you some trouble and prevent you from reworking your boards to get them flat again.

Tricks for Gluing the Top

Gluing up Southern yellow pine can try your patience. The wood is dense and resinous, so it resists glue penetration more than some other pines. The way to get around the resin problem is to remove it

HERE'S A CHEAT: If you're having problems getting your assemblies to mate perfectly, take a couple swipes down the middle with a block plane. This can remove material in the middle that is interfering with clamping.

at the surface by wiping the resinous areas with acetone right before applying glue. The way to get around the density issue is to allow each assembly to stay in the clamps for four hours. This is not arbitrary or overcautious – it's the recommendation from a technical specialist at Franklin International, the company that makes Titebond.

A common complaint that I hear from people trying to treat this construction lumber like a cabinet wood is that it will sometimes come apart at the seams, especially near the ends. I had this happen in an early bench of mine, and it was because I was in a hurry. In our shop we'll clamp up panels for 30 minutes and then take them out of the clamps. That's not always a good idea with yellow pine.

You can fill the splits with epoxy if you like. Or you can rip apart the joint at the glue line and try again. In my instance, I filled the crack. It served as a reminder to slow down a bit.

Apply clamps every 12" or so on your top assembly. Start at the middle and work out to the ends, pushing and pulling your boards into alignment as you go. After all four assemblies are complete, joint and plane them to clean up the faces and edges. Keep them as thick and as wide as you can. Then arrange them as they'll appear in the finished assembly and joint all the edges to get airtight joints.

LOOK MA, NO TENON SAW: The tenons on the legs and stretchers are formed during the lamination process. This saves you from having to cut tenons on the end of a 5'-long stretcher – a real trick to do well.

DON'T BURN A COMMUTATOR: No matter how butch your circular saw is, don't make this cut by starting with a full-depth pass. Make the finished cut in two or three passes; you'll get less burning and it will be easier to clean up the ends.

YOUR 18-GAUGE BUDDIES: The plywood spacers ensure your leg tenons will be exactly 2" long and square. A couple short brads are all the holding power you need for this temporary joint.

KNOCK ON WOOD: A rap with a hammer will loosen the plywood spacers. There might be glue squeeze-out in the corner between the shoulder and cheek. Chisel it out and the tenon is complete.

If you are skilled with a hand plane, I think you'll find this an excellent task for a jointer plane. Two of my three joints for the top needed to be tuned with a hand plane to be at their best. It might seem a daunting task because the edge is so big, but that actually is an advantage because your plane won't tip off the edge. I also did some further tweaking with a block plane.

If you are confident that your joints are sound, you can clamp up the entire top during one big gut-wrenching moment. I did it. I didn't enjoy it. But it worked. If you're not feeling frosty, glue two small sections into one. Then either add a single section at a time to that chunk or glue up a separate hunk of two sections and then join the two hunks.

Be advised that whenever you release an assembly from clamps you should check the edge again before gluing on another chunk. Clamps, glue and – I don't know, the alignment of the stars – can bend a jointed straight edge.

When your top is complete, trim the ends square using a circular saw and a straightedge guide. Or you can use a big handsaw; but that's a lot like working, as an old foreman of mine used to say. If you go the circular saw route, you'll need to cut from both the top and the bottom of the benchtop, so be sure to carry your layout lines around the sides and bottom of the piece. After squaring the ends, clean up your sawblade marks with a block plane. First moisten the end grain with some alcohol and then tidy things up.

Making Tenons Out of Nothing

The next task is to glue up the legs and stretchers. These laminations are easier than the top pieces because they are shorter. But there is another challenge. You're going to leave some of these individual boards a bit longer so that they will become the tenons you need.

You might be asking yourself how you'll get a perfect tenon with these laminations sliding around as you're clamping them. After some

TWO RIPS MAKE ONE TRACK: Make the ½" x ½" chamfer on the long stretchers by simply ripping it on the table saw. Using a chamfer bit in a router is much slower because you will have to make several passes.

TENACIOUS TENONS: With all the legs and stretchers complete, I then dressed the glued-up edges on the powered jointer and then with a hand-plane. This is what the completed and huge tenons look like.

MEASURING WITHOUT MATH: The less you measure, the more accurate you will become. Using the tenon to mark out your mortises reduces the chance of a measuring error. And it is faster, too.

head-scratching I found an easy way to get perfect tenons. First, make sure all your pieces are crosscut square across both the width and the thickness.

Now get some scrap plywood, anything thicker than ¼" will do fine. Cut it so it is as long as your tenons (2" long for the leg tenons; 2½" long for the stretchers). And cut it so it's wider than the assembled lamination (7" wide for the legs; 6" wide for the stretchers).

Before you glue up your legs and stretchers, nail one of these boards to the pieces that will form the tenon's face cheek. Now glue up the layers and butt the two outside laminations against these plywood spacers.

To keep all the leg parts in alignment during glue-up, don't be afraid to put a couple clamps along the length of the leg to align the pieces lengthwise. This extra clamping also guarantees a well-formed tenon. As soon as your clamps are set, knock the spacer off the assembly with a hammer. You don't want the spacer to accidentally get glued to your leg.

If you are particularly worried about the spacer becoming part of the permanent exhibit, then rub some wax or paraffin on the spacer before nailing it down. Wax is an oil; glue is water. That should help.

Before you move to gluing up the stretchers, you need to decide if you want a sliding deadman on your bench. If the answer is yes (and I hope it is), then cut two ½" x ½" chamfers on the long edges of the board that will face the outside of the bench. The deadman will slide on this track. Resist using a groove to guide the sliding deadman, as is done with sliding doors in casework. It can fill up with chips.

Assembling the stretchers uses the same routine as the legs. Use plywood spacers on the ends of the long board in the lamination to properly position the shorter board and create the tenons.

Making Massive Leg Mortises

The mortises in the legs are quite large. As a result, you won't be able to use a mortising machine (at least, not without tremendous difficulty). And making these mortises by chisel alone would also be more work than necessary.

The best solution is, quite honestly, to drill out the mortises and then clean up the corners with a chisel. If you have a drill press and a 1¼" Forstner bit, you're golden. If you are using a brace and bit with an expansive bit, that also will work – just be sure to use a brace with a large swing, 14" is about right.

The first step is to mark out the locations of all the mortises on the legs. Measure up 5" from the bottom of the legs and then use the tenon itself – like a ruler – to lay out the mortise location. This trick reduces measuring errors.

If you're going to drill out these mortises with a Forstner bit, set your drill press for 1,200 rpm (or in that neighborhood). That's a good speed for both clearing chips, reducing burning and getting the job done. When I make mortises with a Forstner, I make many overlapping holes, to the point where I only have the corners to clean up. I do everything I can to avoid chiseling the long-grain walls of the mortise. This is where the joint's strength comes from, and chiseling it almost always introduces a sloppy or irregular fit.

Make each leg mortise a little deeper (I like ⅛") than needed. This means that the two mortises in each leg will meet one another in the

BEGIN THE BOREDOM: Begin the mortise by defining the beginning and ending of the joint with your Forstner bit.

THE BORING MIDDLE PART: Then clean up the waste between as shown above.

HUNT THE HUMPS: Now clean up the little triangles of waste along the long-grain walls of the mortise. The more you bore, the smaller the triangles get.

BORED BOARD: You're done when you can put the bit in the joint and it will slide freely left to right in the mortise.

middle. This is an asset because this gap gives a place for the excess glue to go during assembly.

To complete the joint you can square up the corners with a chisel (as I did) or you can clip the corners of your tenon with a chisel or a coarse rasp. I have found that squaring the corners of the mortise is almost always the faster technique. Your corner work will be more accurate if you begin your cut in the right place. Don't place the chisel where you want the corner to be and wail away. That makes the tool hard to steer. Take a couple smaller bites first and you will be driving the chisel – not the other way around.

Details on the Legs

Before you dive into assembling the base, take care of a few details now to save hassles later. First, plane a ¼" x ¼" chamfer on the bottom edge of the legs. This chamfer prevents your legs from snagging on something on your floor and ripping out some grain when you drag or push your bench to a new location. Yes, even at 350 pounds, you can move this bench around – and you will.

Next up is an important decision. If you're going to install a leg vise in your bench, cut a big notch in the front left leg for the guide that keeps the jaw parallel. If you want my advice, I'd go ahead and

cut this notch, even if you're not sold on the utility of the leg vise. I really like its ability to secure small parts and I find it as tough as many metal-jawed vises I've used. You also should go ahead and drill the 1⅜"-diameter hole in the leg for the vise's screw. Its location is shown in the construction drawing.

The other detail is to drill holes in the legs for your hold-downs. Before you do this, you need to decide on their diameter, and that really depends on which hold-down you purchase.

Assembling the Base

The base is assembled by drawboring the joints together. This technique allows you to assemble the base without any clamps (so you don't have to buy any 6'-long clamps for this job). You can also assemble this base one joint at a time – that's the beauty of this technique. Here's drawboring in a nutshell: Drill a hole through the disassembled mortise. Assemble the joint dry and transfer the hole's location onto the mating tenon cheek. Disassemble the joint and drill the hole through the tenon – but offset it a bit toward the shoulder. When you drive a peg through the completed joint, the peg will draw the bores together, locking them mechanically. It's a bit of 17th-century magic.

CORNERED ANIMAL: A corner chisel is expensive, and it is a trick to sharpen. But when you need one, it's worth the hassle. This operation can be carried out with a standard bench chisel, but it takes longer.

Here are the details for this bench: With the joint disassembled, drill the ³⁄₈" holes through the mortise using an auger bit. Assemble the joint and mark the hole's centerpoint location with a prick of a ³⁄₈" brad-point bit. Remove the tenon and drill the hole for the peg a bit closer to the shoulder of the tenon – ³⁄₃₂" to ¹⁄₈" will do the job. Pick the larger offset if your legs are particularly wet (which means you have more shrinkage ahead of you).

Assemble the joint without glue and twist a drawbore pin into the joint to begin aligning the holes and check the fit of the shoulder. A drawbore pin is a tapered metal drift pin (you can buy them at Sears). The metal pin allows you to check the fit of your components and to deform the wood a bit to prepare a path for a more fragile wooden peg. If, after inserting the drawbore pin, you see any gaps, find the extra material or dried glue that is interfering with a good fit and chisel it out now.

When the joint fits tightly, reassemble it with glue and whittle the ends of two ³⁄₈" x 4" pegs so they look like elongated pencils. For most furniture jobs, I use a ¹⁄₄"-diameter peg when drawboring. But because of the scale of this project, ³⁄₈"-diameter oak stock is far better. (And even better than that is white oak stock that has been rived and is bone dry.)

Twist one of the drawbore pins into one of the two holes and then drive a wooden peg into the adjacent hole. Remove the steel drawbore pin and drive the second peg in. Trim the pegs flush with a saw and chisel. Look ma, no clamps.

SHAVE YOUR LEGS: Before assembly, dress your legs for the final time. They should be straight and true; a smoothing plane removes so little material that it's unlikely to cast your legs out of square.

CHOP THE NOTCH: The notch for the vise is ½" wide, 4" long and runs through the entire leg. The best way to cut it is to saw out the cheeks (I used a band saw) and then use a mortise chisel and mallet to pop out the waste. This is both easy and fun.

POINT TO THE MIDDLE: Assemble the joint without glue and use a brad-point bit to mark the center of the hole on the tenon's cheek.

FOREARM TORQUE: Because of the depth of these holes in your legs, you're going to want to make them with an auger that's powered by a brace and bit. These are powerful tools – and this will get you warmed up for boring out the mortises in the underside of the top.

OK, THIS IS FUSSY: A piece of scrap in the mortise reduces tear-out when you drill into the mortise cheek. It's probably unnecessary to the strength of this bench, but I relish overbuilding joints for workbenches.

And You Thought the Leg Mortises Were Big?

If you've ever built a table before you're probably a bit concerned about how the top connects to the base. Your first reaction might be that this design detail is simply the product of an 18th-century woodworker who didn't understand seasonal wood movement. After all, the top will expand and contract but the base will not. It seems like a disaster waiting to happen.

But it's not.

By tenoning the legs into a top that is a little on the wet side (as yours undoubtedly is), the bench's design is counting on the top shrinking and wracking the base a bit, making it slightly wider at the bottom than at the top and more stable.

If you're skittish about this design detail, here's an option: Make the two mortises for the rear legs an 1/8" wider than necessary to allow the top to move without wracking the base. By widening the mortises for the rear legs only you'll keep the front edge of the top flush to the front legs, a critical detail. If you take this route, you'll still drawbore all four leg joints – the pins won't interfere with wood movement.

The original bench in the Roubo volumes showed the tenons passing all the way through the top. If you are confident enough to attempt this, go forward with my blessing. I made the tenons go only halfway through the top and then drawbored them to the base without glue. This accomplished the same mechanical integration offered by the original design. And yes, this is an authentic Roubo detail. Volume 3 of his book shows a bench with blind tenons (it's plate 279).

Lay out your mortises on the underside of the benchtop by using the base itself. How's that? Turn your top upside down on sawhorses and place the base in position, also upside down. Mark for the mortises. Move or remove the base and bore out the waste using a 3/4" auger bit. If you're going to use an electric drill for this operation, use a

THE OFFSET: Remove the tenon and mark the location of the peg hole in the tenon. It should be closer to the tenon's shoulder than the original mark. All these fussy lines and measuring of offsets is for the beginner. After a dozen joints, you will drawbore through instinct.

corded one. You can cook a cordless drill in short order with this operation.

Clean out the waste with a mortise chisel and use a combination square to confirm that the mortise walls are both square and deep enough to accept the leg tenons. You don't want to fit these joints any more than you have to – the base is about 100 pounds.

If you've opted for the sliding deadman, you'll need to mill a 5/8"-wide x 1"-deep groove in the underside of the top for the deadman before attaching the top and base. After I milled this groove, disaster struck. The top slid off the sawhorses and landed on the corner with the groove. There was a snap, followed by a brief cloudburst of cursing. I vowed to fix the joint with glue (which I did, and seamlessly) and then to reinforce this area with a steel strip (which I didn't). After a couple years of hard use, the edge is solid, and my thoughts about a steel strip diminished.

I drawbored the top to the base, but I didn't use glue in these joints. If I ever need to remove the top, I can drill out the 3/8" pegs to dismantle the assembly. Follow the same drilling and pegging procedure you used to drawbore the joints in the base. The only difference is the length of the pegs; these are 6" long.

PINNED AND PONDERED: Reassemble the joint and twist the drawbore pin into the joint. Check the fit of your components. Don't worry too much about a gap on the inside of the base. Focus on the outside, the show side. After this dress rehearsal, add glue and drive the pegs home.

TRY IT: A try square ensures your holes are straight into the underside of the top. After drilling three of these mortises, you'll have the confidence to do the fourth without the square.

PLACE AND TRACE: Center the top on the underside of the bench and make sure the front legs will be flush to the front edge of the bench. If the top has an overhang at the back you can take care of that after the top reaches equilibrium. Knife around the four tenons. Push the base aside or remove it. Then bore out the waste.

Turn the bench onto its feet. Stand on it. Park a car's engine on it if you like. I've found that this bench is up to any task. Before you start adding the gizmos that hold your work, take an hour or so to flatten the top. A jack plane and a jointer plane are the most effective tools for this operation. See the chapter on maintenance and appliances for more information on flattening a top.

Workholding Details

If you're going to add the crochet to the bench, take care to make sure the grain direction runs straight from the tip to the far corner – this is stronger than making it parallel to the top's edge. I made the crochet by face-gluing three pieces of 1"-thick ash. I cut the shape out on the band saw and then cleaned up the sawblade marks with a spokeshave and a card scraper. Drill clearance holes in the crochet for $1/2$" x 6" lag bolts and $1/2$" washers. Drill pilot holes in the benchtop, using the holes in the crochet as a template. Attach the crochet to the benchtop with the end of the crochet flush to the end of the benchtop. I centered the crochet on the top's thickness. If you use a plow plane in your work, you'll want to lower the crochet a bit so your plow's fence will clear the crochet.

In Woodworking, the Question is often the Answer

There is an old expression that has nothing to do with woodworking, but it has turned out to be one of the guiding principles in my work.

The expression goes something like this: "If you have to ask the question, then you already know the answer."

I know that it sounds like some nonsense that a smooth-talking corporate trainer might spin to baffle you, but allow me to give you a real-world example of how useful it is in the shop.

As I was building the French workbench it came time to attach the massive 230-pound top to the 100-pound base, and I was facing the task of drawboring the four massive joints.

This extra step was going to require a couple hours of work and serious heavy lifting. I was going to have to fit the base into the top, remove the base to bore the holes for the pegs and then fit it again and remove it again to mark and bore the offset holes in the tenons.

It was about 5 P.M., and it would be so much easier to just drop the top onto the base, let gravity hold everything together and call it a day. The question then flashed in my head: "Do I really need to drawbore the top?"

I've found that these questions of expediency are like the old cartoons where the character is getting competing advice from an angel on one shoulder and a devil on the other. Questions such as these always come from the devil on the right shoulder of the cartoon cat (or woodworker).

When You Come to the Fork in the Road, Take it

For years I listened to and agonized over questions such as these. I debated them and tried to see both sides of the argument. However, eventually I realized that all these different questions were really just one question in disguise: Are you going to take a seemingly reasonable shortcut that will save you time now but cause regret later?

· Question: Should I strip the finish off my Morris chair project after the staining highlighted a couple small but disappointing toolmarks near the through-tenons?

· Question: Should I dovetail the rear joints in these drawers for my tool cabinet? No one will ever see them, and a lock-rabbet will be quite a bit faster.

· Question: Do I really need to test-fit this familiar joint before I glue it up?

· Question: Do I really need to check the jointer's fence to make sure it's still 90° to the bed?

In the case of the workbench, I actually asked the question out loud, and all of my fellow editors heard me and chimed in with advice. One editor said that gravity was more than enough to hold everything in place and that drawboring the top was likely an act of ridiculous excess.

The other editors were on the fence and so we assembled the bench and put it on its feet. The bench looked good all put together like that. It seemed rock solid, like I could park my old Volkswagen on it. I was ready to go home and have a beer.

ASK YOURSELF: I seem to mutter to myself a lot while making chairs, and I also find myself remaking the complex curved parts quite a bit. The two things are related.

Then one of the editors went up to the end of the bench and gave it several king-size hip checks. Something caught my eye. I looked closely at where the legs met the top as the editor gave it a few more hip checks.

Though it was slight, the bench base was wracking with every shove. After years of planing on this bench, this wracking would become a problem. So I fetched my drawbore pins from my tool chest and got ready for a long evening. I had already wasted an hour testing out a question to which I already knew the answer.

As I drove home later that evening (ready for two beers), I wondered if this philosophy could become immobilizing for some. That is, every question could lead to a fussy downward spiral of extra work that resulted in nothing ever getting done.

But I don't think so. Every project is a series of operations, many of which are familiar and don't generate these questions. But when we stumble into new territory, these questions are the angel on our left shoulder telling us to first slow down and figure things out.

And if we listen, then the next time we encounter the same problem there won't be any questions – just action.

A TRENCHER: Mill the groove for the deadman using an upcut spiral bit in your plunge router. An edge guide makes this operation a snap. This groove is deep to allow the deadman to be removed or modified.

HOOKED ON THE HOOK: Here you can see the proper grain direction for a crochet. This feature and the shape of the crochet allows it to grab your work and wedge it against the benchtop. It is surprisingly effective.

DEAD ON: To cut the trench on the bottom edge, mark out the shape on the front edge of the deadman, then set your table saw's blade to 45° and line things up with your marks. Make one pass, turn the deadman around and make a second pass to finish the cut. Clean up the work with a chisel.

The planing stop is one of the most important parts of the bench. It is simply a piece of 2" x 2" x 12" ash that is friction-fit into a 2" x 2" mortise in the benchtop. You knock the planing stop up and down with your mallet. Roubo shows two kinds of planing stops. One is wood only, and the stop has a slight bevel on the four edges of the top. This is an important detail. If you leave it flat you'll damage the edges with your mallet eventually. The slight dome shape ensures your mallet blows will land on the center of the stop.

The leg vise is a simple affair to make if you purchase an inexpensive metal vise screw. The vise comes with a threaded metal collar that you screw to the inside of the leg, centered on the 1¼" hole you drilled before assembly.

The jaw has a slight coffin shape as shown in the drawings. And I planed a chamfer on three edges to soften the look. The chamfer on the top edge is the only critical one. It allows better access to your work when working at an angle with a plane, chisel or rasp.

The parallel guide is tenoned and pegged into the jaw. It is probably the part of the vise that is most unfamiliar to our 21st century eyes. The parallel guide is drilled with two offset rows of ⅜" holes on 1" centers. By placing a ⅜" steel pin in one of the holes in front of the leg and advancing the bench screw, the peg will then jam against the leg and pivot the top of your jaw against your work. This provides tremendous workholding power, equal to a metal vise as near as I can tell. The only downside is that you have to move the pin around for different thicknesses of work. It's a small price to pay for the small price (and great benefits) of the bench screw.

I made my own vise handle with a piece of 1" x 1" x 15" ash left over from the crochet. I planed it to an octagonal shape and then secured it in the bench screw by driving ⅜" pegs (left over from drawboring) through each end. You could buy a vise handle, but this one is much more tactile and appropriate. Then I asked Senior Editor Bob Lang to carve the year into the vise jaw. The font, by the way, is authentic. We took it from a clock face made circa 1780.

The sliding deadman is a gizmo that you can add now or wait on. You might not find your work needs it, however it's so quick to make you should give it a try. First plow out the triangular trench on the bottom edge of the deadman using your table saw. Then cut the ⅝" x 1"-long tenon on the top. Tweak the tenon's thickness and shape until the deadman fits up into the groove and then onto the track below.

Once the deadman fits, cut the curved shape on the long edges. The curve allows you to get your hand between the deadman and leg when the deadman is pushed up against the leg. Then drill the two rows of offset holes on 2" centers. You can make a dedicated peg to place in these holes or you can make the holes the same size as the shaft on your holdfast and use one of those to support your work.

Finally, you want to drill holes in the top for holdfasts. Their location isn't arbitrary. The hole near the planing stop allows me to put a batten in front of the planing stop and secure it with the holdfast, which allows me to plane wide panels against the batten.

The holes along the back edge allow me to secure thin battens up against the long edges of long boards. These are ideal for controlling your stock from the side, which is helpful when planing at an angle to the grain or across the grain. My advice is to drill these few holes

NOW WITH A SHELF: I didn't have time to make the shelf below the bench when I first built it. One afternoon I fixed that situation. I haven't actually seen the shelf for a couple years – it's covered in parts, tools and appliances.

TONGUES & GROOVES: You could simply butt the edges of the shelves together, but a tongue-in-groove shelf is stronger, traditional and nicer.

FIT THE END: Shown is one of the shelf pieces for the end with its notches cut. You also can see the ledgers beneath the shelf pieces.

and add more when needed. With the holes drilled, you can finish the bench if you please. I applied a couple coats of an oil/varnish blend. Then I added some wax to the top so it would resist glue penetration.

When I completed the bench I soon realized something unexpected. Though building the bench itself was an adventure, the real journey began when I started using the bench. With the holdfasts, crochet and battens in my arsenal I found new ways to work just about every time I stepped up to the bench.

A Flexible Bench

You do not have to add all the bench accessories shown to create a working bench. In fact, you might want to try this bench in its purest form first: a crochet, planing stop and holdfast holes. You can accomplish every major workholding task with this setup (plus one clamp).

The leg vise and sliding deadman are nice additions. The leg vise helps hold small work. And the deadman offers quick and flexible support when holding wide boards or doors on edge.

Another ugrade I recommend is the shelf shown in Roubo's volume. When I built the bench, I had a deadline based on when the photographer had to take a picture of it. An hour before show time I was still building the bench – putting the finishing touches on the leg vise to be exact. I had always meant to put a tongue-and-groove shelf below the workbench like the original, but I simply ran out of time. One day during lunch I resolved to correct that omission.

I stopped by the home center and picked up enough Southern yellow pine for the job – two 8'-long 2x12s for the shelves and one 8'-long 2x6 for the ledgers beneath the shelves. This was 30 percent more wood than I needed, but it gave me clear, straight stock.

First joint and plane all the stock down to 1¼" thick. Rip the ledgers from the 2x6 and the shelf planks from the 2x12s. Crosscut the ledgers to length after double-checking your measurements against your bench. Clamp them in place on the stretchers so that the bottom edge of each ledger is flush with the bottom edge of its mating stretcher. Screw the ledgers to the stretchers with #10 x 2" screws. I used four screws in each long stretcher and two in each end stretcher.

Shelf for the French Workbench

NO.	PART	SIZES (INCHES)			MATERIAL
		T	W	L	
☐ 2	Long ledgers	1¼	1¼	56	Yellow pine
☐ 2	Short ledgers	1¼	1¼	14	Yellow pine
☐ 6	Shelf planks	1¼	11	19	Yellow pine

Fig. 15.

CROCHET AND VISE: This isn't a traditional setup but it is an effective one. I like using the crochet and leg vise in tandem. Nothing ever slips.

CLAMPING PLATFORM: One of the best features of the French workbench is also the least obvious: the top. The thick, stiff top is a superb clamping surface, especially with the lack of aprons below it.

WORKING ON EDGES: Holdfasts in the legs and a scrapwood ledger support the work from below. The crochet wedges the work against the benchtop and legs.

Now you can crosscut your shelves easily and fit them on top of the ledgers and between the stretchers. Now plow a $^1\!/_2$" x $^1\!/_2$" groove along one long edge of each shelf plank. I used a dado stack in my table saw. Now reduce the height of the dado stack to $^3\!/_8$" and cut the rabbets on the opposite long edge that will create the tongue. The fit between the tongue and its groove shouldn't be too tight. You want the pieces to slide together easily.

Plane your shelves flat. Chamfer the long edges of each shelf. A small $^1\!/_8$" x $^1\!/_8$" chamfer will make the long edges more robust. Place five of the shelves on the ledgers and center them between the legs. You should have about a $4^1\!/_4$" gap between the shelves and the end stretchers. Measure this gap and then rip your sixth shelf. One piece will go on one end; the other will go on the other end.

My wood was pretty wet (15 percent moisture content). So these boards will shrink up a bit as they come in equilibrium with the shop. So I didn't leave much of a gap between the shelves, just $^1\!/_{32}$" or so. Now place the shelf pieces for the ends up against the legs and lay out

the notches that will allow each end piece to fit around the legs. Cut the notches and clean up your work with a chisel.

With everything fit in place, you can then secure the shelves to their ledgers. I used Miller Dowels without glue. These stepped and tapered dowels are great if you ever need to knock something apart to move it. A couple coats of oil/varnish blend and you're done.

Shop Testing the French Workbench

I'm often asked how I like my French workbench, or if I'll ever come to my senses and simply buy a continental workbench like the rest of the world. This French bench has been the center of my work for more than two years now, and I cannot imagine ever getting rid of it.

I've made changes. I added a wagon vise in the end-vise position plus a matching row of dog holes. I made this modification to help me work across the grain of boards with my hand planes (mostly my jointer and fore planes). A wagon vise is faster than using the battens-plus-holdfasts method – but it's not better.

PIERRE, MEET JACK: Though a sliding deadman isn't original to the French bench (that I can find), it is a highly recommended addition to the bench. When your French friends come for a visit you can remove it.

SAWING TENONS: A leg vise offers a wide expanse of gripping surface. You can clamp your work, assume it will stay put and focus on cutting to your knife lines.

WORKING ON FACES: Holdfasts and battens keep the work from skittering around on your benchtop.

The wagon vise is worth a few sentences of explanation. I found a drawing of it in an early 20th-century French woodworking catalog. And it pops its head up every once in a while (most recently I saw it in an issue of *Woodsmith* magazine). But the wagon vise has never been nearly as popular as the classic tail vise.

Because my wagon vise was a retrofit, it also was a compromise. I first hacked out a large through-mortise in the benchtop and installed a small metal vise screw in the mortise. (This screw is usually used in making homemade veneer presses, but it is more than stout enough for this application). I attached the end of the vise's screw to a wooden block that had a couple holes bored through it for round bench dogs.

Once I added a little track below the bench to keep the vise block steady, I thought I was in business. I was mistaken. The vise screw was applying a lot of pressure to the 2" block of end grain at the end of the

bench. I got a little worried that the whole thing would self-destruct if someone applied a lot of pressure to the vise screw. And so I added a thick end cap to the bench using 6"-long carriage bolts and washers. That seemed to make everything really tight and sturdy. But was it worth all the trouble? I think the jury is still out. The biggest advantage the wagon vise offers over a Wonder Dog system is the ability to plane thin stock with ease. Plus the wagon vise is a bit faster to use. So think carefully before you make this modification to your bench. It helps, but it is not a cure-all.

One more note: If you simply screw the wagon vise's threaded casting to your bench (instead of bolting it through the benchtop) it will be great for applying pressure to pinch stuff between the dogs, but it will be ineffective for disassembling things. Using the dogs of the wagon vise to pull apart a frame assembly is more likely to pull the

The French Workbench

vise's threaded casting right out of the bench, screws and all. I know that it sounds like I don't like my wagon vise – but that's not true. I use it all the time. I like it. I just don't want to sell it to you as the most perfect solution of all time. If it were, then what you are holding in your hands would be a pamphlet instead of a book.

I think that I learned a lot about building vises after making several of them. The rules I outlined earlier in this book for workbenches should have one special caveat for woodworkers making vises. Remember the rule about overbuilding your workbench? When it comes to making your own vises, there is no such thing as overbuilt. Make all the components of a homemade vise as stout as possible with thick, tough woods.

Other modifications to the stock French bench: I've messed with the sliding deadman during the last couple years so that it uses the Stanley No. 203 bench bracket instead of a wooden peg. That change was in the name of science, not necessity. I wanted to know how the bench bracket compared to the wooden peg. The No. 203 is cool and helps out in some situations by stabilizing your work. But is it a do-or-die modification that you should make? Not really.

In fact, there's only one modification I've made in the last two years that I think is essential: Add some leather to the jaws of the leg vise. This makes the vise grip even better with less pressure.

Apart from that $15, 15-minute fix, I think you can build this bench as is. After working on it you might come up with modifications that suit your work. And this is the true beauty of this bench. Its open architecture allows you to add vises or other workholding devices with little fuss. Want a quick-release vise? No problem – there are no aprons to restrict the bars of the vise. How about adding a twin-screw vise in the end-vise position? Again – not a problem.

This bench is like an empty canvas or a lump of clay. It is designed to be altered. And because you won't be the same kind of woodworker in 10 years time (this I guarantee) you're going to want a bench that will change with you. This bench just might save you from building another bench (or even two) as your skills deepen and your workholding needs become more complicated.

PLANING PANELS: Secure a batten (of any thickness) against your planing stop with a holdfast and you can work wide stock with ease.

SAW PANELS OF ANY WIDTH: The deadman, leg vise and a bar clamp (or two) will allow you to hold any panel for sawing.

"I have a friend who was involved a few years ago in the construction of a nightclub in Mexico. Much of it was cast concrete. The forms were made of timbers sawn to order on the spot by a couple of guys with handsaws and big arms. You wanted a 2x8? They would cut it from a larger timber right then and there. No pit saw, no power saws. "Got to tell you, boys and girls, I like hand tools and am very interested in saws and saw skills, but there comes a limit. For something like that I'd rather have a Skil Saw than saw skill."

— Joe Sullivan, quoted on the Knots forum, March 11, 2007

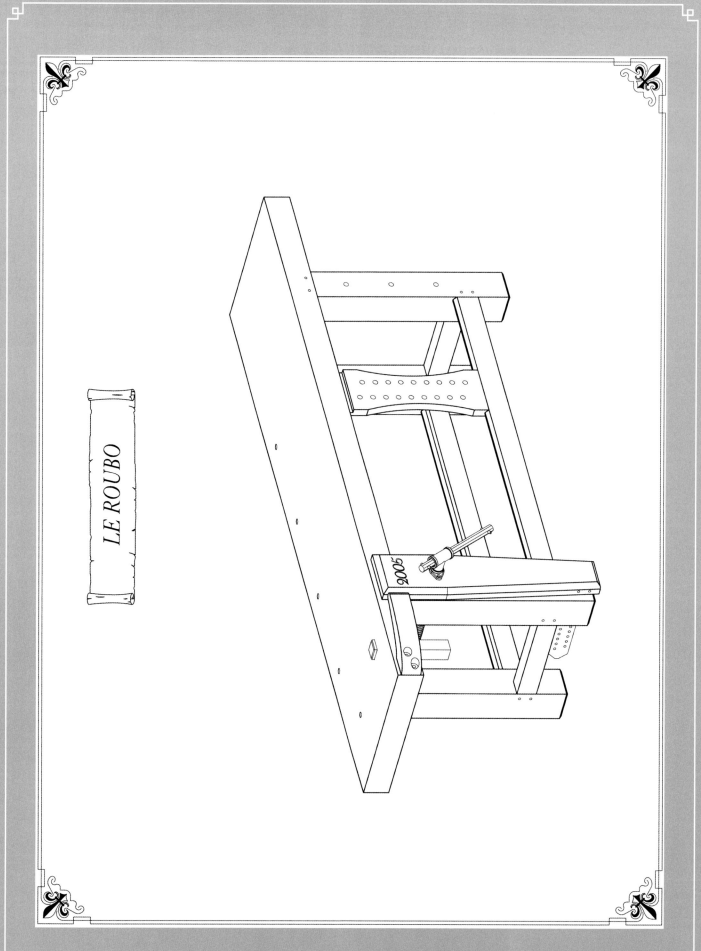

LE ROUBO

2005

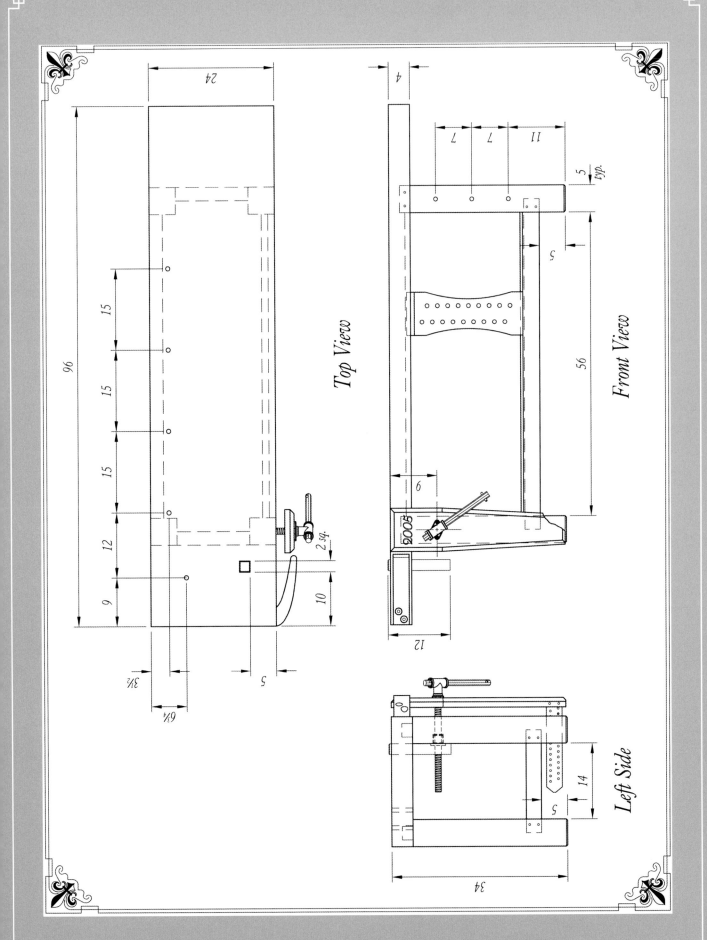

Top View

Front View

Left Side

24

96

15

15

15

15

12

9

3½

6¼

5

2 sq.

10

4

7

7

11

5 typ.

5

56

6

2005

12

34

14

5

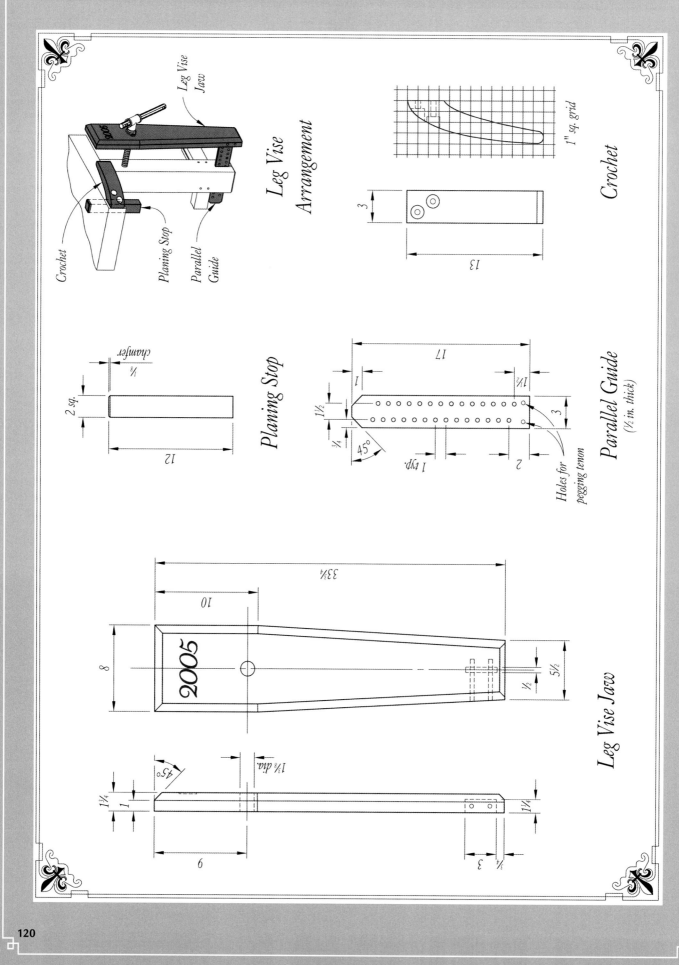

Leg Vise
Arrangement

Leg Vise Jaw

Crochet

Planing Stop

Parallel Guide

Crochet

1" sq. grid

3

13

Planing Stop

¼ chamfer

2 sq.

12

Parallel Guide
(½ in. thick)

17

1

1½

1½

3

¾

45°

1 typ.

2

Holes for
pegging tenon

Leg Vise Jaw

33¾

10

8

2005

5½

½

45°

1⅝ dia.

1¼

1

6

3

¼

1¼

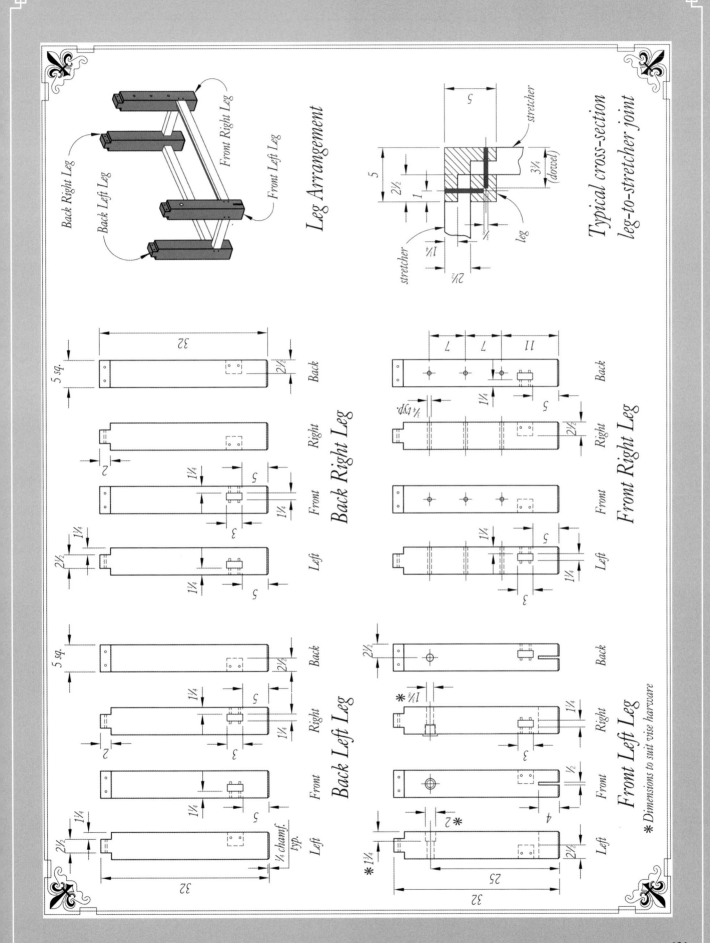

Leg Arrangement

Back Right Leg
Back Left Leg
Front Right Leg
Front Left Leg

Typical cross-section
leg-to-stretcher joint

Back Right Leg

Front Right Leg

Back Left Leg

Front Left Leg

* Dimensions to suit vise hardware

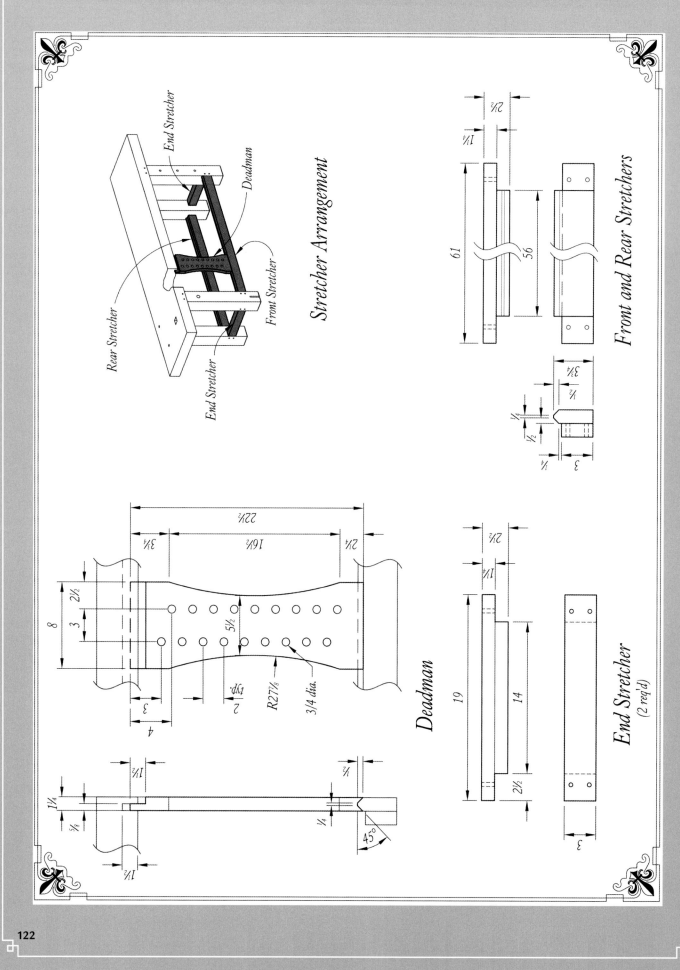

Stretcher Arrangement

Rear Stretcher

End Stretcher

End Stretcher

Deadman

Front Stretcher

Front and Rear Stretchers

61

56

2½

1¼

3¾

½

½

¼

¼

3

Deadman

22¼

16½

3¾

2¼

8

2½

3

5½

4

3

2
typ.

R27⅛

3/4 dia.

1¼

1¼

5/8

1½

¼

½

45°

End Stretcher
(2 req'd)

19

14

2½

2½

1¼

3

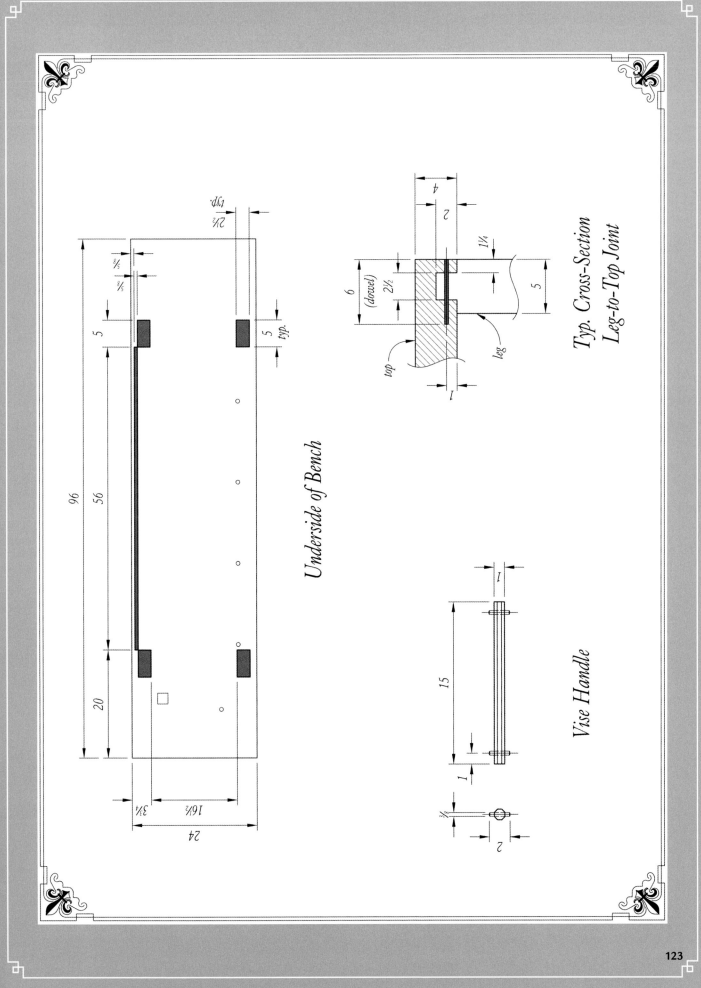

Underside of Bench

Typ. Cross-Section
Leg-to-Top Joint

Vise Handle

HAPPILY EVER AFTER: Building a good bench is key, but what you do with it after it's complete is just as important. A flat benchtop will make your work predictable. And a handful of appliances (but not too many), will make your tools more accurate.

Chapter Seven

Maintenance & Appliances

Like any tool or machine, a workbench requires accessories (jigs, fixtures, appliances) and occasional maintenance to actually do anything of great value. A bench without a bench hook is a dining table. A bench with a cupped work surface is an exercise in bewilderment and wasted effort.

There are many appliances you can build for specialty work. Instead of my filching them from Robert Wearing's masterpiece, *Making Woodwork Aids & Devices* (Guild of Master Craftsman), I implore you to seek out his book, purchase it and read it. Later in this chapter, I will show you the basic woodworking appliances that every bench needs. But before you can build any appliance, you need to tend to one important chore: truing your benchtop.

There are a variety of ways to go about this, including some that are patently nuts. But before I march down that list of your options, I ask: Does the top need to be flat?

Whenever I'm in an old barn, workshop or even an antique mall, I can't resist poking around the guts of any old workbenches I find. When we take the kids on a hayride, I end up in the chicken house checking out the 18th-century wooden screws on a face vise. When we visit living history museums, the kids are chasing the animals, and I'm asking the guy dressed like a cooper if I can poke around the undercarriage of his bench.

I've found little evidence that these benches were flattened regularly. Many of them bear toolmarks that are deep and of varying ages. I've seen benches that are so worn from use that the edges look as round as a pillow. One bench was so worn away in one spot that the bench's 3"-thick top was less than an inch thick.

And when I check the 19th- and early 20th-century books, there's very little attention given to the workbench top. While there is detailed instruction on sharpening, tool maintenance and the act of building a bench, flattening its top isn't often listed as routine shop maintenance. At most, they'll say the top should be flat.

There are several explanations:

1. Workbench flatness is overrated and a product of our modern obsession with granite plates and dial calipers.

2. Early woodworkers would use *planing trays* – a disposable workshop appliance that attached to the bench and allowed woodworkers to plane cabinet-scale parts at a variety of angles. (If you've never seen one of these, you will in this chapter.)

3. Or a flat workbench was so important to those who handplaned panels and furniture components that its flatness was a given.

I don't have the answer, but I suspect that all three are true to some degree. If you've ever done any handwork on a bench that was cupped, bowed or twisted, then you know that it's not a good way to work. The downward pressure from a hand plane (particularly wooden-bodied planes) can bend your work into a low spot in the bench. When using long planes in particular, a low spot will prevent you from ever planing the board flat.

You can use small wooden wedges under your stock to support it and prevent it from bending into a low spot on your bench, but the problem is that you will have difficulty knowing when your board is flat. A workbench top that is fairly flat is also a fair gauge of the flatness of other boards.

Two Solutions for Tops

So my recommendation is that if you can wield a handplane (even just enough to be trouble), then you should either use a planing tray or strive to keep your top fairly flat. You can overdo this. It's not necessary to flatten the top using methods that involve a machinist's straightedge and feeler gauges. And I would ward you away from methods that use a router that runs on a carriage suspended over your bench. I've watched people do this, and it is a lot of trouble to build these devices.

I think there are two smart paths: Learn to use a jointer plane (flattening a workbench top is the best practice for this) or remove your benchtop and take it to a cabinetshop that has a wide-belt sander.

> *"While we don't necessarily need more objects, we just might benefit from more making"*
>
> — John Dunnigan, from the essay "Understanding Furniture" in *Furniture Studio: The Heart of the Functional Arts* (The Furniture Society)

IN THE RIGHT LIGHT: Move your bench so that one end points to a window. This makes it easier to read your winding sticks as you look for gaps underneath them and alignment across their lengths.

LOOK FOR WARP: My winding sticks here are 36"-long aluminum angle. Place one winding stick at the far end of your bench and the other one about 24" away. Sight across them both, looking for high and low spots. Move the second winding stick another 24" and repeat.

CUP OR BOW? Now that I know the geography of the top, I'll drag one stick all along the top and watch the gap under the stick. This quick check confirms my suspicions about where the high spots are (and they are usually along the long edges of the top).

STOP SPELCHING: Before I get down to business, I'll cut a small chamfer (1/16" to 1/8") on the long edges of the top. This will prevent the grain from blowing out (the British call it spelching) when I plane cross-grain.

(Side note: Some workbench designs can be flattened using home woodworking machines. One such design has a benchtop that is made of two thick 10"-wide slabs with a 4"-wide tool tray screwed between them. Simply remove the screws and run each 10"-wide slab through your portable planer. Reassemble! Side, side note: I dislike tool trays, aka hamster beds.)

I can hear the workbench purists squirming from where I perch. Won't sending a workbench top through a wide-belt sander embed it with grit that will mar the work pieces of future projects? Not in my experience. Once you dust off the top and put a finish on it, such as an oil/varnish blend, the grit becomes part of the finish.

Plus, even if there is a little #220-grit in my benchtop, that's a lot kinder to my workpieces than what else gets embedded in my bench during my normal work: bits of dried glue, dyes, pigments, occasional stray metal filings.

Flatten it With a Handplane

Because I don't have a wide-belt sander, I prefer to use a hand plane to do the job. It's a 30-minute job – and cheaper and easier than carting my top across town. The first time I ever tried to flatten a benchtop with a hand plane (years ago) it was 100 percent successful, and I just barely knew what I was doing.

Flattening a benchtop is like flattening a board on one face. First you remove the high spots. These high spots could be at the corners or there could be a hump all along the middle (though I have never had one of these in my benchtop). Find the high spots using two winding sticks – parallel lengths of hardwood or aluminum angle that are longer than your bench is wide.

Mark the high spots (if you have any) in chalk and work them with a bit of spirited planing using a jack plane or fore plane set to take an aggressive cut using its cambered iron. Get things close. Check your results with your winding sticks.

Fetch your jointer plane and work the entire top using diagonal strokes that overlap. Repeat that process by going diagonally back the

other way across the top. After each pass, your shavings will become more and more regular. When your shavings are full length, your top is flat (enough). Now plane the entire top with the grain and use slightly overlapping strokes. It should take two or three passes to produce regular full-length shavings. You are finished. So finish it with some oil/varnish blend and get back to work.

Need details? Visuals? I've prepared a pictorial essay of the process that should help you get started. My digital camera codes each photo with the time it was taken. The first photo was snapped at 10:46 A.M. By 11:44 A.M. I was done. And remember: I'd stopped to take 26 photos about the process, and each photo had to be illuminated with our photographic lights. I think the photography took longer than the actual work.

Appliances for the Bench

There are a galaxy of gizmos out there for you to make or buy for your bench. The ones I discuss are the essential appliances for building casework. I have a whole pile of them for making chairs and finishing that I won't deal with, plus more piles of one-off jigs that get recycled into smaller and smaller one-off jigs with every project.

The first one doesn't guide your tools. It holds them. If you position your workbench against a wall, I recommend you build a tool rack that can hold a high density of tools right in front of you. I have worked out of tool chests, hanging cabinets, tool walls and roll-around bathroom cabinets (seriously!) and nothing beats a simple tool rack above the bench.

Here are the particulars: My rack is made using two sections of 3/4" x 4" base moulding that we used to use in photo shoots at the magazine to hide ugly industrial vinyl base moulding. The two pieces of moulding are glued together with four 1/2"-thick spacers separating the two. The 1/2"-thick space between the mouldings holds a remarkable array of hand tools. The 1/2" allows most tools to slip between the mouldings and stop at the ferrule of the handle.

IN MY CUPS: In general, my tops become cupped in use. So I remove the two high edges by working directly across the grain. In this instance the cup is slight, so I started with a jointer plane. If the cup is acute, start with a jack plane so you can take a thicker shaving.

ACROSS AND DOWN: Every stroke across the top should overlap. The shavings will give up easily (though I am told that the iron will dull more quickly). Work from one end of the top to the other. Then back down. Repeat until the plane's cutter can touch the hollow in the middle.

DIAGONAL MAKES A DIFFERENCE: Work across the top diagonally now, overlapping your strokes as before. Take care at the starting corner and stopping corner – your plane's sole won't have much support. You can proceed with speed during the middle strokes.

AND THE OTHER WAY: Switch directions and work diagonally the other way across the top. Repeat these two types of passes until you can make shavings at every point in a pass.

FINISH PLANING: Now reduce your depth of cut and use your jointer plane along the grain of the top (cutting cross-grain allows you to take a heavy cut). Overlap your stokes and repeat your passes until you are getting full-length shavings.

FOR THE OBSESSED: You don't have to smooth-plane your bench-top, but it's good practice with a large laminated surface. You can begin smooth-planing with the grain, there is no need for cross-grain or diagonal strokes.

CROSS-GRAIN SHAVINGS: When setting up your planes, here's what to shoot for. When working across the grain, this is what your shavings should look like. Take the heaviest cut you can manage and keep your work under control.

DIAGONAL SHAVINGS: Full-length shavings taken at 45° will look like thick ribbon. Shoot for a thickness of .006", perhaps a bit more.

FOR THE OBSESSED II: If you smooth-plane your benchtop, set your tool to take a shaving that is .002" or less. You can take even more if your top is behaving and you used a mild wood.

WIPE ON, WIPE OFF: Rag on two coats of an oil/varnish blend. When everything is dry, a coat of wax will help your top resist glue, but it will make it slippery (a bad thing – hand tool users don't want their stock sliding everywhere.

RIGHT AT HAND: An over-the-bench tool rack is an ideal and easy way to work at the bench. If I could get away with it in our shared shop, I'd also put router wrenches and a few select bits up on this rack.

Across the front of the moulding I added large Shaker pegs (you can get them at Rockler and even some home centers) on 4" centers. Then, between several of the large pegs, I centered a smaller Shaker peg. I placed the tool rack high enough so that my longest tool hung about 4" off the benchtop (you don't want your planes crashing into your hammers when planing across the grain of a wide panel).

I hung my large saws above the rack (also on pegs) and now everything is right where I need it. Some tools I can grab without even looking up from my work. It's a right-powerful way to prevent you from walking all over the shop, opening drawers and toolboxes.

Leather-faced Dogs

If you've made it this far in the book, you know that I like to add little bits of leather to my vises to increase their grip. Wooden bench dogs are part of a vise and so they don't escape my leather fetish either. Gluing rectangles of leather to the faces of your wooden dogs just might make you think twice before buying steel dogs.

Holdfast Pad

This is a trick I picked up from blacksmith Phil Koontz, who makes hand-forged holdfasts. Like the leather-clad canines above, this improvement falls into the category of small tricks that also help protect your work. When using a holdfast you should protect your work with a wooden pad. Hold fasts can leave an impression. This little pad is always right where you want it and swung out of the way if need be. The pad should be about $^3/_8$" thick, wider than the pad of your holdfast and longer than the reach of the holdfast. The hole for the pad should be about $^1/_4$" larger in diameter than the shaft of your holdfast.

Bench Hook

Two huge misconceptions about sawing: Freehand sawing requires great skill. Immobilizing your work for sawing requires a serious vise. Both are false, thanks to a bench hook. These three pieces of wood are so essential to good woodworking that I think you should finish read-

CRASH AT MY PAD: This pad never has to be fished from the garbage and is always the right size. I have been surprised by how much I use it.

ing this section, put down the book and go down to your workshop and build a bench hook.

With a bench hook, you can saw (and sometimes plane) workpieces anywhere you have a stable top. I have used a bench hook on a kitchen counter, a dining table, a table saw wing, a stair tread and a cinderblock.

Here's why they get my vote for the most ingenious shop device ever: The *hook* of the bench hook braces against the edge of your work surface. The fence of the bench hook immobilizes your work with the assistance of a little bit of hand pressure from your off hand and the cutting force of the saw itself. The fence also assists you in sawing square crosscuts by guiding your eye.

The bench hook lets you quickly position your work, hold it without clamps and saw pieces of any size. No more cutting 1" off a $^1/_4$" dowel on your 12" miter saw. Once you have a bench hook and a backsaw, you will stop with the foolish jiggery needed to cut small parts or just the foolish foolishness (which is what usually happens).

ULTIMATE SAWING ACCESSORY: A bench hook and a sharp backsaw will change your woodworking. Saw cuts that seemed like they might require a maestro are within your grasp. Saw cuts that seemed foolhardy are simple and safe.

HOOKED: The second bench hook slides along the benchtop to support long work. You could put a fence on it, but if you don't position it perfectly, it could interfere with holding your work against the fence of your other bench hook.

My bench hook is the deluxe model. The fence and the hook are trimmed off the ends of a $^5/_8$" x 5" x 12" piece of ash. The fence and the hook are $1^1/_2$" long. I glued the hook to the underside of the jig as shown. I trimmed a $^1/_2$" off the width of the fence and glued it to the top of the jig. This avoids cross-grain construction, which is what causes these jigs to self-destruct or go out of true after a while. Then, to further add to the de-luxe-ness of the jig, I marked out a small scale on the fence between 0" and 3" in $^1/_8$" increments. I use a spring clamp as a fence when cutting small parts.

I also use the bench hook as a planing accessory. I brace small parts against the fence, using it at a planing stop. I also use it as a quick shooting board for trimming end grain. Flip the bench hook over. Use the fence as the hook against the benchtop. Place your work against the full-width hook (now used as a fence) and place your plane against the edge of the bench hook. You can now shoot the end grain of small pieces: dowels, muntins to perfection.

As you are making your bench hook, also make a second one without a fence. The second fence-less bench hook is used with the bench hook to support long stock on your bench.

Shooting Boards

Shooting boards are like bench hooks. They hold the work so you can concentrate on guiding the plane through the cut. There are many kinds of specialty shooting boards. The three most common include

one that looks like an oversized bench hook (for shooting end grain), a miter shooting board (for shooting 45° cuts) and a long shooting board designed for shooting long edges of boards.

I don't think you need to build the shooting board for long edges. You only need one of those if your workbench cannot hold pieces on edge to work them. It's far simpler (and smarter) to either clamp a board in your vise and shoot the edge than it is to build a big shooting board that has to be dragged out and set up every time you shoot an edge. Plus, many need to be adjusted for different widths of boards being trued.

As you can guess, I see little use for these long shooting boards for edges. Build a good bench and they are like your appendix or vestigial gill slits.

The other shooting boards are useful, however. The one for shooting end grain is built just like a bench hook, but it's longer and wider. I like to use plywood for these shooting boards for its dimensional stability and (relative) flatness. When attaching the fence, strive to get the fence dead square to the working edge of the shooting board. You can make the fence adjustable if you like. Mine is. The fence is screwed to the bed using pan-head screws I drove through oversized holes (Note: the screw hole near the fence is not oversized. I use it as a pivot point for the fence.)

The underside of the fence has sticky-back sandpaper adhered to it. This works fairly well to keep the parts aligned.

SHOOTING ENDS: Use a heavy plane that is easy to grasp for shooting. This shooting board has a separate track for the plane. If your benchtop is flat you can just run the plane on the benchtop.

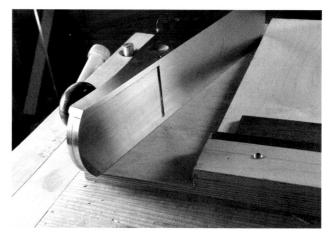

TINY RABBETS: The first time you use a shooting board the iron of your plane will cut into the long edge of the appliance, cutting a small rabbet. After a couple strokes the sole at the side of the mouth will stop the plane from cutting. Note to user: Don't use a rabbeting bench plane for shooting because it will never stop cutting the shooting board.

A couple important details about shooting: People ask how you prevent the plane from cutting the side of the shooting board. You don't. The first two or three passes with a plane removes a tiny corner of the shooting board. Then the edge of the mouth (by the sidewall of the plane) prevents the tool from cutting the shooting board any more. Try it, you'll get it as soon as you do.

When I shoot, I work to a knife line. I cut it close with a saw and then use the shooting board to take the end down. The first strokes are rough. Then the shavings will become more regular. When you get to the knife line, stop planing.

Here's what the mechanics feel like: Brace the work against the fence only – I don't like to press it against the sole of the plane. Immobilize the work with your weight. Use your right hand to push the plane forward into the cut. Your right hand should focus your efforts on keeping the tool pressed both down and against the shooting board.

Practice with some narrow scraps. Soon you will be able to shoot those so you are reducing the length of your board in .001" increments (try that with a table saw). Then move to the wider stuff.

Miter shooting boards are great if you can get them in alignment and keep them that way. They shoot a perfect 45° after you saw a less-than-perfect 45°. That's dang handy.

With my miter shooting board, the 45° fence is actually cut from a square piece of stock that is sliced across its diagonal, making two triangular pieces. If the piece started square, then the triangular section will be at 45° – or at least complementary angles to one another.

Mortise the fence block into the bed of the shooting board. You should leave a little play in the mortise to adjust the fence at the end. Other than that, the mechanics of the miter shooting board works just like the end-grain shooting board: Brace, slice, repeat.

Sticking Boards

Sticking boards are useful for forming rabbets and mouldings. They were designed for use with moulding planes and rabbet planes, but they also work with routers. A sticking board is a long section of stout wood with a low fence along one long edge. It also has some kind of restraint or stop at one (or both) of its ends.

SHAVE YOUR MITERS: This traditional design for a miter shooting board allows you to trim miters going either direction, which reduces the times when you will get tear-out on a moulded, show surface.

After you secure your sticking board to the bench (there are many ways to go about this) you nestle your work in the rabbet created by its bed and fence. Then you adjust the stop of the sticking board so that it will restrain your work without interfering with the cutter or fence of your tool.

My sticking board uses four screws. I move the screws up and down (or remove them) to accommodate different mouldings. Then you plane or rout the work. Note that with a moulding plane you will plane from right to left. With a router, you will rout from left to right. So you might need stops at both ends if you use both kinds of tools.

Shopmade Planing Stop

There are many ways to restrain your work with a planing stop. Planing stops come in many sizes and materials. I prefer one that crosses the width of the benchtop (so I can plane panels) and is thin (just shy of ¼" thick) so I can plane thin stock.

BEGIN AT THE END: When planing moulding, you begin with short strokes up by the far end of the moulding. Gradually increase the length of your strokes. This process creates a track for your plane to ride in and makes cleaner profiles. Note that my left hand pushes the tool against the fence. My right is pushing forward. Each hand has but one job.

SIMPLE STICKING BOARD: My sticking board is immobilized by other accessories on my bench. At the end, my planing stop holds it, and the dogs brace the sticking board from the side. As a result my sticking board is two pieces of wood and four screws. Note I'm using only one screw to cut this ³⁄₁₆" beading profile in some walnut.

Here are the details: The stop itself is ¹⁄₄" x 8" x 24". Why so wide? To add stiffness to the stop so it can be that thin. Glue and screw one end of the stop to a sort section of scrap that you can secure in your face vise. I used pan-head screws – a countersunk screw hole would split the thin stop.

This stop is adjustable, quick to make and dirt simple – all the things I like about good workbench appliances. Woodworking author Nick Engler once told me he never wanted to build a jig that had more than 10 parts. I agree.

Mortising Board in a Vise

This "jig" is taken directly from Robert Wearing's book *Making Woodwork Aids & Devices*, but I have found it so handy for hand-mortising that I feel compelled to show it to you.

I put jig in quotes because it's just a single board that you clamp in your face vise with one long edge proud by 2". Then you clamp your door stiles or legs to this board, stand yourself at the end of the bench and waste out your mortise. You can get a clamp directly across the end of the stile to help prevent splitting, and because of the position of

THROUGH THICK OR THIN: What I like about this stop is that it is thin enough to restrain small pieces of work (top). And you can tip it up to stop thick boards. The width of the stop (8") and its stout nature (oak) allow this to really work.

MORTISING MADE EASIER: This simple board holds your work on your benchtop and allows you to clamp it right where you should.

HALF FRAME; HALF SHUTTER: The planing board is an odd assembly. The slats float free in a 3⁄8" x 3⁄8" groove. The tenons on the rails are glued into the stiles.

your face vise, you're mortising right where you should be: off the end of the bench and right over a stout leg of your bench.

Planing Boards

A planing board is useful if you have a thin benchtop, a warped benchtop or no benchtop at all. It offers a flat and stout surface with stops that you can plane against. Some planing boards are pieces of plywood with a thin lip all around. This works great (as long as the plywood is flat). The planing board can raise your work off the bench a bit if your bench is low. It also can raise your work too high.

Make your planing board large enough to accommodate your work. If you are going to build cabinetry, make it about 24" wide and 36" long. That will accommodate most case sides. Just as with your sticking board, you can come up with a variety of ways to secure your planing board to your bench. I recommend a hook on the front edge of the tray and then some sort of way to restrain it from sliding off the end: a holdfast or a bar clamp across the benchtop.

I made a planing tray with the theory (unfounded) that benchtop flatness is a red herring. If you work a lot on a bench that isn't flat, you'll see it affect your work. A low spot in the top will prevent you from planing the middle of a board. You'll only be able to plane the ends of the board.

One solution to this problem is that woodworkers who toiled on less-than-ideal benches would use a planing board. I first stumbled on the idea in *Modern Practical Joinery* (1902) by George Ellis.

I made a planing board using Ellis's description and text, and it works quite well. It's an unusual piece of work: It's a frame assembly that contains seven slats that float in grooves and can be slid a bit back and forth. Here's where it gets a bit odd: The frame's rails and stiles are 1³⁄8" thick; the slats are 1¹⁄2" thick. The slats are proud on the bottom of the planing board. The top of the planing board is cleaned up flat and flush all around.

The differing thicknesses, I believe, might keep the whole thing flatter in the end. The center of the planing board will always be planted on the benchtop. You can easily true the underside because it is proud and then flip the thing over and true the whole thing. That's a working theory. I have a few others as well.

PORTABLE PLANING: I use a planing tray when I'm headed someplace where I know I'm going to need to plane things but I'm not sure about the workbench. My planing tray hooks over any work surface, and I can constrain it with one or two bar clamps across my work surface.

There are two planing stops at the end that adjust up and down. You can also restrain work for cross-grain planing by inserting wedges between the slats and pushing the work against the wedges.

And how do you keep the planing board on your bench? The book is quiet on this. I have mine pinched between dogs and against a dog at the back of the bench. I'm going to change this arrangement this weekend. I plan to put a hook on the front edge (just like on a bench hook for sawing). And then I'll push the thing against a planing stop in use. There's no need to have a tail vise here.

After dressing your stock, plow a ³⁄8" x ³⁄8" groove down one long edge of each stile. Cut ³⁄8"-thick x 1¹⁄4"-long haunched tenons on the ends of the rails. Cut matching mortises in the stiles. Cut the ³⁄8" x ³⁄8" stub tenons on the ends of the slats.

Bore the two ³⁄8" x 2" through-tenons in one rail for the planing stops. Dry-assemble the frame, clamp it up and make sure the slats will move when the assembly is put together. If everything works, glue up the frame and clamp it. When the glue is dry, dress the underside of the planing tray flat. Then flip it over and dress the entire top surface flat. Fit your planing stops and get a few wedges you can insert between the slats.

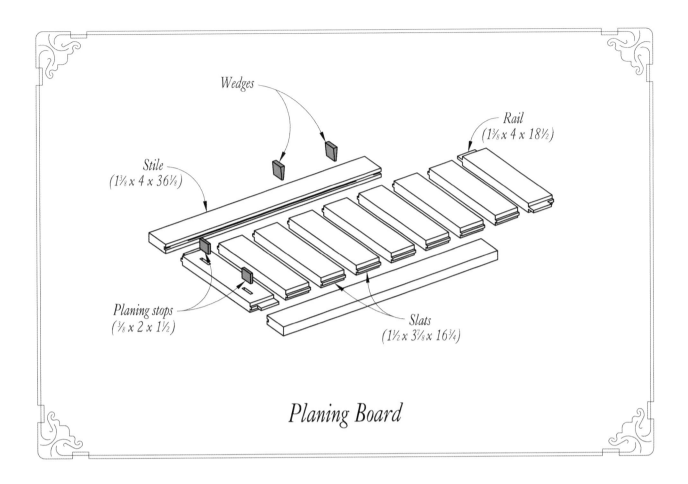

Wedges

Rail
(1⅜ x 4 x 18½)

Stile
(1⅜ x 4 x 36⅛)

Planing stops
(⅜ x 2 x 1½)

Slats
(1½ x 3⅞ x 16¾)

Planing Board

INGENIOUS WEDGES: The slats move so you can press wedges between them. The wedges allow you to hold your work in a wide variety of ways fore and aft. The more wedges you have, the more you can do.

NO CLAMPS; NO BATTENS: Working cross-grain is always tricky. With a planing board, small wedges between the slats prevent the board from skittering across the bench.

Planing Board

	NO.	PART	SIZES (INCHES)			NOTES
			T	W	L	
❑	2	Stiles	1⅜	4	36⅛	⅜ x ⅜ groove
❑	2	Rails	1⅜	4	18½	1¼ tenons
❑	7	Slats	1½	3⅞	16¾	⅜ x ⅜ tenons

ANOTHER SUNDAY IN THE SHOP: These joiners had a lot in common (vests and pocket watches), but they had different benches. The man on the left has no tool tray, whereas his partner had a large one (that's filled with junk, I might add). Sadly, we don't get to see their vises.

Chapter Eight

Epilogue: Invent Nothing

I lost confidence a couple of times while writing this book. Not in the writing itself. Or in the workbenches I've built. Instead, I lost heart in the idea that a good workbench is an essential part of good woodworking.

In 2002 I got to visit Sam Maloof's new workshop and home in Southern California. We were expecting a tour of the place by one of his assistants. But instead, Sam himself took us around the establishment and spent hours showing us all the inside corners of his curvaceous furniture, plus his workshop and his cave-like wood-storage sheds filled with wood that you never see in Southern California.

Sam's whole place is arranged like a walled compound, but there is nothing closed about it. The Maloof homestead is filled with pieces of his work you can touch and sit on, from his early days as a struggling woodworker to some of his modern designs that fetch breathtaking prices. In all of his pieces, even the early ones that Sam would call primitive, the level of craftsmanship is quite high.

So when we took a walk through his shop, I was bewildered by his benches. The main workbench looks like a dining room table. Seriously. Take off the Emmert patternmaker's vise, plop it in a SoHo loft and the goateed hipsters would gladly nibble some Brie around it and use words like *ennui*.

The bench is about 30" high and hugely rectangular. There are four tapered dining-table legs. Four wide aprons under its thin maple top. Stretchers below support a shelf that was stacked so full of chair parts that you would never be able to clamp anything to the top.

The bench disobeyed every single rule in this book. And it bore the marks of heavy use. On the day I visited they were assembling a settee on it. The seat and legs were together; the spindles were yet to come. The work was fresh from the rasp and sandpaper that Sam's shop assistants (*the boys* as they are called) use to fair the work.

In other words, this dining bench wasn't just for assembly (they had low carpet-covered trestles for that) and it wasn't just a cart for parts (they actually used a continental-style workbench for that – ha!). This was a working workbench.

At first I thought: Sam Maloof builds chairs. So he doesn't need much in the way of traditional workholding. But his house is filled with cabinetwork as well as chairs. A lot of world-class woodworking had passed over this bench while under the hands of Sam Maloof.

So, I considered, perhaps workbenches are vestigial to the modern woodworker. They are remnants of a time when we needed bench dogs and bench planes, tail vises and sash saws. Old bench designs survive in the same way that professional woodworkers who have never used a hand plane will put a picture of one on their logo or business card.

After all, the best woodworking I've ever seen in my lifetime was built on the worst workbenches I've ever seen.

But my own experiences with workbenches since I was a boy kept me typing, reading and building for most of a year. And as I got to visit shops all over the world and delve into private tool collections (which always have a bench or two) I saw many patterns in the old forms of benches, echoes of cultural migration and tool evolution.

Modern-day workbenches, however, usually seem to fall into two patterns: the poorly conceived commercial brand of bench and the individualistic design made by someone who was more interested

"Every contrivance of man, every tool, every instrument, every utensil, every article designed for use, of each and every kind, evolved from very simple beginnings."

— Robert Collier (1885 - 1950)
author, publisher

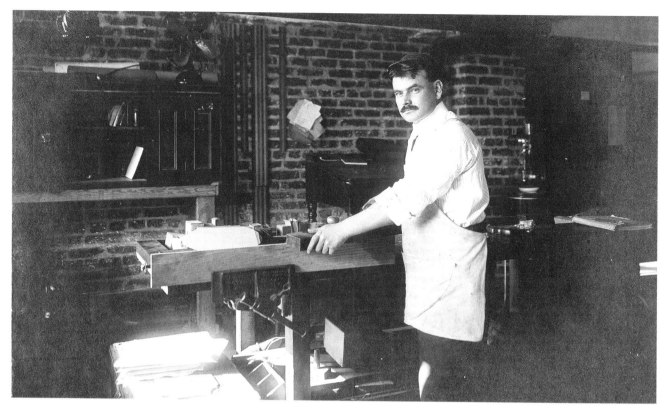

A BASEMENT SHOP: I suspect this guy was a professional woodworker, based on his bench. Manual training benches from this era tended to be spindly.

in getting something knocked together than in poking through old woodworking books. Great modern benches exist, but they're rare.

Most modern benches usually fail to satisfy the three basic workholding tasks that all benches should do with ease: to be able to quickly hold boards so you can work on their broad faces, long edges and recalcitrant ends. Why are our modern workbenches so bad? Perhaps we don't need them.

A planer's serrated feed rollers are the 21st-century equivalent of the wrought iron holdfast. A power jointer's flat bed is the requisite flat worksurface required to try and true your cupped boards. Random-orbit sanders don't need boards that are secured with bench dogs. Dovetail jigs can be screwed to an old kitchen table and churn out tight tail after tight tail.

It's enough to make you stop typing, I can tell you.

But then I visited Brian Boggs shop in June 2006. Boggs, in my mind, is the Kentucky equivalent of Sam Maloof. His chairs are exquisite, and he also builds tables and casework in his shop in Berea, Kentucky. The back of his shop looks like a laboratory more than a shop. He's assembled a robotic army of router jigs built using extruded aluminum 80/20 hardware. He's built a machine that turns hickory bark into a flexible seat material that, when woven, can endure hundreds of years of Thanksgiving dinner abuses.

But at the front of his shop are two huge traditional workbenches – one old, one new. Both of them see heavy use. The Ulmia workbench is about worn out from all the work Brian and his employees give it. The replacement, a Lie-Nielsen bench, is only a year old but looks about 10 years old and Brian fears he is starting to wear out the bearings in one of the vise screws.

When he works on these benches, it's like watching two dance partners. Boggs is at ease. The vises spin in and out. He secures the work without a glance and begins to saw, plane or file. This is exactly how I feel when I'm at my workbench. Workholding is easy, leaving me to worry if the surfaces are true or if my joints fit. I almost never have to stop and ask: How will I hold this part to work on it? This freedom makes me less of a jigger and rigger and more of a joiner. And that I like.

So here's the message I leave you with today: No matter what sort of projects you build. No matter what sort of tools you use. No matter what your skill level. No matter what kind of joints you use. A good workbench will make every workholding task easier.

And here's the best part: You don't need to invent anything, patent anything or manufacture anything to create a workbench that's better than what's lurking in the aisles of many stores today. Workbench designs evolved into their highest form more than 300 years ago. And they are just waiting to be rediscovered by anyone who can understand that though things are always changing, that doesn't mean they are always improving.

Christopher Schwarz
February 2007,
Fort Mitchell, Kentucky
christopher.schwarz@fuse.net

Sources of Bench Supplies

Diefenbach Workbenches
33498 E. U.S. Highway 50
Pueblo, CO 81006-9460
800-322-3624
www.workbenches.com
Workbenches & accessories

Galena Village Blacksmith
P.O. Box 288
Galena, AK 99741
907- 656-2328
www.galenavillageblacksmith.com
Hand-forged holdfasts

GarrettWade Co., Inc.
5389 East Provident Drive
Cincinnati, OH 45246
800-221-2942 (U.S. and Canada)
www.garrettwade.com
Workbenches & accessories

Grizzly Industrial
P.O. Box 3110
Bellingham, WA 98227-3110
800-523-4777
www.grizzly.com
Benches, hardware, plans, vises, workbench
tops & accessories

Highland Hardware
1045 North Highland Ave. NE
Atlanta, GA 30306
800-241-6748
www.highlandwoodworking.com
Benches, hardware, plans, vises, workbench
tops & accessories

Lee Valley Tools
P.O. Box 1780
Ogdensburg, NY 13669-6780
800-267-8735 (U.S.)

P.O. Box 6295, Station J
Ottawa, ON K2A 1T4
800-267-8761 (Canada)
www.leevalley.com
Benches, hardware, plans, vises, kits
& accessories

Lie-Nielsen Toolworks
P.O. Box 9
Warren, ME 04864-0009
800-327-2520 (U.S.)
207-273-2520 (international)
www.lie-nielsen.com
Benches, hardware, vises, & accessories

Perfect Plank Co.
P.O. Box 3007
Paradise, CA 95967
800-327-1961
www.perfectplank.com
Custom workbench tops

Rockler Woodworking & Hardware
4365 Willow Drive
Medina, MN 55340
800-279-4441 (U.S.)
763-478-8200 (international)
www.rockler.com
Benches, hardware, plans, vises,
& accessories

Tools for Working Wood
27 West 20th St. Suite 507
New York, NY 10011
800-426-4613
www.toolsforworkingwood.com
Holdfasts, plans, vises, & accessories

Woodcraft Supply
1177 Rosemar Road
P.O. Box 1686
Parkersburg, WV 26102
800-225-1153
www.woodcraft.com
Benches, hardware, plans, vises
& accessories

Woodworker's Supply
1108 N. Glenn Road
Casper, WY 82601
800-645-9292
www.woodworker.com
Hardware, plans, vises & accessories

TIGHTEN UP: Drawboring is a simple and fundamental skill that will radically transform your joinery. The few extra steps it requires will virtually eliminate gaps in a mortise-and-tenon joint – even if the wood still needs to reach equilibrium with its environment. Plus, drawboring reduces clamping and the need for a perfect fit.

Drawboring Resurrected

Drawboring is one of the simple reasons that so much antique furniture survives today, some of it as sound as the day it was made.

What is drawboring? It's a technique that strengthens a mortise-and-tenon joint, transforming it from a joint that relies on glue into a joint that has a permanent and mechanical interlock. In essence, you bore a hole through both walls of your mortise. Then you bore a separate hole through the tenon, but this hole is closer to the shoulder of the tenon. Then you assemble the joint and drive a stout peg through the offset holes. The peg draws the joint tight.

Drawboring offers several advantages compared to a standard glued mortise and tenon:

· The joint will remain tight. A common problem with mortise-and-tenon joints is that the joint can open up and develop an ugly gap at the shoulder. Sometimes this is caused by the wood shrinking as it reaches equilibrium with a new environment (such as your living room with its forced-air heat). Sometimes this gap is caused by simple seasonal expansion and contraction, especially with woods that tend to move a lot, such as flat-sawn oak. The peg in a drawbored joint keeps the tenon in tension against the mortise during almost any shrinkage.

· The joint can be assembled without clamps. Drawboring is excellent for unusual clamping situations. Driving the peg through the joint closes it and clamps are generally not needed. Chairmakers use drawboring to join odd-shaped pieces at odd angles. It's also an excellent technique when your clamps aren't long enough. Or when you don't have enough clamps. Drawboring also allows you to assemble a project one piece at a time if need be.

· The joint can be assembled without glue. There is good evidence that drawboring allowed early joiners to assemble their wares without any glue. This is handy today when you're joining resinous woods (such as teak) that resist modern glues or when you're assembling joints that will be exposed to the weather, which will allow water to get into them and destroy the adhesive.

· The joint doesn't have to be perfect. The mechanical interlock of drawboring means that your tenon's cheeks don't have to have

a piston fit with your mortise's walls. In fact, you might be surprised at how sloppy the joint can be and still be tight after hundreds of years. Drawboring requires you to be careful only when fitting the tenon's shoulder against your mortised piece. The other parts of the joint are not as important. And while I never argue against doing a good job, drawboring ensures that every joint (even the less-than-perfect ones) can be tight for many lifetimes. For this reason, I think drawboring is an excellent basic skill for beginning woodworkers.

So why has drawboring become an almost-lost art? It's a good question, and one that I cannot fully answer. I suspect that modern glues and machine-made joinery made the technique less necessary, particularly for manufactured furniture. Drawboring does require several extra steps, and the benefits of it — particularly the long-term durability of the joint — is not something that is apparent to a customer.

Another reason the technique has fallen out of favor, I suspect, is that manufacturers have stopped making drawbore pins. These tapered steel tools allow you to temporarily assemble the joint to check the fit and to ease the path that the wooden peg will later follow. You can drawbore without drawbore pins by relying on the peg (and luck) alone. But once you use a proper set of drawbore pins, you will wonder why they are not in every tool catalog.

"(Drawbore pinning) is chiefly confined at the present time to rough outside work, or imitation mediaeval joinery, as it is neither so effective or of so good an appearance as a glued and wedged joint."

— George Ellis
Modern Practical Joinery (Linden)

Drawboring Basics

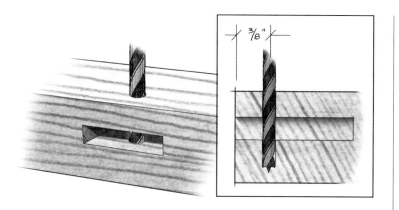

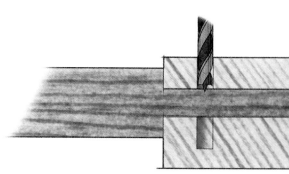

1 Bore a ¼"-diameter hole through both mortise walls. The center of the hole should be ⅜" from the edge of the mortise.

2 Assemble the joint. Mark the hole's center on the tenon using a ¼" brad-point bit.

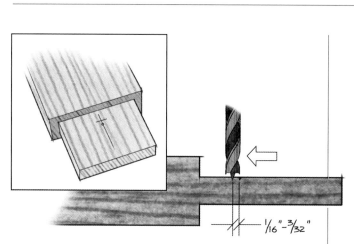

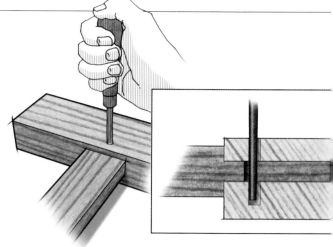

3 Remove the tenon and shift the mark closer to the tenon shoulder – ¹⁄₁₆" to ³⁄₃₂". Use the same bit to bore a ¼"-diameter hole through the tenon at the offset mark.

4 Reassemble the joint. Twist the drawbore pin into the joint to check the fit. Ensure there are no gaps in the joint.

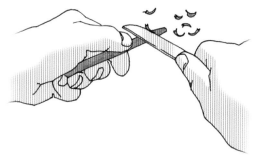

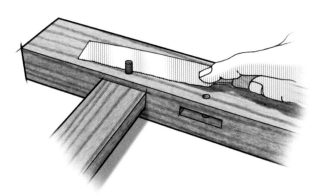

5 Whittle the end of a ¼" peg to about ⅛" diameter at the tip. Add glue to the joint and peg. Assemble the joint and hammer the peg through the offset holes.

6 Saw (or chisel) the protruding peg material flush with the work.

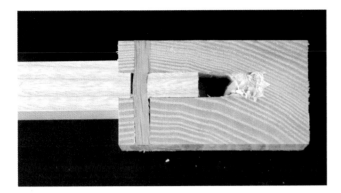

INSIDE THE JOINT: I sawed apart a drawbored joint to show how the oak peg bends through the offset hole. This was a ³⁄₃₂" offset in ash.

Joint Details

I have drawbored many joints during the last five years or so and have found the methods described to be highly effective. My method is based on historical descriptions of the process from the 17th century as well as my own work.

The first detail to tend to is the size and location of the hole through the mortise. I have found that a ¹⁄₄"-diameter hole is good for cabinet work. For larger-scale work (workbenches, doors and windows for homes) a ³⁄₈"-diameter hole is better because the peg is stouter. In general, place the hole ³⁄₈" from the opening of the mortise in furniture work and ¹⁄₂" in larger work. Make the hole as deep as you can. Usually this requires boring it through the assembly, though the hole can be stopped in thick stock. The goal is to ensure that the untapered part of the peg passes into the other wall of the mortise.

Historically, many of the drawbore pins I've encountered are a diameter that's best suited for a ³⁄₈"-diameter hole and peg. Entryway doors and large windows are appropriate for this larger hole and peg. I have encountered (and own) a set of old pins that work with a ¹⁄₄"-diameter hole, however, so this approach is historically accurate.

The next thing to consider is how much to offset the hole in the tenon. The bigger the offset, the sounder the joint, but the bigger the risk that you'll destroy the tenon or peg during assembly.

The traditional joiner was advised to offset the holes by the width of a shilling, according to Joseph Moxon's *Mechanick Exercises*, a 17th-century how-to book on woodworking. I had difficulty locating a shilling from the middle to late 17th century (I did try), but according to one knowledgeable collector of English coins, a 17th-century shilling would be about ¹⁄₁₆" thick.

An offset of ¹⁄₁₆" will always work and is easy to assemble. But I've found that it's sometimes not enough to get the job done. Some of the joints I assembled with this small offset were just a bit wiggly. For furniture-scale work, I prefer a ³⁄₃₂" offset. For big-scale work, I'll push that offset to almost ¹⁄₈" if the parts of the joint are large and the wood is a tough species, such as ash or elm. Experience will be your guide. Begin with small offsets in a sample joint and gradually increase them. You'll know when you've found the sweet spot.

Marking the offset on the tenon must be done with care because small changes can make a significant difference and cause the tenon to split in fragile woods, such as cherry. If you mark the offset with a slightly dull pencil, it can shift your mark by ¹⁄₃₂" or so. I recommend you use a sharp mechanical pencil or (even better) a knife.

HOMEMADE TOOLS: Making your own drawbore pins is easy using an inexpensive alignment pin and a scrap of sawn (or turned) hardwood.

The shape of the peg is important, too. I whittle mine so the last ¹⁄₂" tapers to an ¹⁄₈" tip. In almost all cases, I use straight-grained white oak for my pegs. It must be completely dry; wet pegs will shrink in time and allow the joint to loosen up. Typically I'll split out my pegs from some dry oak using a pocketknife and mallet. This is called *riving*, and it is a technique used by chairmakers to produce durable chair parts. Wood that is shaped by riving is stronger because it splits along the wood's grain lines. Sawing cuts across the grain lines, which can create a more fragile peg in some cases.

I then whittle the pegs round or roughly octagonal. Another option is to pound them through a steel plate with the correct-size hole bored in it. When pressed for time, I'll use dowel stock, which I have found to be satisfactory as long as I choose dowels with straight grain.

When you knock the peg home, you'll sometimes create a small gap between the hole and the peg as the peg leans into one side of the mortise as it makes its path through your joint. If this gap is unsightly, try a different strategy on your next joint. Whittle your pegs slightly larger in diameter and switch to an octagonal shape. Again, a bit of practice in a couple sample joints will help you get it right.

Despite everything I know about drawboring, I still glue most of my joints and even coat the peg with glue before driving it in. It cannot hurt. But I do take great satisfaction in knowing that when that modern glue has given up, the peg will still keep everything in place and the joint will be just as tight as the day I made it.

Index